IMAGES
of America

WILLIAMS COUNTY

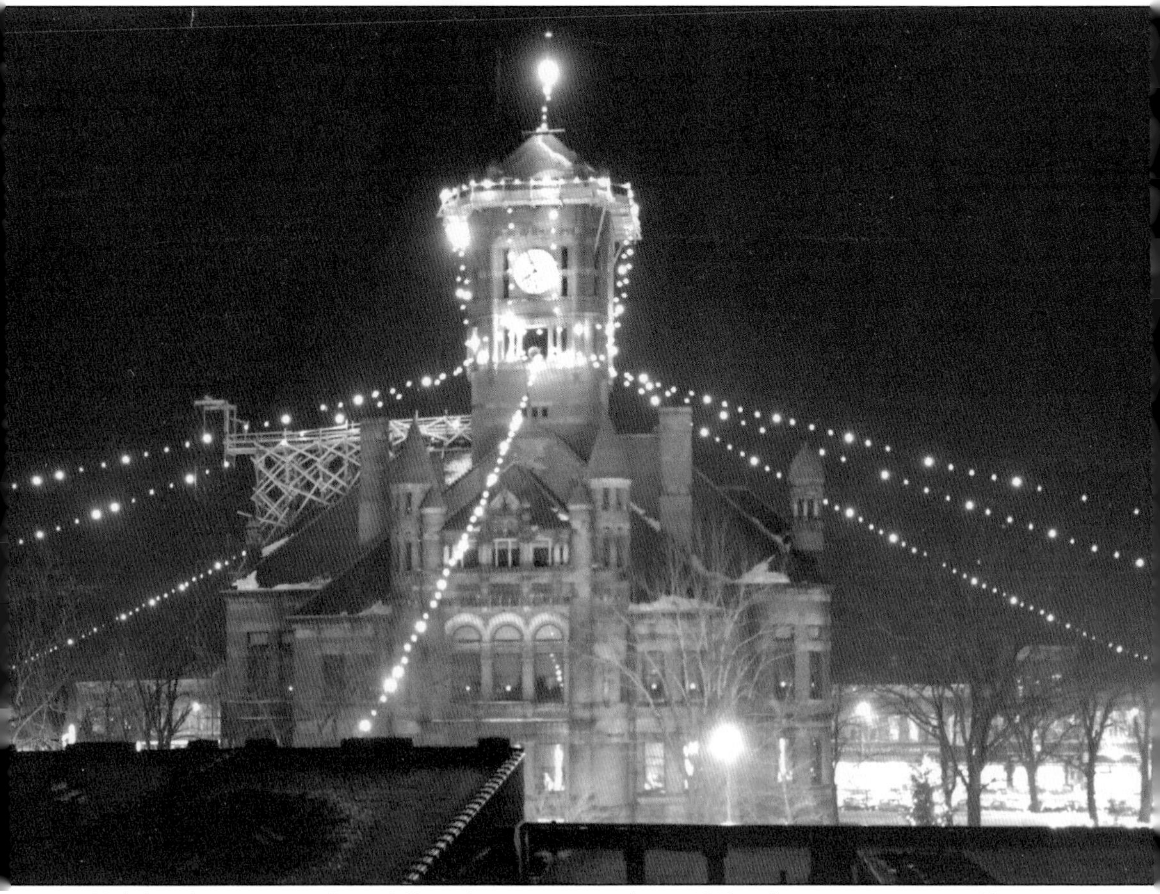

Holiday decorations adorned Bryan's square as early as 1913, when a community Christmas tree graced the courtyard. In 1947, 1,500 colored lights were strung from the courthouse, and passing trains slowed to allow passengers a view of the display. In 1950, the Weaver Construction Company repaired the courthouse roof and tower. The company's scaffolding is visible on the north side of the historic county building in this December 1950 photograph. (Williams County Public Library Photographic Archives.)

On the cover: The automobile forever changed the way Williams County residents lived, worked, and played. This c. 1910 photograph, printed from a glass plate negative, shows a group of automobile enthusiasts with a Model 10 Buick on North Michigan Avenue in Edgerton. (Author's collection.)

IMAGES
of America

WILLIAMS COUNTY

Kevin M. Maynard

ARCADIA
PUBLISHING

ISBN 978-0-7385-6195-0

Published by Arcadia Publishing
Charleston SC, Chicago IL, Portsmouth NH, San Francisco CA

Printed in the United States of America

Library of Congress Catalog Card Number: 2008927819

For all general information contact Arcadia Publishing at:
Telephone 843-853-2070
Fax 843-853-0044
E-mail sales@arcadiapublishing.com
For customer service and orders:
Toll-Free 1-888-313-2665

Visit us on the Internet at www.arcadiapublishing.com

To my family: Bernie and Josephine Maynard, Cerelle Loftus, Margo Straman, Sabrina Armstrong, Andrea Vestal, Kim Maynard, and Marquita Schaeffer

Contents

ACKNOWLEDGMENTS

First and foremost, I thank the Stryker Area Heritage Council for sponsoring this pictorial history and for its efforts to preserve our local heritage.

Many of the photographs featured in this publication are from the Williams County Public Library (WCPL) Photographic Archives, an incredible source of images of Williams County's past. A debt of gratitude is owed the many individuals and organizations who have donated or allowed historic photographs to be copied for this archival collection and also to the library for preserving this critical piece of local history for present and future generations to enjoy and to learn from.

Jane Kelly and Joyce Yoder of the Williams County Public Library helped select and scan vintage images, researched needed information, and provided community outreach. This book would not have been possible without their invaluable assistance and interest.

Don Allison, Richard L. Cooley, Jane Kelly, Eldon Smith, and Joyce Yoder reviewed this publication to help ensure historical accuracy and readability.

Charles Bates and the Allen County, Ohio, Historical Society granted permission to reprint the Melbern depot photograph from their collection.

Don Wetzel, the engineer who set the North American rail speed record through Williams County in 1966, granted permission to use his photograph of the M-497 in this publication and has been wonderfully supportive of local efforts to commemorate this important event.

Kelly Michael provided a history of the George Kollar residence/Wertz Hospital in Montpelier.

Finally, this pictorial history would not have been possible without the unwavering support, patience, and understanding of my family—Teresa, Austin, Jennifer, and Nathan. I love you.

INTRODUCTION

Williams County was created by the Ohio legislature in 1820 and named after Revolutionary War hero David Williams, one of three captors of British spy Maj. John André. André was carrying plans supplied by Benedict Arnold as part of a plot to surrender the American fort and garrisons at West Point to the British. Williams died in 1831, and there is no record that he visited the county that bears his name.

When Williams County was created in 1820, it was a large rectangle of land containing about 720 square miles, compared to its present area of roughly 420 square miles. Williams County's southern border was about 12 miles farther south, encompassing most of what is today Defiance County, until that county was established in 1845. Williams County's eastern boundary was a north-south line until parts of Millcreek and Brady Townships were transferred to Fulton County upon its creation in 1850.

In 1824, the Ohio legislature organized Williams County, allowing local residents to create a county government. The county seat was established at Defiance. Court was held in a two-story warehouse along the Maumee River and at other Defiance locations until a small, two-story brick courthouse was completed on Wayne Avenue in 1832.

There is no record of settlers within present Williams County boundaries in 1824. The county's first permanent resident is believed to be Samuel Holton Jr., who settled along Fish Creek in St. Joseph Township in 1827.

In the early 1830s, settlers began pouring into Williams County, primarily farm families seeking inexpensive land and new lives on the frontier. Many were European immigrants or the children of immigrants willing to perform the backbreaking labor necessary to clear the forests and convert them into fertile farmlands.

In 1840, the county seat was moved to a more central location at the future site of Bryan. A two-story log courthouse was built on North Main Street, which was replaced by a two-story, brick Greek Ionic–style courthouse on Bryan's square in the mid-1840s.

The first settlers' homes were log structures, which could be quickly constructed using felled trees and hand tools pioneers brought with them. The furnishings of these log homes were simple but functional and well-suited to life on the frontier. Log residences were replaced by larger frame or brick houses as farms and communities became established.

The first roads were trails cut through the woods or laid out along old American Indian trails. In 1831, the Bellefontaine Road became the first road formally surveyed through Williams County, running from Bellefontaine through Defiance, Brunersburg, Ney, Williams Center, Denmark, and into Indiana.

Many roads and bridges were constructed prior to the Civil War, but the dirt roads became so muddy or rutted that travel was next to impossible certain times of year, even with horses or oxen. In winter, sleighs and bobsleds were often used to transport people and goods.

Williams County's first rail line was the Michigan Southern and Northern Indiana Railroad, which was extended from Toledo to Stryker in 1854. The following year the railroad was constructed westward through Bryan, Edgerton, and into Indiana.

The railroad's arrival had a dramatic impact on the county's growth and prosperity. It provided a great improvement in transporting people and goods, opening new markets for local farmers.

With an outlet for manufactured goods and abundant raw materials, small factories began springing up. Stryker, Melbern, and Edgerton were surveyed next to the railroad and quickly became bustling frontier towns.

The area's earliest business enterprises included water-powered sawmills and gristmills to provide building materials, flour, or cornmeal. These were later replaced with steam-powered mills and elevators that served as collection points for locally grown grain.

Salespeople, travelers, and prospective settlers visited the area, and numerous small hotels did a thriving business. Blacksmith shops, harness shops, and livery stables provided support services while horses were a primary means of transportation.

The first schools were often held in homes or simple log or frame buildings. By 1862, there were 141 schools in Williams County, most of them one-room rural schools. As the population increased and compulsory education laws were adopted, larger schools were required. In the early 1900s, school districts began consolidating, but one-room schools continued to operate in Williams County until 1957.

The first settlers had diverse religious backgrounds representing many denominations. Congregations frequently met in homes or schoolhouses until strong enough to construct church facilities. Early churches were often small log or frame meetinghouses with simple interior furnishings. Services were commonly conducted in a native tongue such as German or French until older members of congregations passed away.

Although work occupied much of pioneer life, there was still time for entertainment. Pastimes included swimming, hunting, and fishing. Carnivals, circuses, and parades have long been attractions. Nearly every town had a brass band that played on Saturday nights and during community events. Fairs have been held since 1856, and fraternal organizations such as the Grand Army of the Republic (GAR), Masons, Grange, Knights of Pythias, and the Independent Order of Odd Fellows provided fellowship, entertainment, and services to their members and communities.

The late 1800s witnessed many local improvements and changes. Two additional railroads breathed new life into existing towns and created others. The Wabash Railroad was built through Williams County in 1880–1881, eventually touching Montpelier, Edon, West Unity, and Kunkle and giving birth to Blakeslee and Alvordton. In 1887, the Cincinnati, Jackson and Mackinaw Railroad was extended through Bryan, Pulaski, West Unity, and Alvordton.

Williams County became more prosperous, and its courthouse built in 1888–1891 reflected this progress. Villages began installing electric, water, and sewer systems, and telephone lines soon connected many areas. Improved fire protection and public libraries also appeared during this time.

After 1900, the automobile brought still greater change. Improved roads became a priority; villages laid brick pavement, and rural roads were graded, graveled, and ditched. Wooden covered bridges were replaced by steel spans. The automobile's popularity also led to new support industries such as service stations, automobile insurance agencies, tourist camps, and motels.

Improvements in agriculture allowed farmers to till more and more acres and produce greater yields. Small family farms began disappearing as labor migrated to villages to work in factories. Many local industries trace their roots to this period, including Bard Manufacturing, Winzeler Stamping Company, Ohio Art Company, Spangler Candy Company, and Hause Machines. Others, such as the Van Camp Packing Company/Pet Milk Company, Delite Manufacturing Company, Challenge-Cook Brothers, and Holabird Company, thrived for years before falling victim to changing times.

The strong work ethic, faith, entrepreneurial spirit, and sense of community that has characterized the people of Williams County—past and present—has worked a wonderful transformation, turning a wilderness into fine farms and communities with modern public facilities and services, numerous businesses and industries, and offering a high quality of life in a rural setting.

One

Main Street

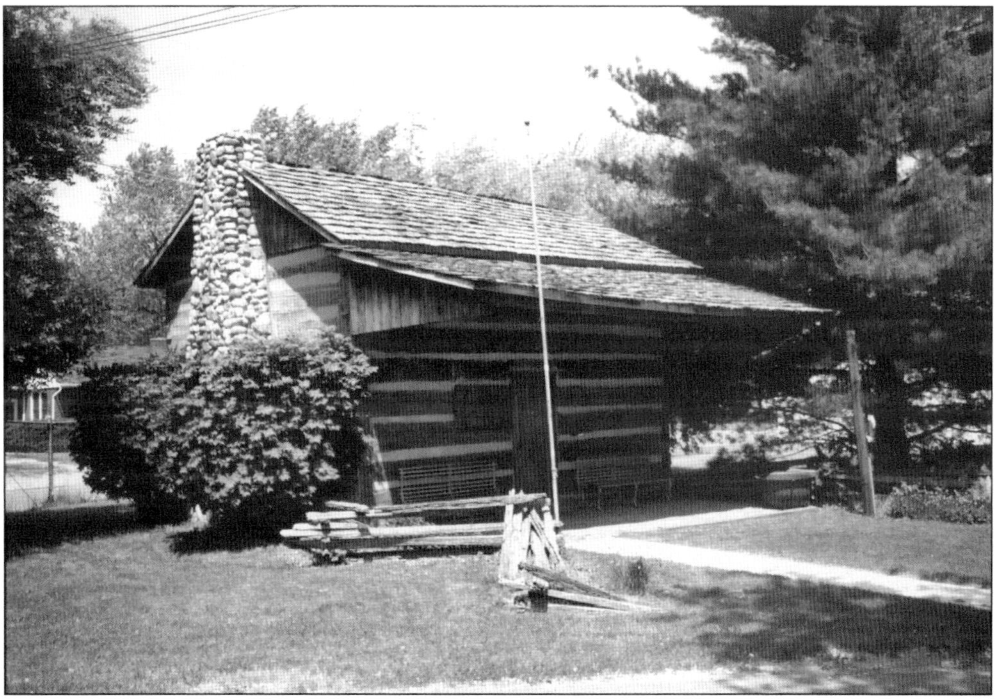

The area's earliest settlers constructed log houses using hand tools. An excellent example of a local log residence has been preserved by the Williams County Historical Society. The Lett Log House above was built three miles south of Edgerton around 1850–1851 by George Lett. In 1962, the log structure was relocated to the Williams County Fairgrounds and restored.

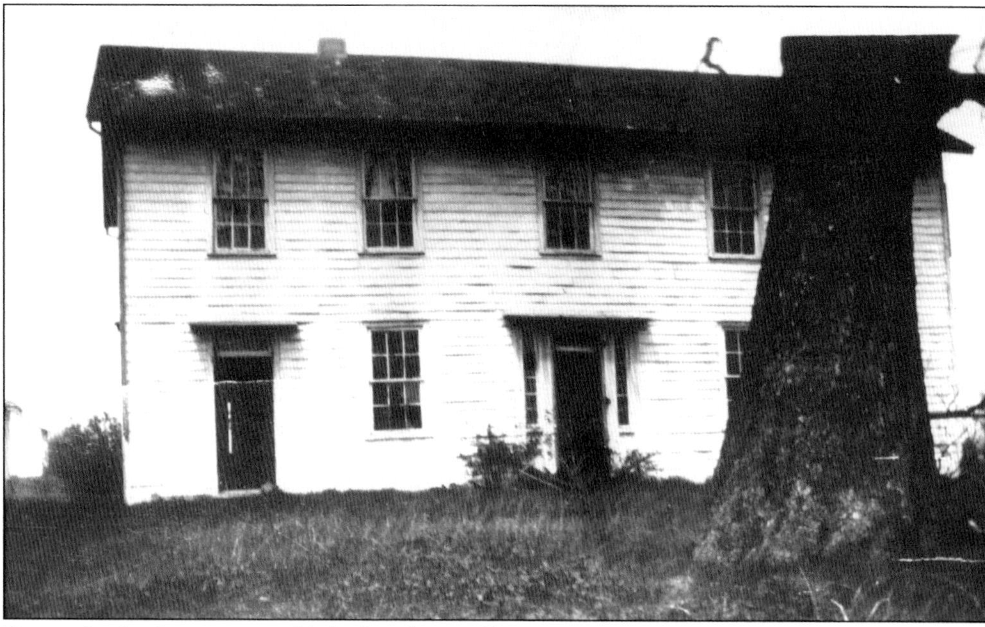

Denmark, the first town established within Williams County's current boundaries, was surveyed on December 25, 1834, next to the St. Joseph River in St. Joseph Township. Denmark contained 93 town lots, with 88 more surveyed in 1836. About 1835, town founder Judge Payne C. Parker built this two-story building to house his tavern, inn, and store. Part of Denmark's plat was vacated in 1841 and the remainder in 1861. (Richard L. Cooley.)

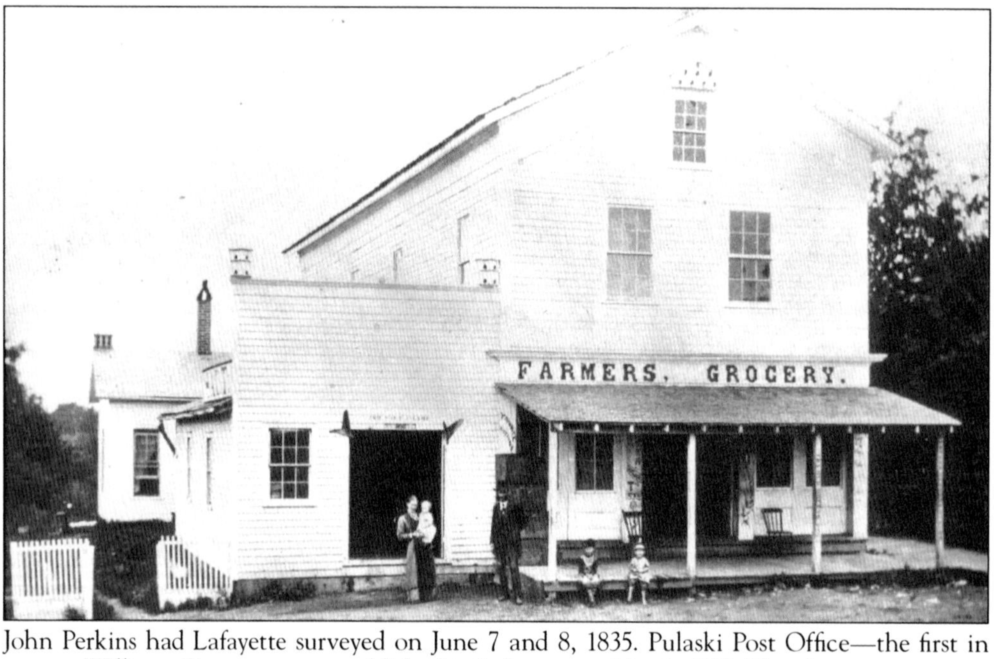

John Perkins had Lafayette surveyed on June 7 and 8, 1835. Pulaski Post Office—the first in present Williams County—was established in Lafayette on May 1, 1837. This disparity in names was not uncommon in the 1800s and was resolved in 1857, when the court approved residents' request to rename the village Pulaski. W. J. Carroll's Farmers Grocery stood on North Street west of High Street (U.S. 127) in Pulaski. (WCPL Photographic Archives.)

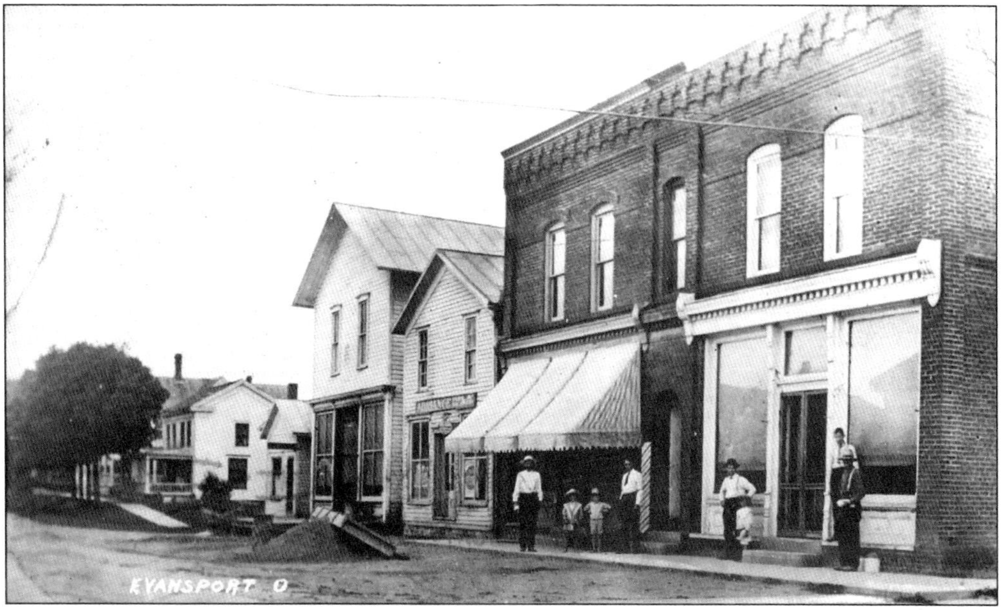

Evansport was surveyed next to the Tiffin River just south of the Williams-Defiance county line for Jacob Coy, Amos Evans, and Albert G. Evans on December 14, 1835. Evansport Post Office was established on May 1, 1837—the same day as Pulaski Post Office. This *c.* 1908 photograph shows the west side of Main Street looking south from Evansport's main intersection.

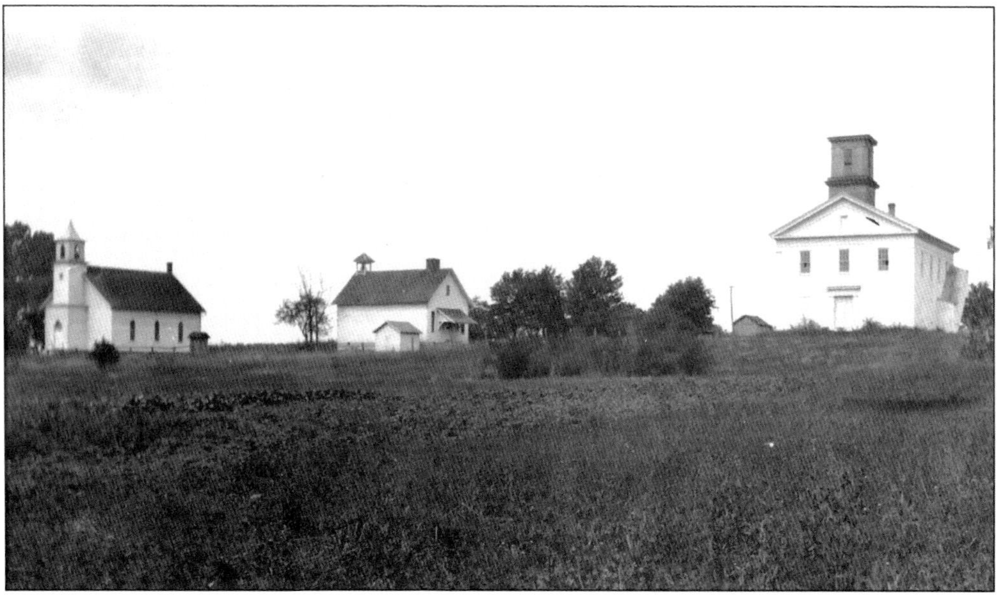

On January 23, 1836, Centre was surveyed near the geographic center of "old" Williams County for Dr. John Evans of Defiance. Over time the village became known as Williams Center, the name of its post office established in 1839. This photograph shows the United Brethren Church (destroyed by fire in 1947), the town's one-room schoolhouse, and the building that served as the Center Institute from 1858 to the 1870s.

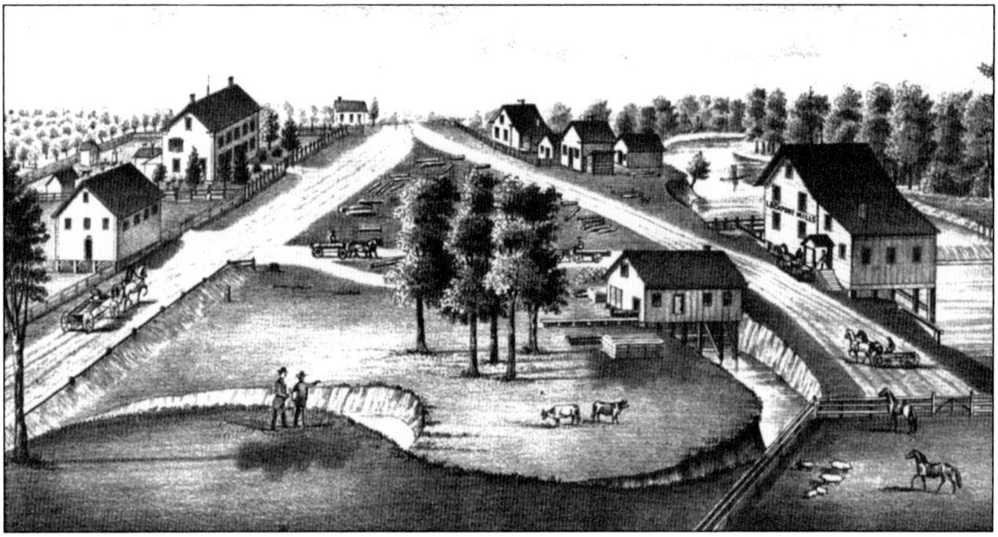

On February 26, 1836, Dr. John Evans (Centre's founder) had Lockport surveyed next to the Tiffin River in Brady Township. Lockport quickly became a trade center with stores, a post office, schoolhouse, sawmill, and gristmill. After the railroad reached Stryker in 1854, Lockport began its decline. This illustration shows Lockport in 1874, including its water-powered sawmill and gristmill on the right. (Williams County atlas of 1874.)

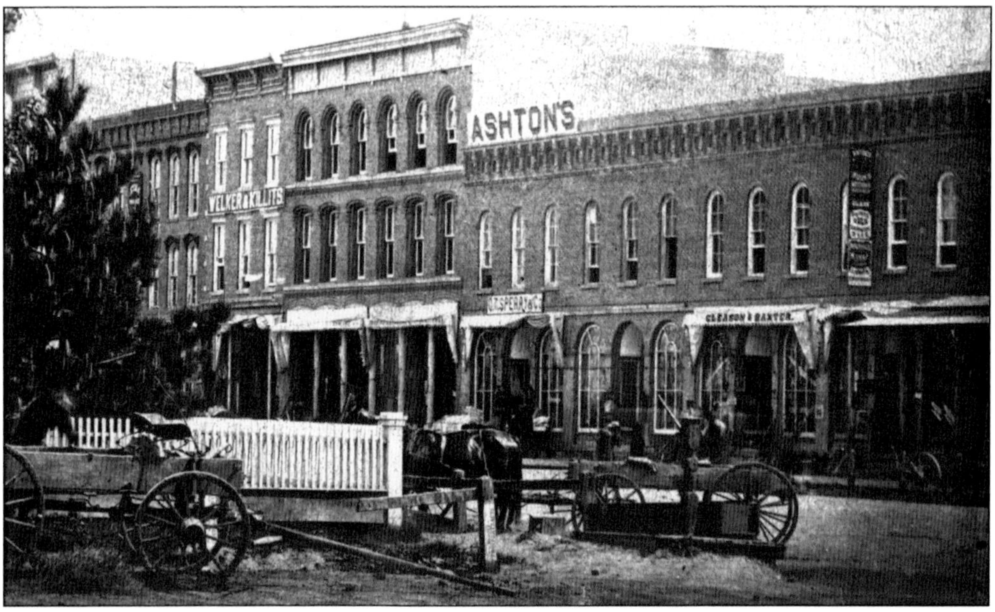

Bryan was surveyed as the new Williams County seat on July 14, 1840, for John A. Bryan of Columbus. The town once had so many flowing artesian wells that it became known as the "Fountain City." On March 7, 1849, Bryan was incorporated by the Ohio legislature. The east side of Bryan's square (Main Street) is shown in this c. 1865 photograph. (WCPL Photographic Archives.)

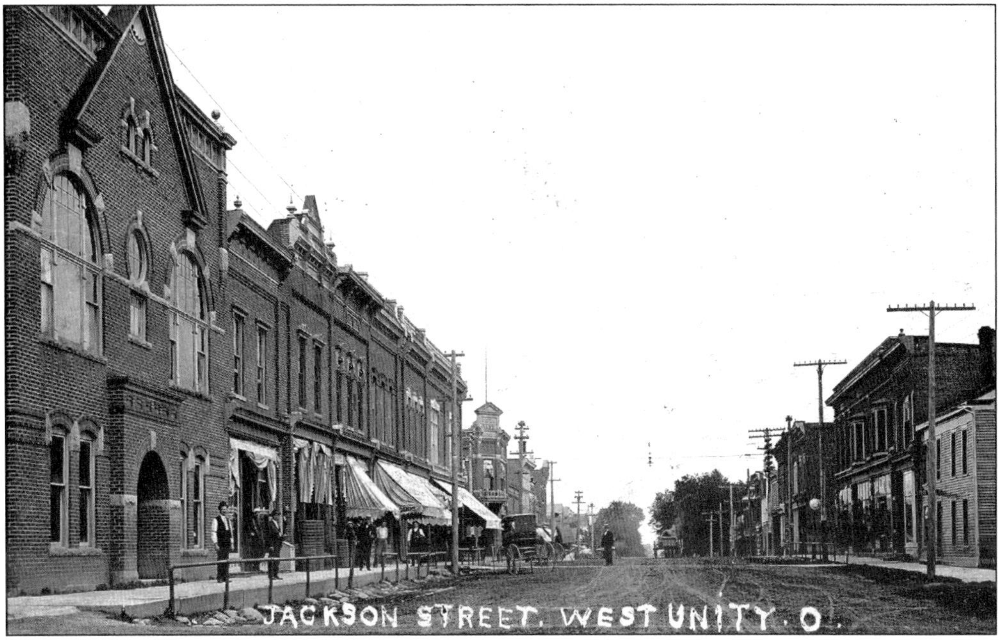

West Unity was surveyed for Brady Township pioneers John Rings and William L. Smith on June 14, 1842, and named after Pleasant Unity, Pennsylvania. This *c.* 1907 photograph was taken looking east from the intersection of Jackson and High Streets. The town hall, built in 1894–1895, is on the left.

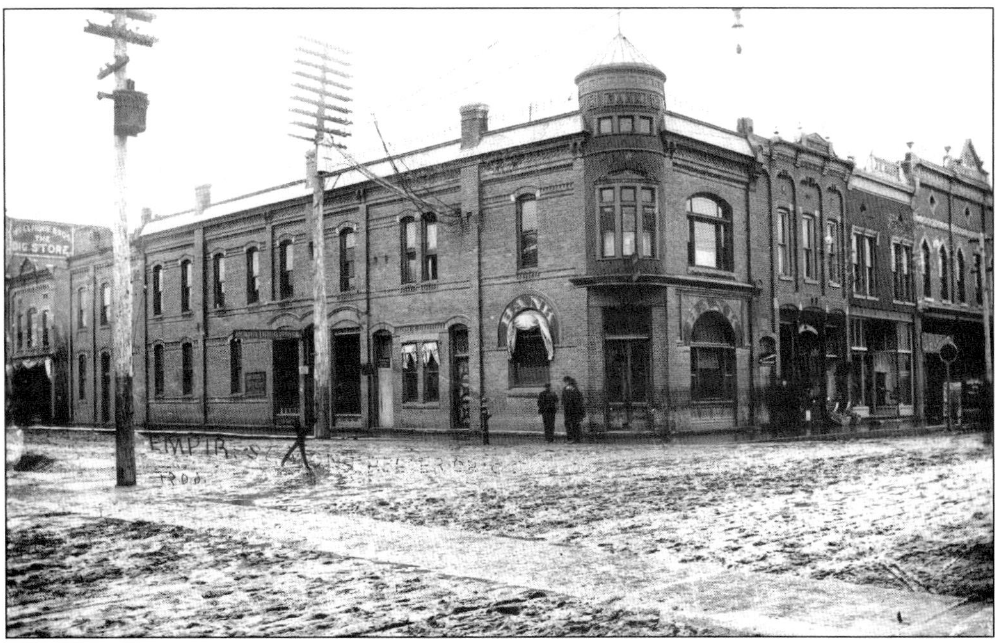

By 1845, John K. Bryner and Jesse Tucker constructed a water-powered mill on the St. Joseph River in Superior Township. On May 25, 1845, Bryner and Tucker had Montpelier—consisting of 41 lots and a public square—surveyed south of their mill. Local tradition holds that the village was named after Montpelier, Vermont. This undated photograph shows the intersection of Main and Empire Streets. (WCPL Photographic Archives.)

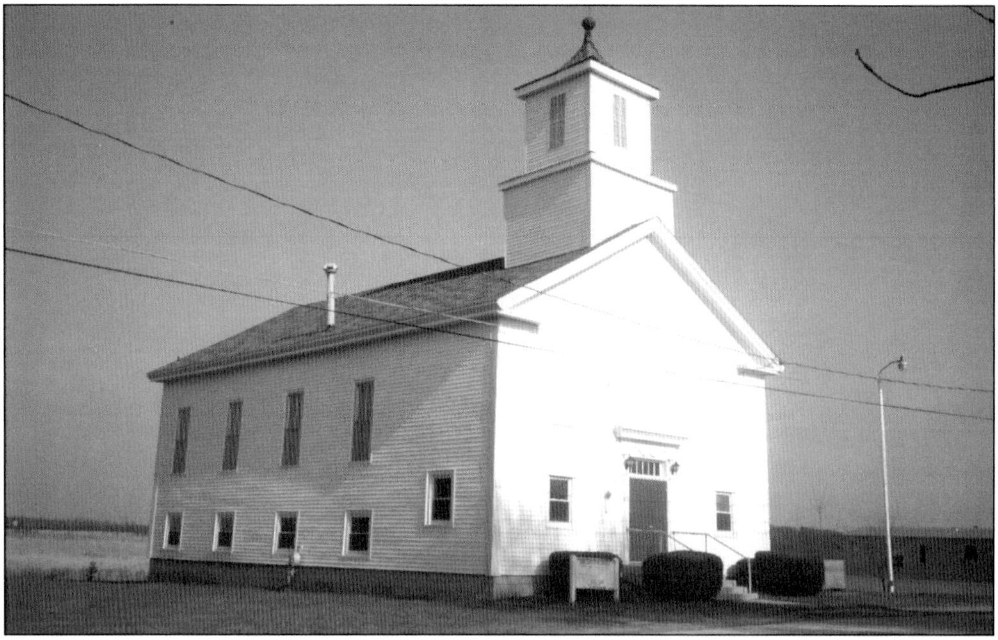

West Jefferson was surveyed on December 14, 1849, for Jonathan and Jeremiah Gilbert, George Dorshimer, and Elias H. Brown. The town plat contained 96 lots and five streets. West Jefferson's Zion Lutheran Church was formally organized on February 11, 1859. The congregation completed this frame church later that year. It is believed to be Williams County's oldest church building used for regular worship services.

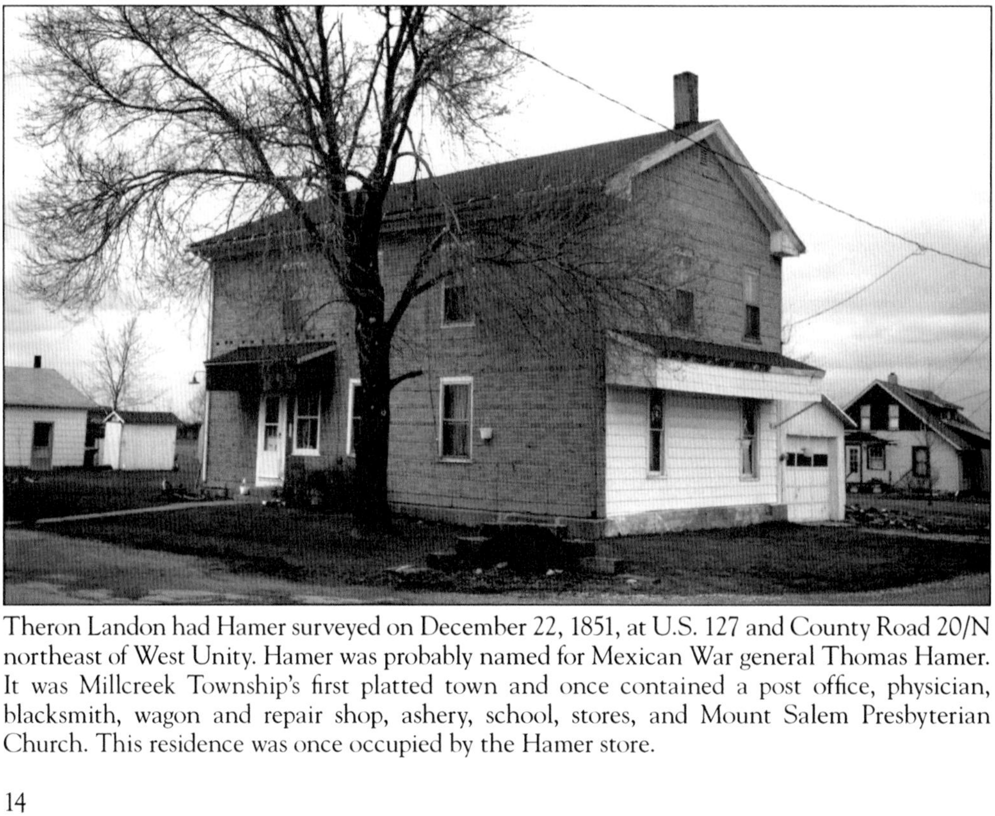

Theron Landon had Hamer surveyed on December 22, 1851, at U.S. 127 and County Road 20/N northeast of West Unity. Hamer was probably named for Mexican War general Thomas Hamer. It was Millcreek Township's first platted town and once contained a post office, physician, blacksmith, wagon and repair shop, ashery, school, stores, and Mount Salem Presbyterian Church. This residence was once occupied by the Hamer store.

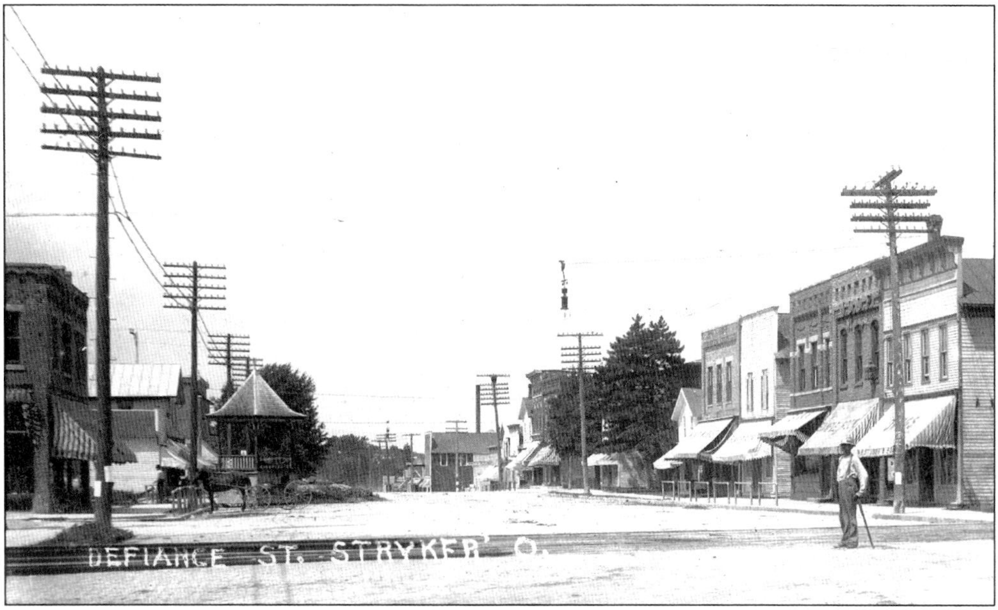

Stryker was surveyed on September 19, 1853, beside the proposed Michigan Southern and Northern Indiana Railroad by John H. Sargent, Epaphras L. Barber, and Jesse McCart. The village was named for Rome, New York, attorney and railroad executive John Stryker and was the first Williams County community with rail service. This *c.* 1910 photograph was taken looking north on Defiance Street from the railroad.

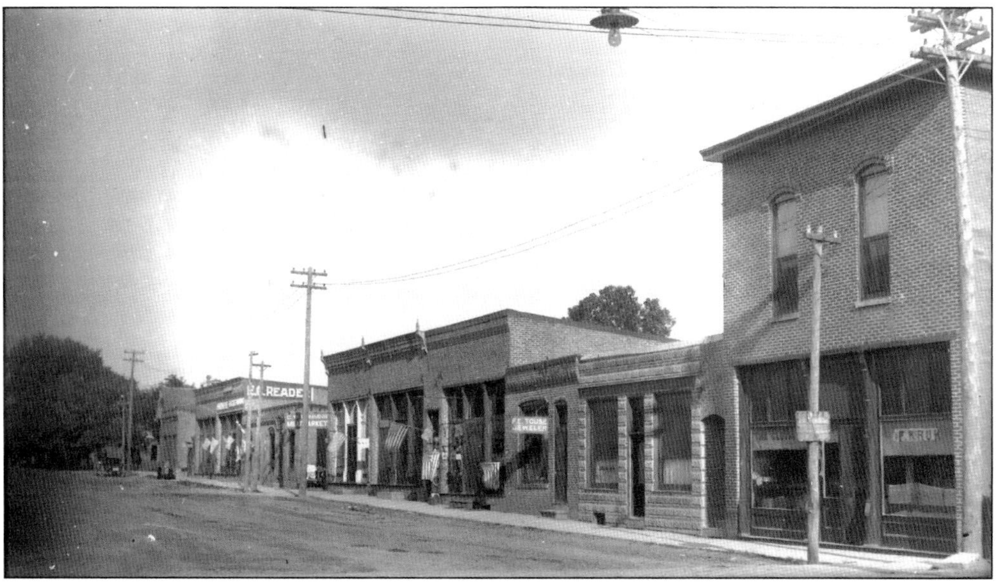

On April 16, 1851, the Pioneer Post Office was established with Philetus Walter Norris, who later served as second superintendent of Yellowstone National Park, as postmaster. On October 13, 1853, Norris had the village of Pioneer surveyed. The village was incorporated in 1876. This *c.* 1900 photograph of the south side of Baubice Street was printed from a glass plate negative. (WCPL Photographic Archives.)

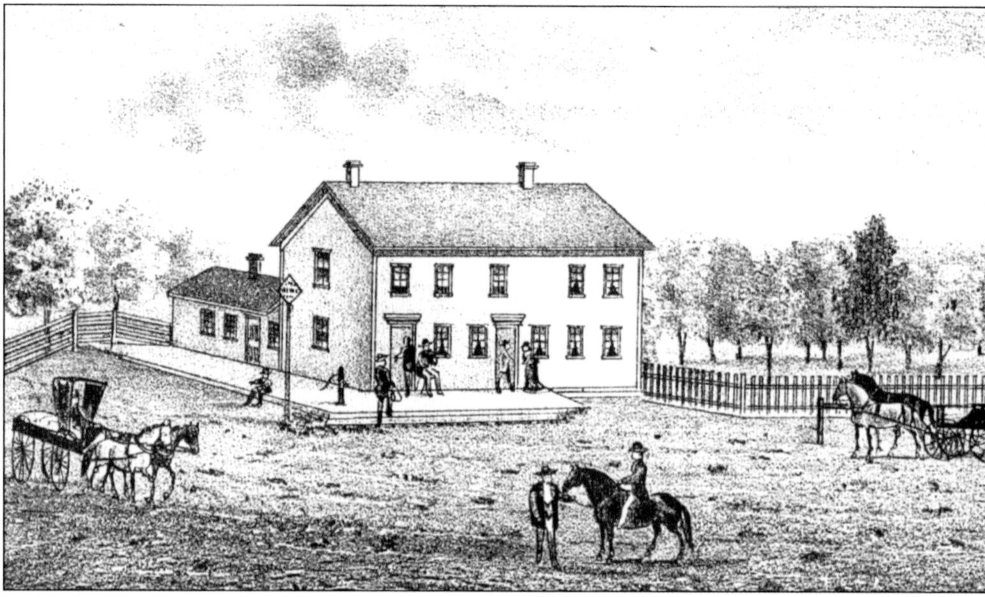

Columbia was surveyed on February 13, 1854, by John R. McConnell, William Rannels, and Alfred D. Gambell and is Northwest Township's sole platted town. An 1864 map shows Columbia was home to four stores, four physicians, a hotel, sawmill, cabinetmaker, photographer, wagon maker, blacksmith and gunsmith, tannery, school, and cemetery. The Columbia Hotel, above, stood on the southeast corner of Main and Water Streets. (Williams County atlas of 1874.)

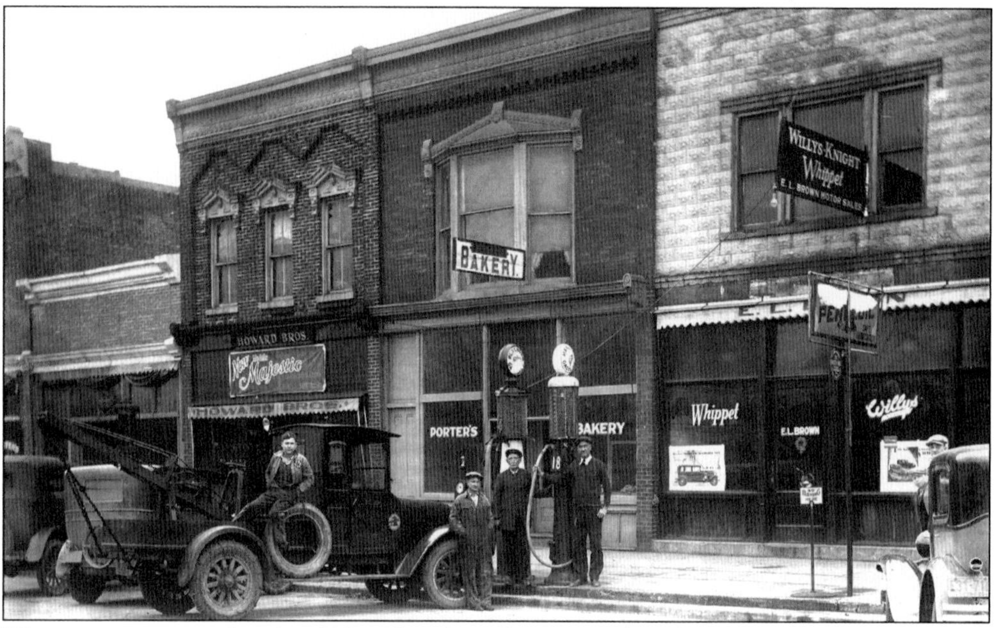

Edgerton was surveyed on April 22, 1854, where the proposed Michigan Southern and Northern Indiana Railroad crossed the St. Joseph River by John H. Sargent, acting chief engineer and superintendent of the railroad extension. The village was named after Alfred Peleg Edgerton, a local land agent, Ohio senator, and U.S. representative. The village was incorporated in 1865. This c. 1930 photograph shows Day Brothers' Garage on East Indiana Street. (Edgerton Historical Society.)

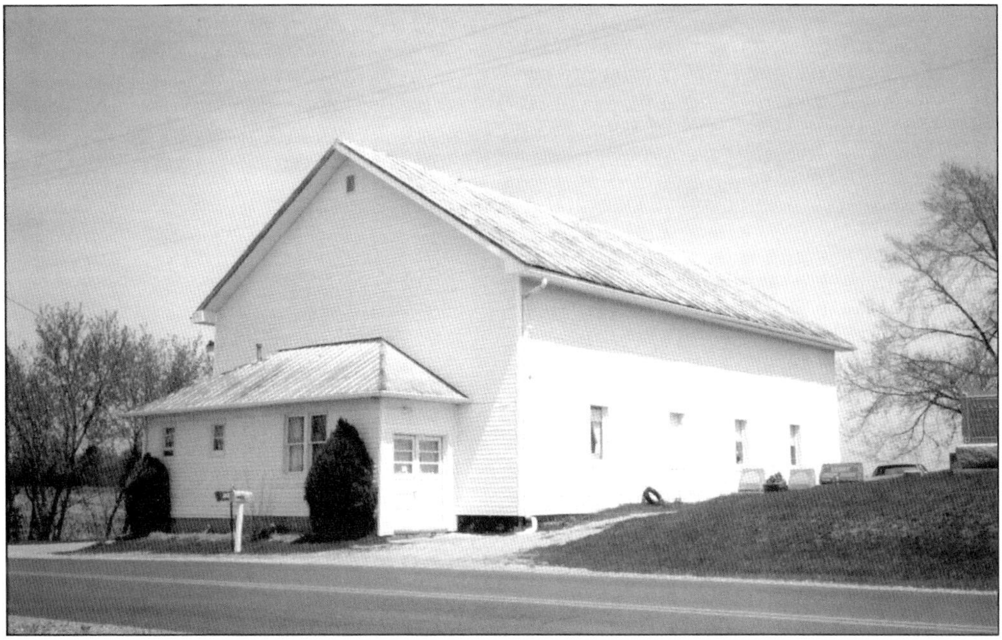

Primrose was surveyed on May 25, 1866, for 11 local landowners at County Roads R and 20. An 1864 map shows Alvord and Skiles' Store, a Universalist church, ashery, blacksmith shop, steam sawmill, post office, two cooper shops, Rev. Stacy Saye, and Drs. J. J. Struble and A. Netz at the future site of Primrose. In 1888, Walnut Grove Church of the Brethren erected this frame church south of Primrose.

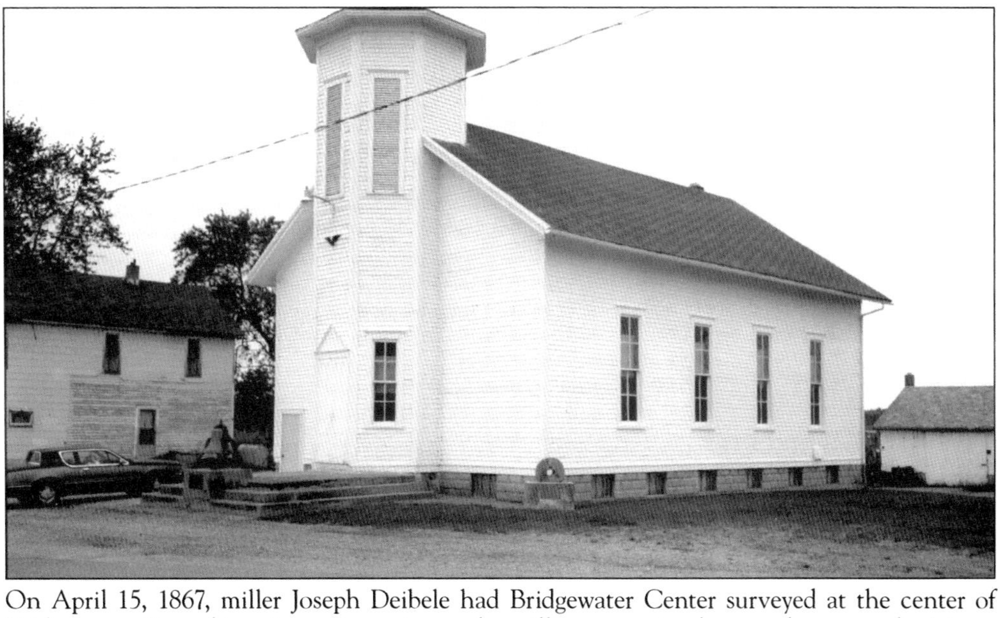

On April 15, 1867, miller Joseph Deibele had Bridgewater Center surveyed at the center of Bridgewater Township. At various times, the village contained general stores, physicians, a sawmill, gristmill, ashery, blacksmith shop, post office, township hall, town band, wagon shop, barbershop, Grange hall, Gleaners hall, and school. The Bridgewater Center Methodist Episcopal Church above was constructed in 1875. The building was sold to Bridgewater Township in 1929.

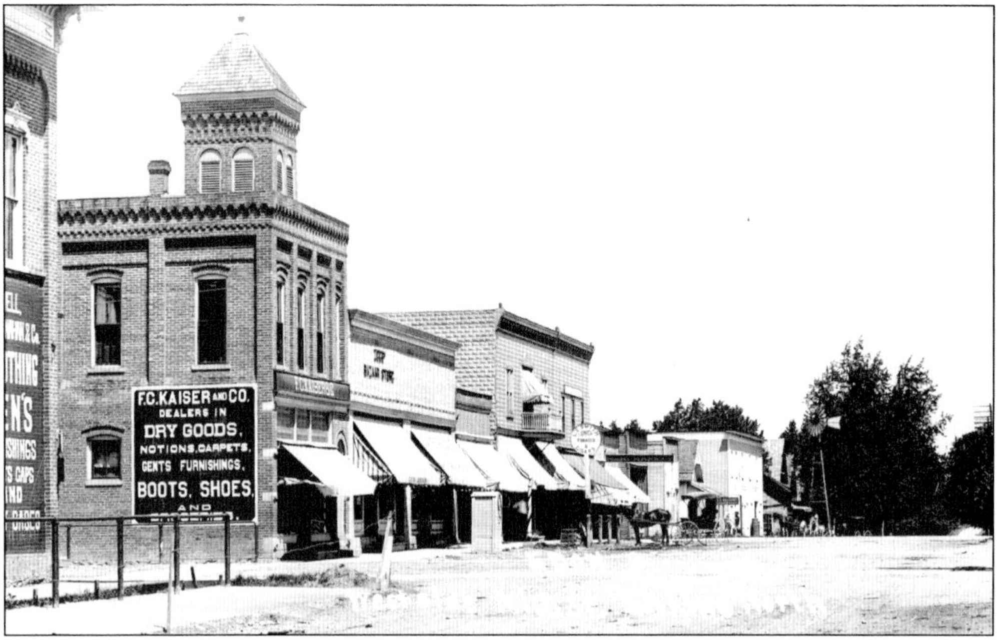

On September 21, 1867, Weston was surveyed in Florence Township by 12 local landowners. In 1874, the village was incorporated and its name changed to Edon, the name of the post office established in Weston in 1867. This c. 1900 photograph was taken looking north on Michigan Street from Indiana Street. (WCPL Photographic Archives.)

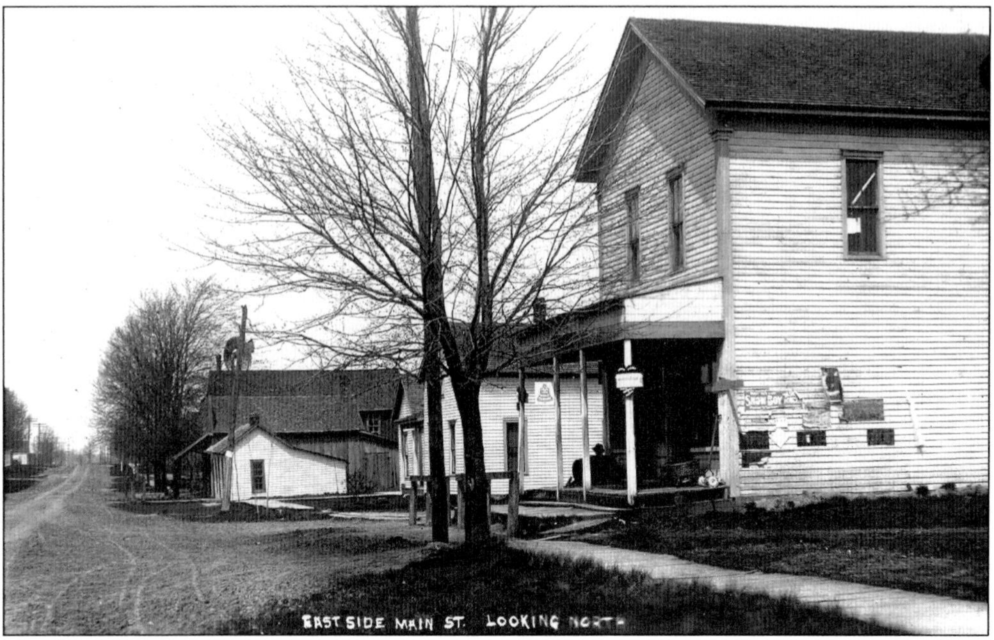

Melbern was platted on June 27, 1856, as Kansas on the north side of the Michigan Southern and Northern Indiana Railroad by William Shafer, John Neihardt, Jacob Neihardt, and John Fritch. On August 21, 1869, Kansas was replatted as Melbern, the name of the post office established in Kansas in 1866. This c. 1910 photograph shows the east side of Main Street looking north.

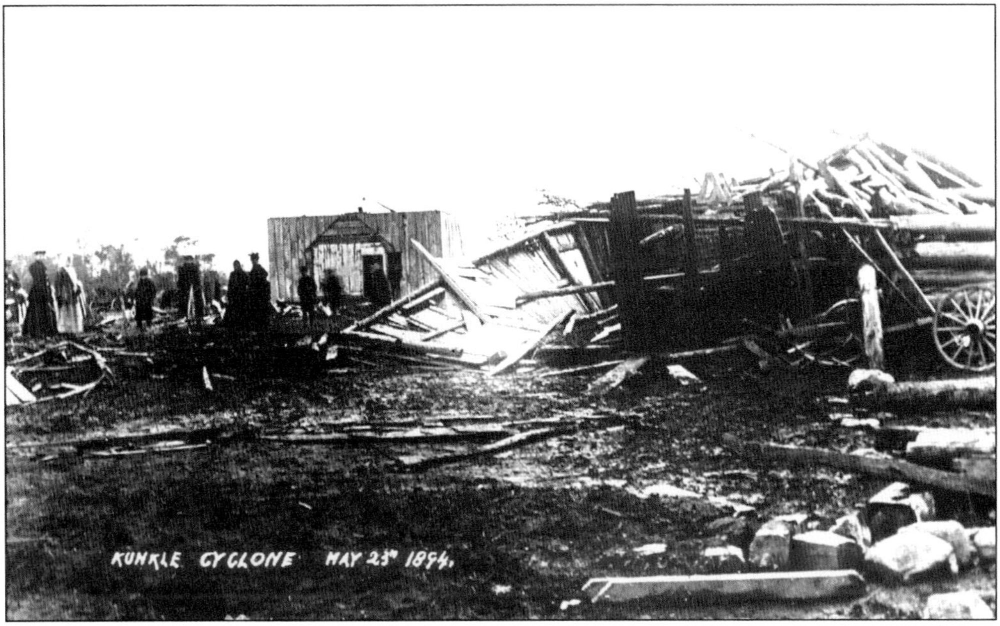

Kunklesville (later shortened to Kunkle) was surveyed on December 8, 1875, and was Williams County's smallest platted village with a mere eight lots. The village was named after its founders, Henry and Matilda Kunkle. On May 17, 1894, a tornado south of Kunkle killed four people, injured several others, and destroyed or damaged numerous buildings. (WCPL Photographic Archives.)

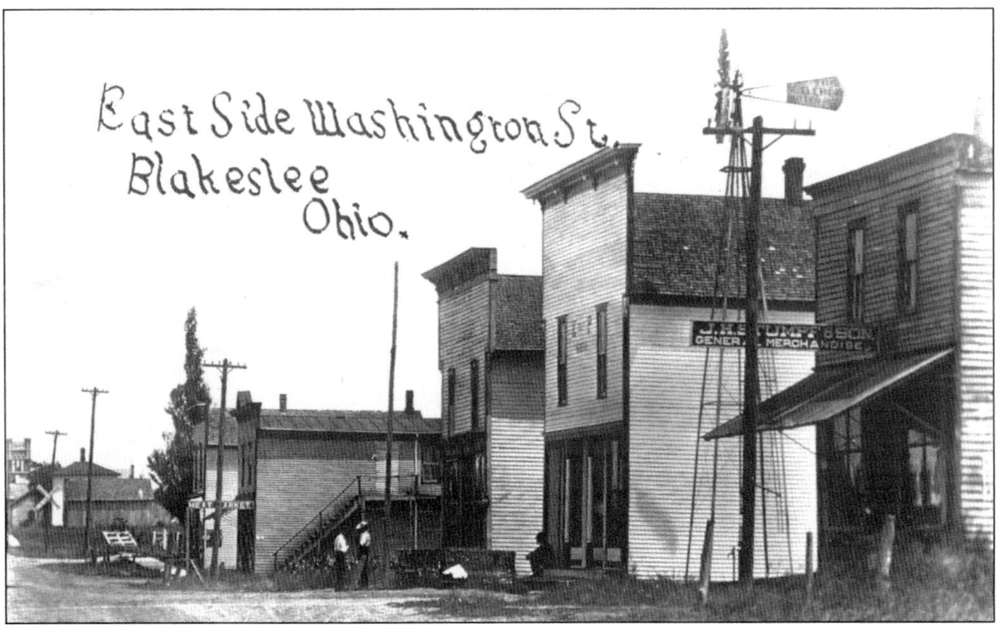

In 1880, Blakeslee Post Office, named after Bryan attorney Schuyler E. Blakeslee, was established at John Chilcote's Florence Township store. When the Detroit, Butler and St. Louis Railroad (later the Wabash and today the Norfolk Southern) was surveyed through John Boman's farm, he platted 56 lots on November 8, 1880, and christened the town Blakeslee. This *c.* 1909 image shows the east side of Washington Street looking north.

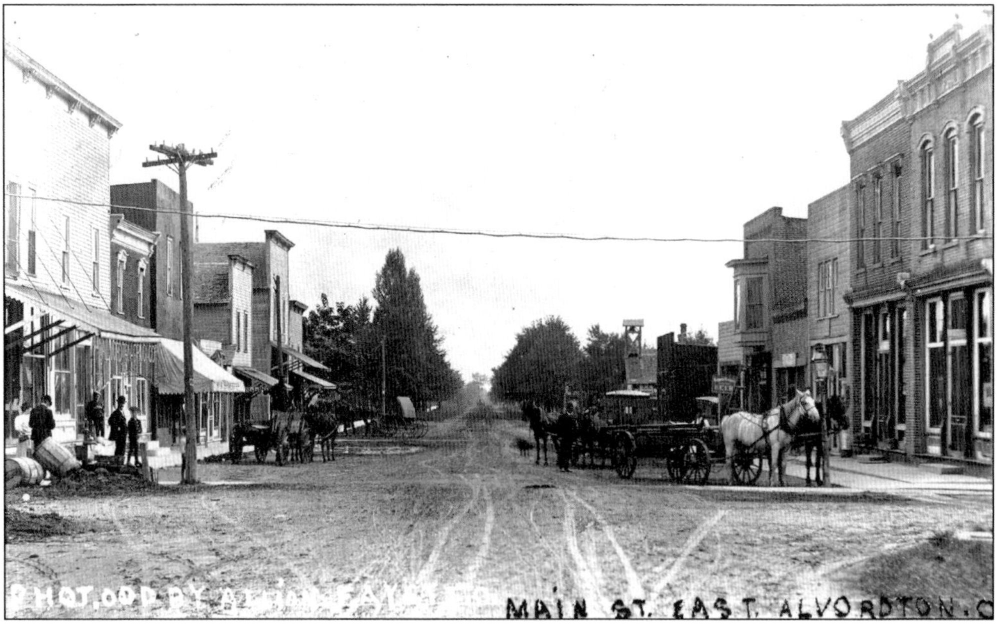

In 1854, Millcreek Center was surveyed near the center of Millcreek Township. It was replatted as Alvordton by Henry D. Alvord on February 18, 1881. Construction of the Wabash Railroad in 1881 and the Cincinnati, Jackson and Mackinaw Railroad in 1887 boosted Alvordton's fortunes. Alvordton was incorporated in 1891; its citizens revoked incorporation in 2007. This c. 1908 photograph was taken looking east on Main Street from Michigan Avenue.

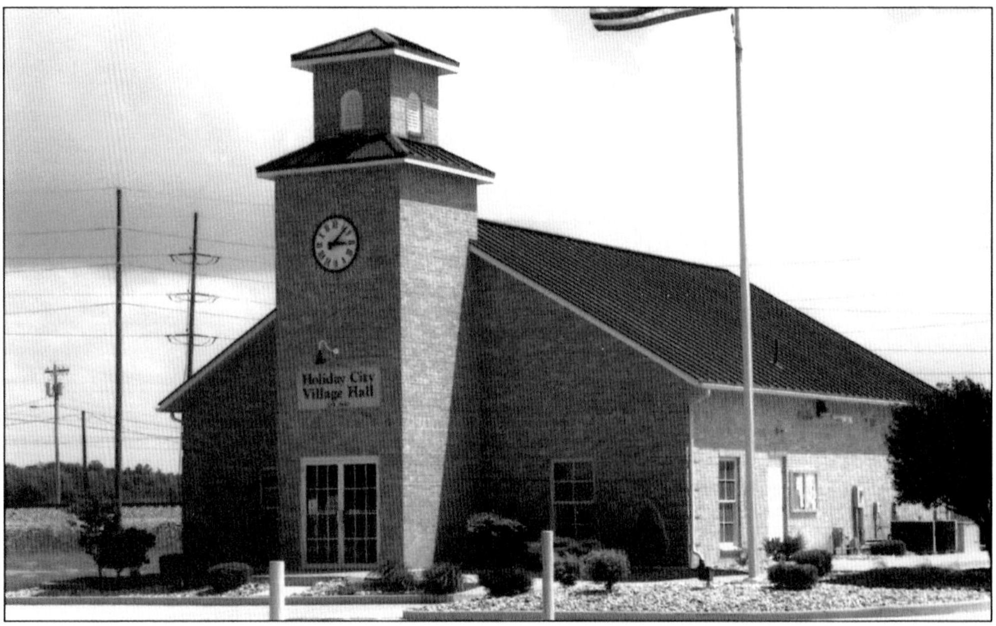

Williams County's newest village is Holiday City, created by local residents and business representatives as a means of establishing a municipal electric utility. In September 1991, Williams County commissioners approved incorporation of the village, but legal challenges delayed this action until June 24, 1997. In 2003, this village hall was completed south of County Road M west of Ohio 15. (Mike Damschroder.)

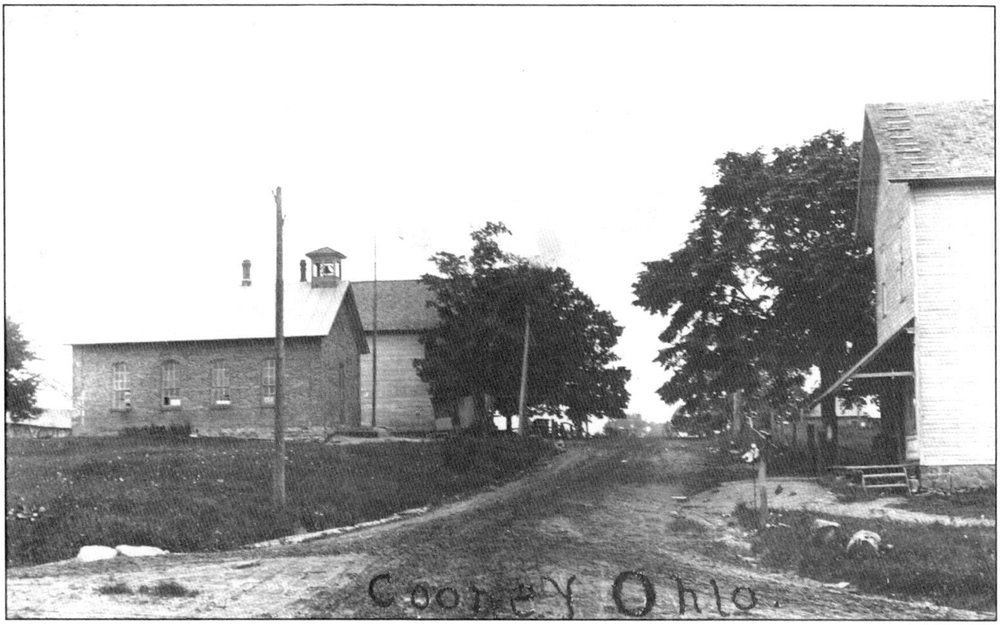

Cooney was a rural economic center at Ohio 49 and County Road P.50 in Northwest Township that was originally known as Northwest Center due to its location. This *c.* 1905 photograph taken looking north on Ohio 49 shows, from left to right, Cooney's one-room brick schoolhouse, Northwest Lodge No. 722 Independent Order of Odd Fellows, and Northwest Grange No. 413.

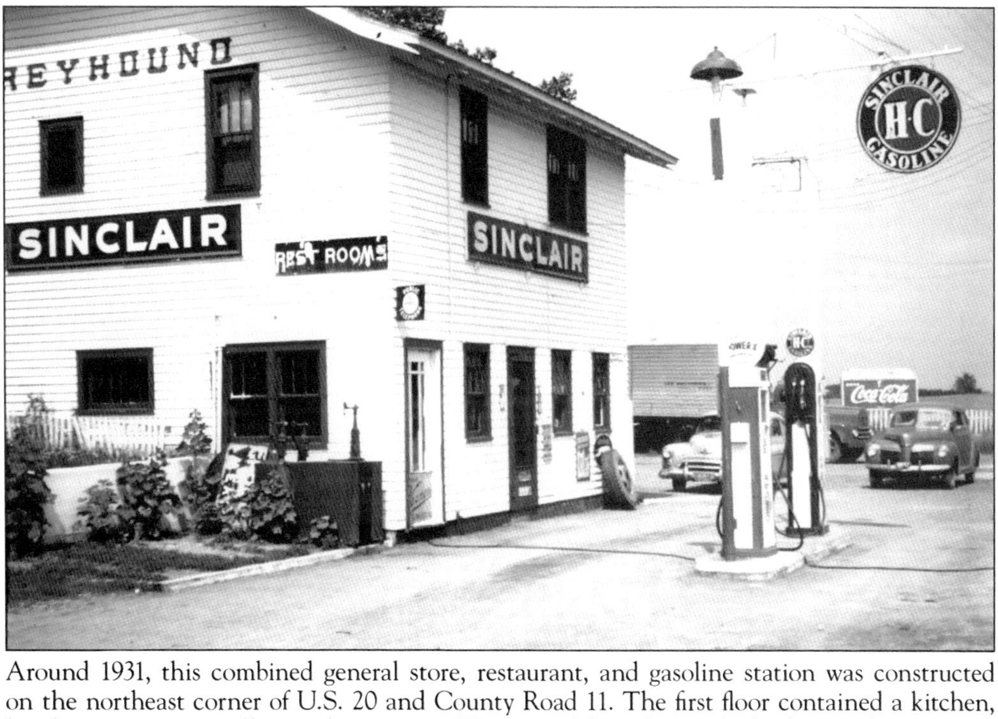

Around 1931, this combined general store, restaurant, and gasoline station was constructed on the northeast corner of U.S. 20 and County Road 11. The first floor contained a kitchen, lunchroom, grocery, office, and restrooms. The second floor featured a bathroom, living room, dining room, and two bedrooms. By 1941, the crossroads became known as Greyhound because of its bus stop. The business closed about 1978. (Alan Benjamin.)

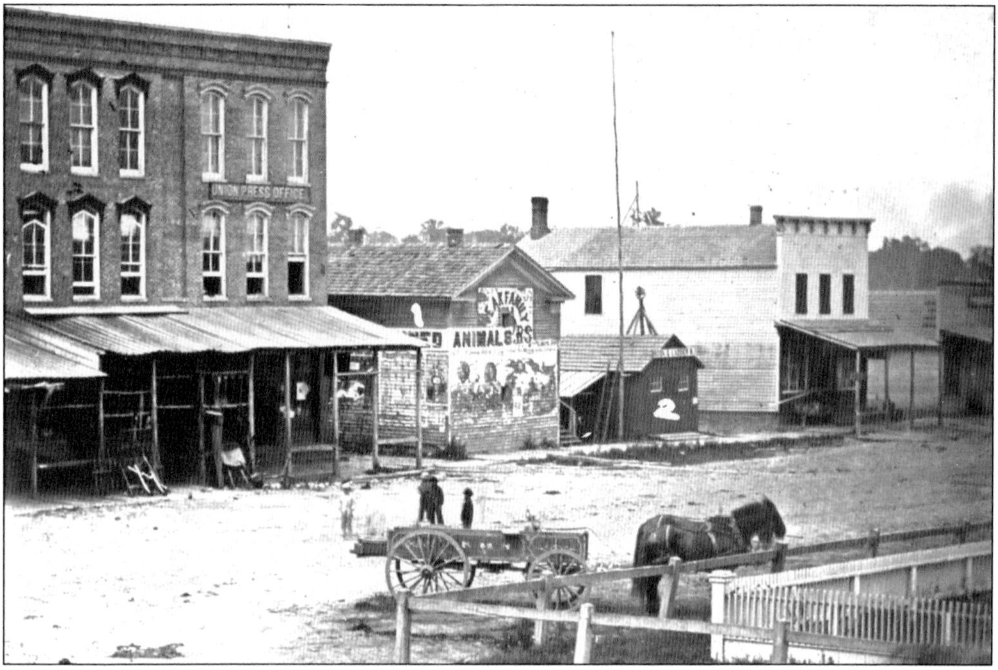

This is the north side of Bryan's courthouse square in 1864–1865. The brick Union Block was constructed in 1859 and still stands. The building plastered with posters is the Williams County jail, built of logs covered by wooden siding. The small building housed the equipment of Bryan's first fire department, Hook and Ladder Company No. 1. The two frame buildings on the right are groceries.

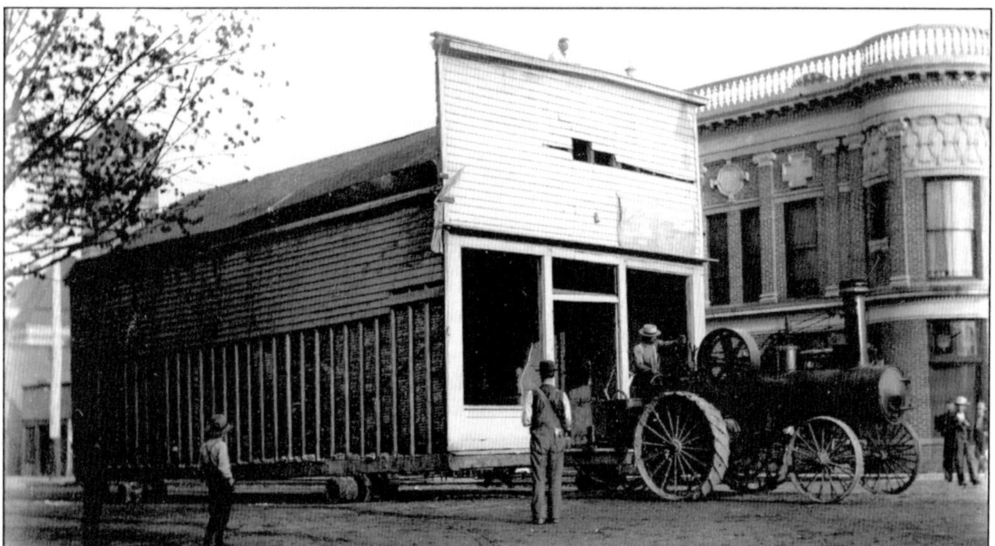

One of Bryan's features during its "Fountain City" period was wide dirt streets leveled by horse-drawn scrapers. This *c.* 1900 photograph shows a steam-powered traction engine moving a building past the Hotel Williams—later known as the Hotel Elder—at the southeast corner of High and Beech Streets. The Williams County Courthouse tower is visible through the branches on the left. (WCPL Photographic Archives.)

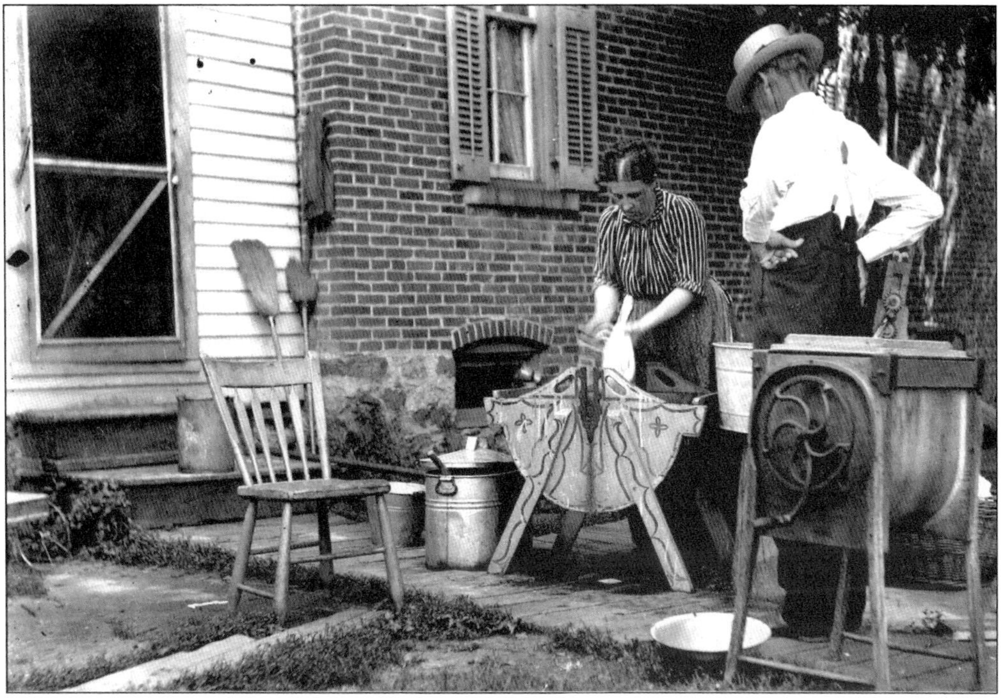

Before modern appliances, housework was much more labor intensive and time consuming. In this *c.* 1900 photograph taken on Bryan's West High Street, a woman washes clothes using a manual washing machine. (WCPL Photographic Archives.)

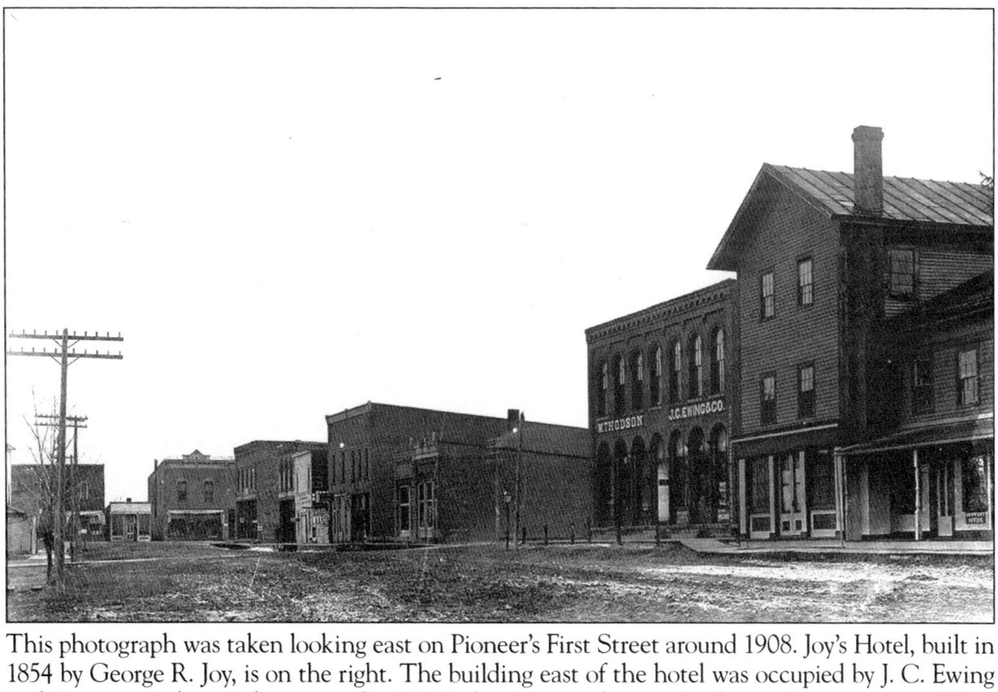

This photograph was taken looking east on Pioneer's First Street around 1908. Joy's Hotel, built in 1854 by George R. Joy, is on the right. The building east of the hotel was occupied by J. C. Ewing and Company's dry goods store and M. T. Hodson's general store. At the southwest corner of First and State Streets was Hadley's, which sold dry goods, shoes, and clothing from 1868 to 1963.

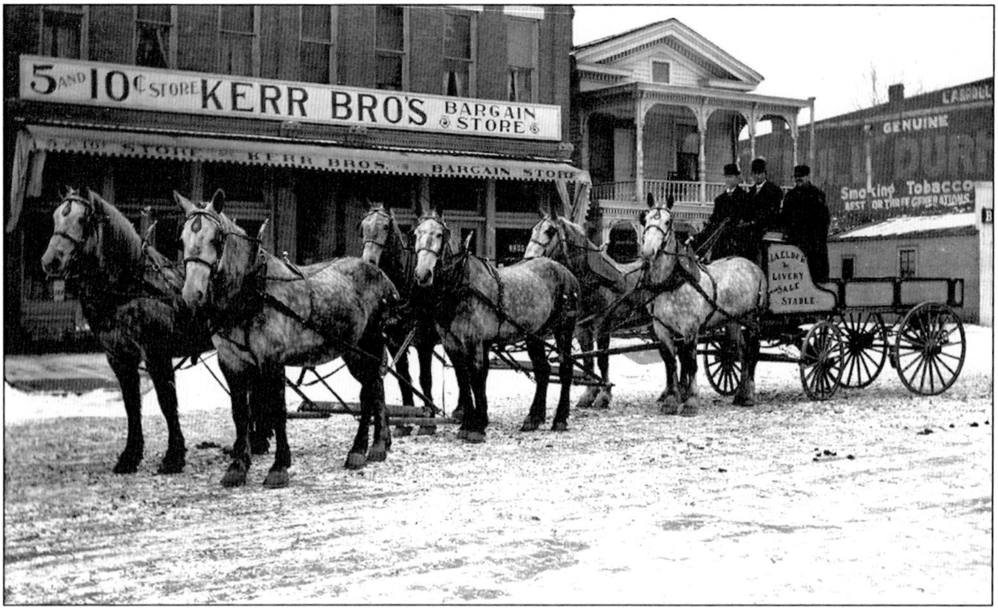

A six-horse hitch from James A. Elder's livery and sale stable pauses on the west side of Bryan's square (Lynn Street). The house to the right of Kerr Brothers' bargain store was built in 1844 and occupied for many years by attorney Schuyler E. Blakeslee. When the Bryan Theater was built on the site in 1940, the house was moved to 530 South Cherry Street. (WCPL Photographic Archives.)

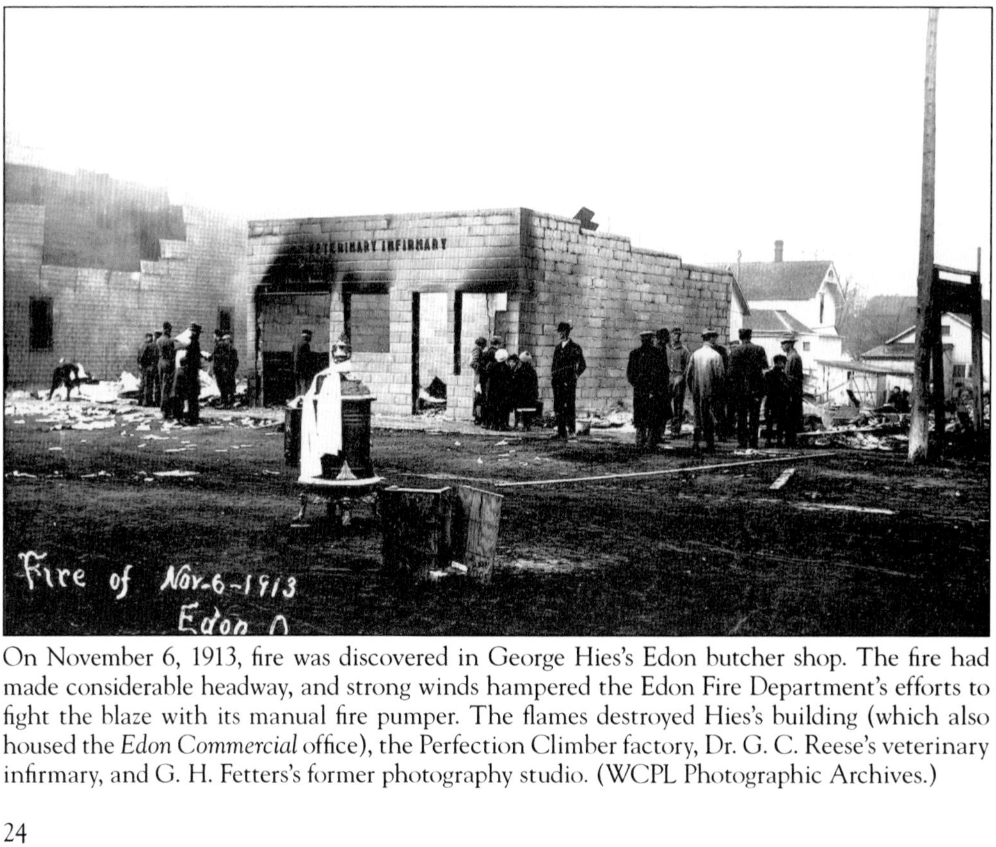

On November 6, 1913, fire was discovered in George Hies's Edon butcher shop. The fire had made considerable headway, and strong winds hampered the Edon Fire Department's efforts to fight the blaze with its manual fire pumper. The flames destroyed Hies's building (which also housed the *Edon Commercial* office), the Perfection Climber factory, Dr. G. C. Reese's veterinary infirmary, and G. H. Fetters's former photography studio. (WCPL Photographic Archives.)

Two

AGRIBUSINESS

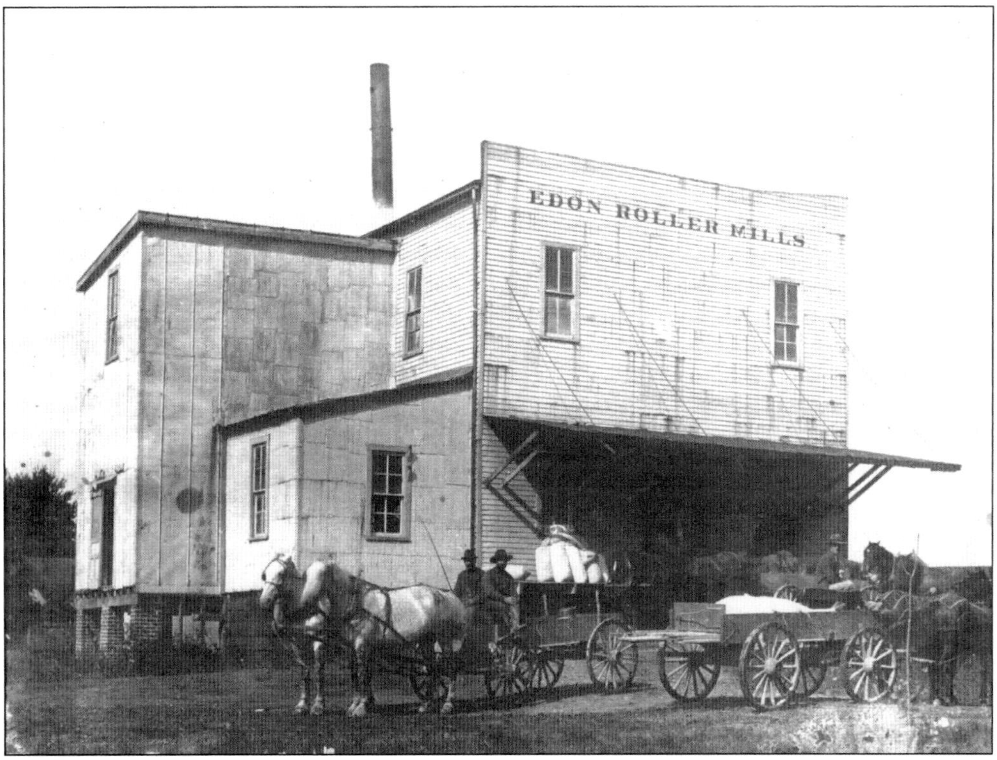

Mills were among Williams County's first businesses and helped tame the wilderness. Sawmills supplied lumber that was used to replace crude log structures with frame buildings. Gristmills offered a market for locally grown grain and produced cornmeal and flour. Mill products were considered valuable commodities. Early mills harnessed the power of creeks or rivers; later boilers, gasoline engines, and electricity were used. By the 1880s, roller mills that used metal rollers to produce finer, more consistent flour began to appear. This *c.* 1910 photograph shows the Edon Roller Mills.

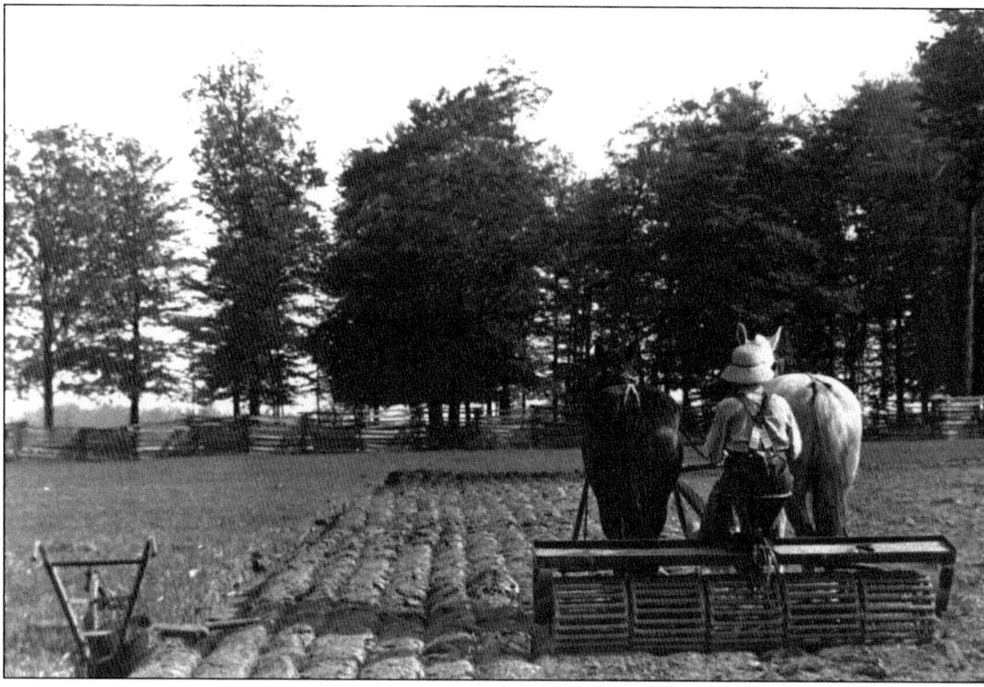

Before motorized equipment, farmwork was performed manually or with the aid of oxen or horses. Millcreek Township farmer LeRoy Blaker's team pulls a cyclone land roller in this May 1911 photograph, while a horse-drawn walking plow rests in a furrow on the left. Blaker recalled that farmers walked eight miles while plowing each acre and could plow two acres in 10 hours with two good horses. (Williams County Historical Society.)

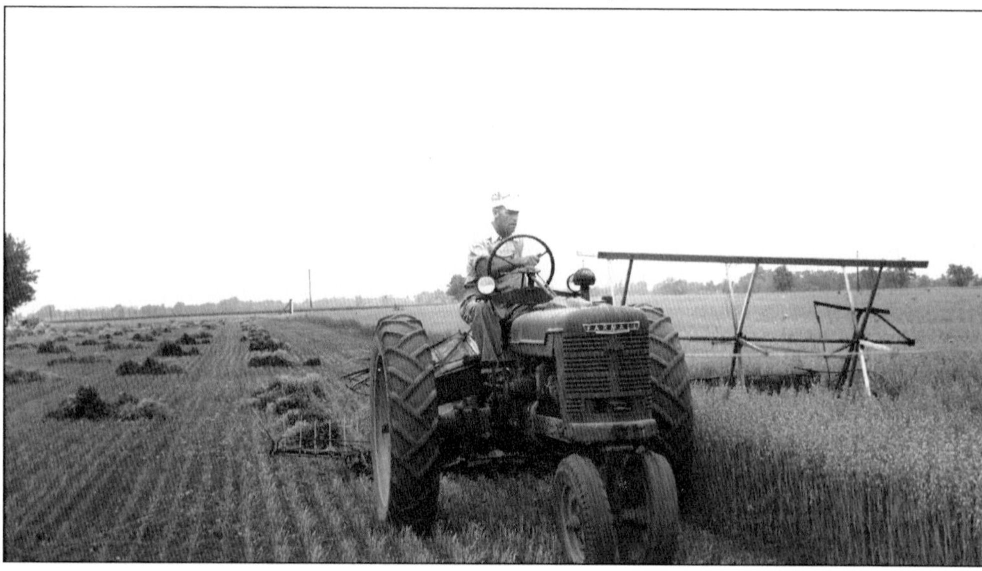

The area's first settlers used sickles, scythes, or grain cradles to harvest grain by hand. Horse-drawn reapers that cut grain were demonstrated in Williams County by the 1850s. In the 1880s, farmers began using horse-drawn binders, which cut grain and bundled the stalks for threshing. In this *c.* 1953 photograph, a farmer pulls a left-handed binder using a tractor. (WCPL Photographic Archives.)

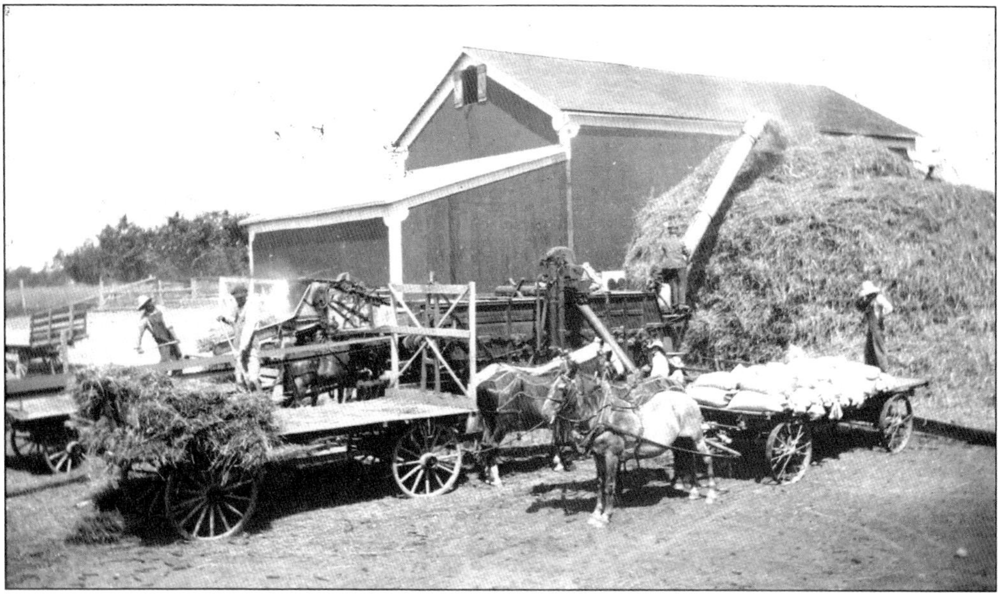

Local pioneers separated grain from straw and chaff with flails or trampling by animals. By the late 1800s, threshing machines powered by steam engines were common. In this *c.* 1915 Edgerton area photograph, farmers use pitchforks to unload wheat bundles from a wagon into a threshing machine. The thresher filled bags with grain on the right and blew straw into a stack at the rear.

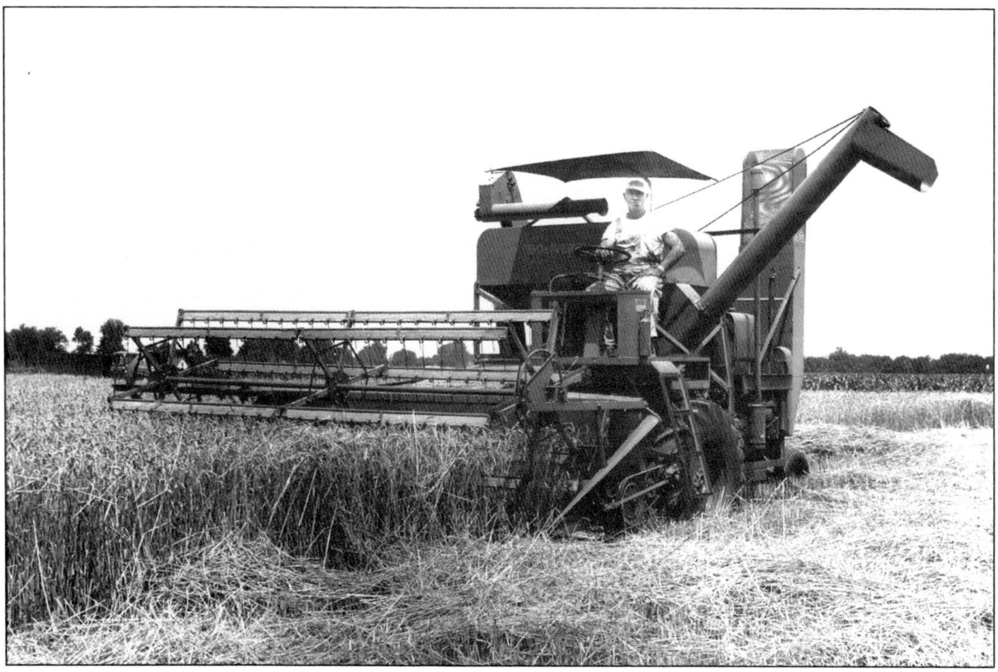

By the 1930s, combines—so called because they combined the functions of a reaper and threshing machine—were used locally to harvest grain. Early combines were drawn by tractors; this *c.* 1953 photograph shows a self-propelled Oliver combine. (WCPL Photographic Archives.)

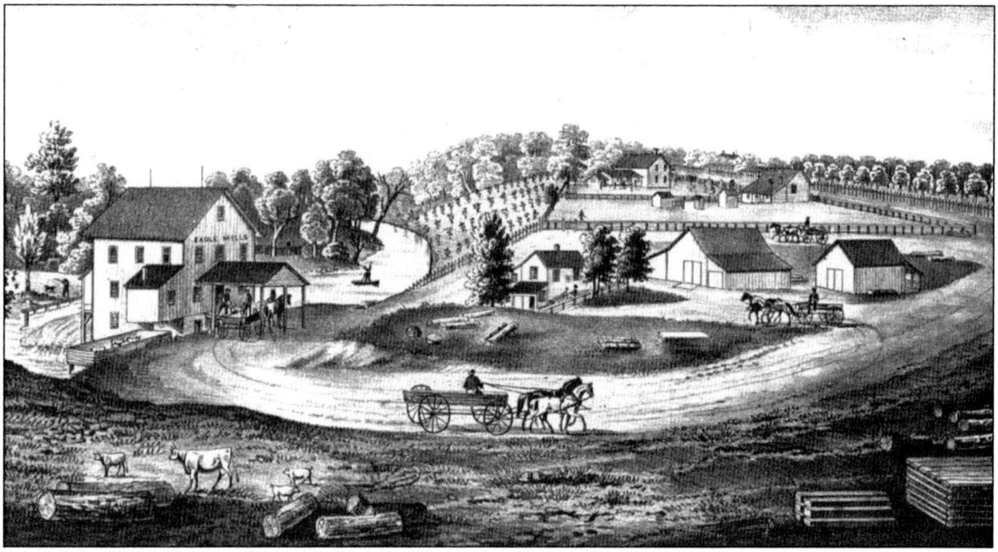

Around 1864, John Chappuis built this water-powered gristmill and sawmill on the Tiffin River south of Ohio 34 and County Road 20.50 in Springfield Township. Chappuis, like many Stryker area settlers, was born in France. Chappuis sold the mill in 1870, and it operated under various owners and names—including Eagle Mills—until destroyed by fire on July 1, 1883. (Williams County atlas of 1874.)

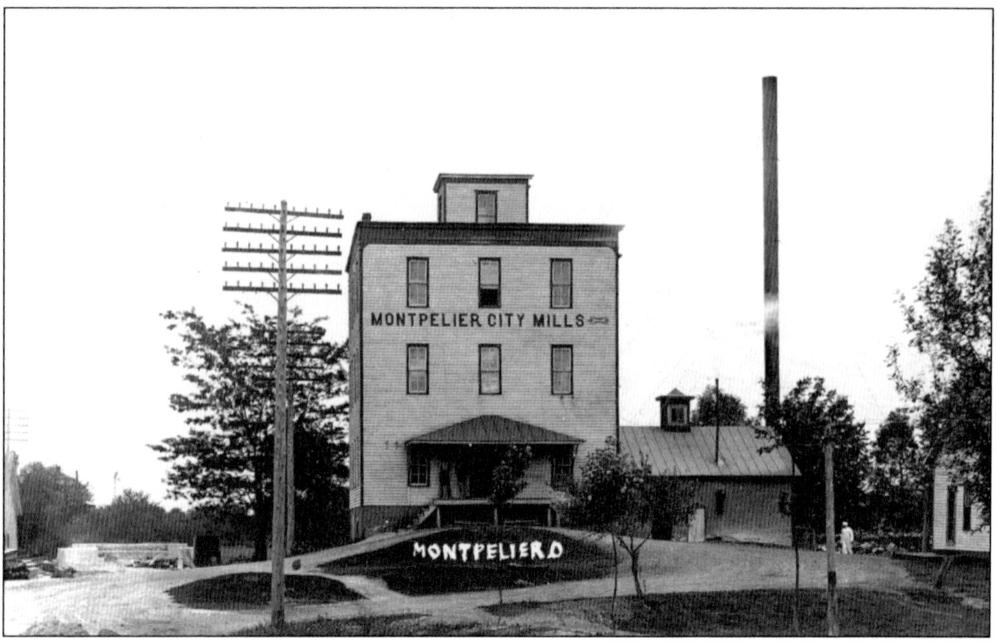

Mills were an important part of Montpelier's early economy and development. By 1845, a water-powered gristmill was constructed on the east side of Monroe Street near the St. Joseph River. In 1883, Joseph Deibele built this steam-powered gristmill near the old mill. The mill building was dismantled in 1927.

Philip and Gustave Christman constructed this mill and elevator on the west side of Walnut Street south of the Lake Shore and Michigan Southern Railroad in Bryan, replacing a mill that burned in 1896. It was one of the largest operations of its kind in this part of the state with a capacity of 125 barrels of flour per day. Fire destroyed the Christman Mill and Elevator in December 1918. (WCPL Photographic Archives.)

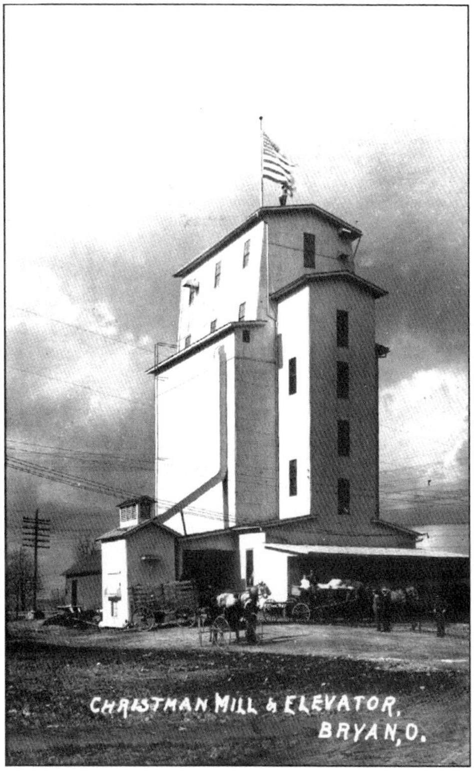

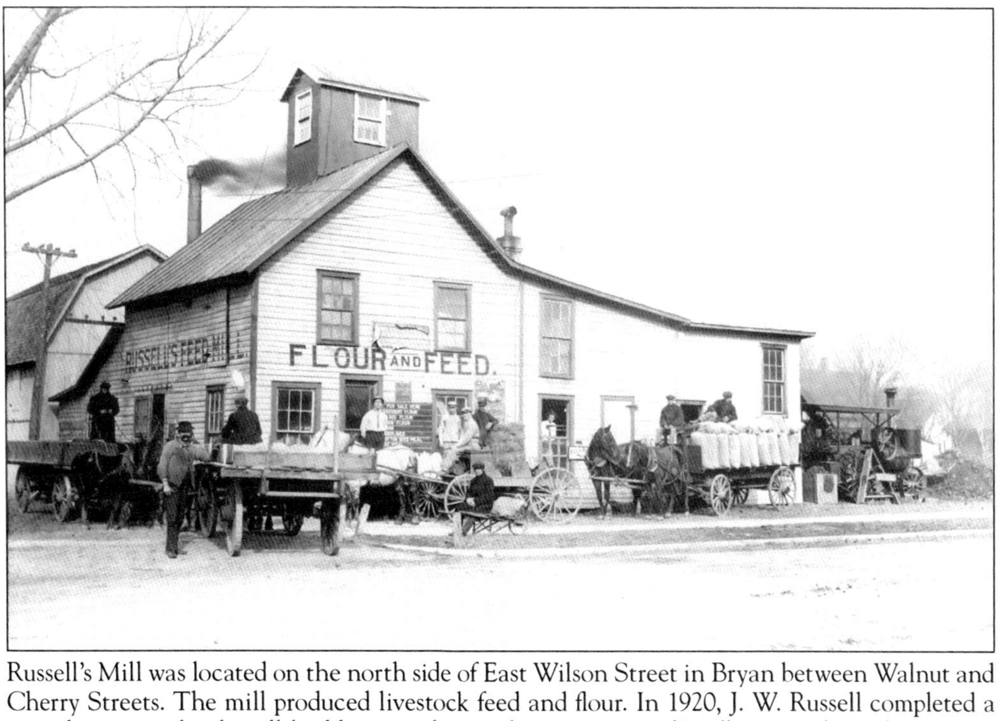

Russell's Mill was located on the north side of East Wilson Street in Bryan between Walnut and Cherry Streets. The mill produced livestock feed and flour. In 1920, J. W. Russell completed a new three-story brick mill building on the southwest corner of Mulberry and Garden Streets next to the Cincinnati Northern Railroad. (WCPL Photographic Archives.)

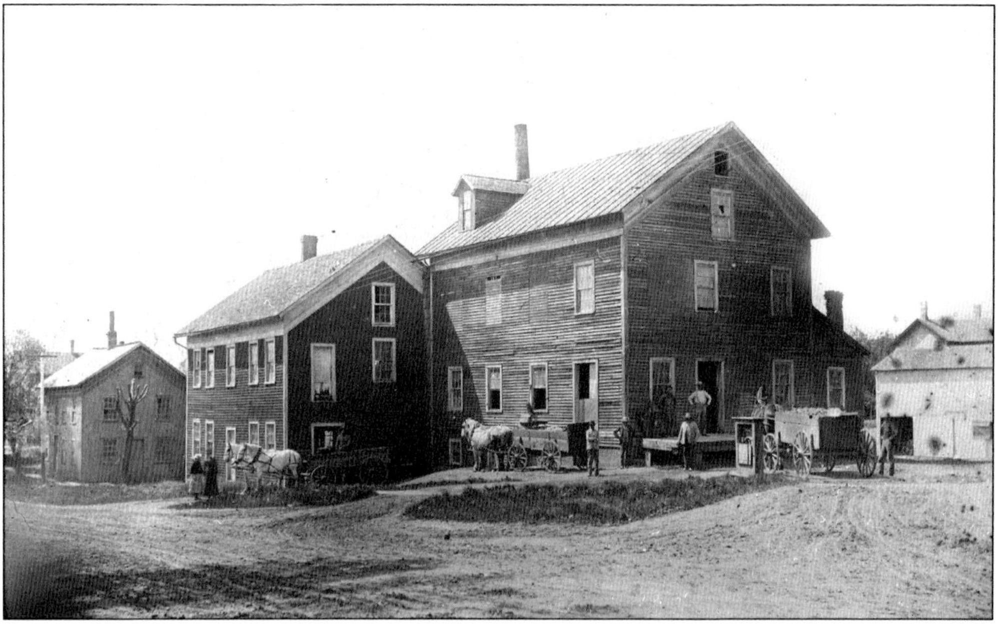

John Zimmerman operated the West Unity Flouring Mills at West Jackson Street and U.S. 127 from 1905 to 1935. The mill was originally equipped with millstones and later converted to the roller mill process. Zimmerman delivered his "Favorite" brand flour to area families, grocers, and bakers. The *c.* 1905 photograph above shows a team and wagon leaving the mill scales with another waiting to be weighed. Below, Zimmerman (left) and an unidentified worker are shown inside the building next to the roller mills. (WCPL Photographic Archives.)

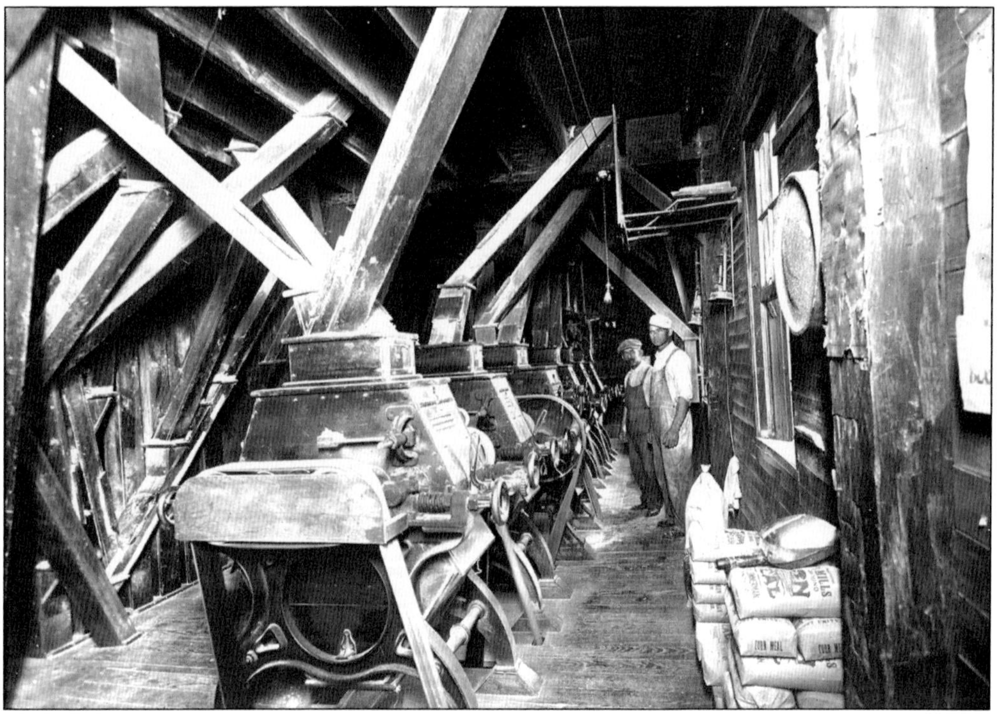

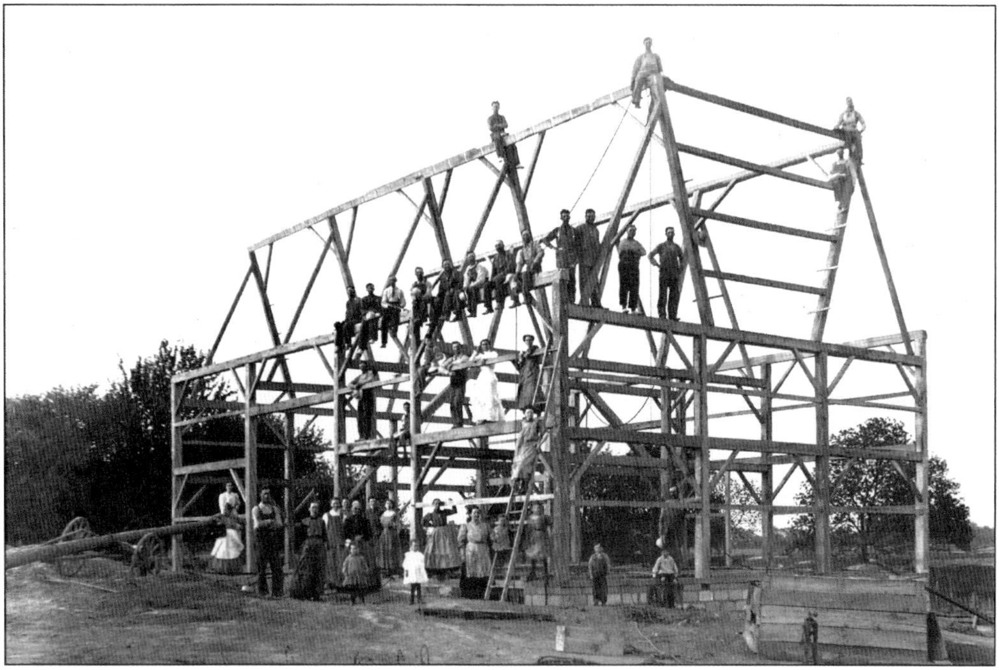

Local farmers have long used barns to shelter livestock and store hay, straw, grain, and farm equipment. This May 1911 photograph shows a barn raising on the Wade Rethmel farm south of Evansport. Barn raisings were community events—neighbors, friends, and family members of all ages gathered to construct a barn. While men built the barn, youngsters carried water and fetched needed items, and women prepared bountiful meals for participants.

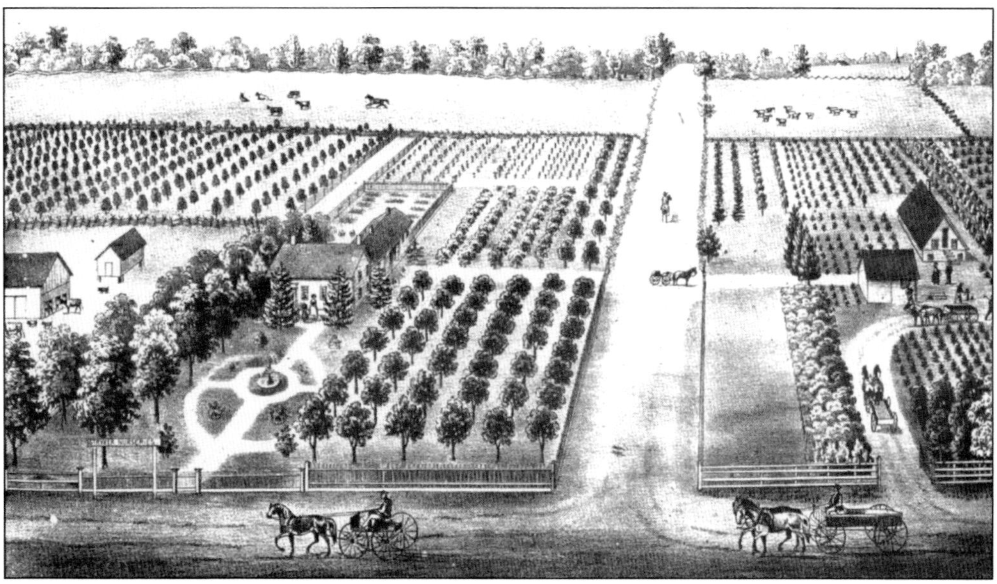

By 1861, Joseph Boynton established the Stryker Nurseries on about 20 acres at Ohio 34 and County Road 20.50. Boynton's business prospered, and by 1871, he had a remarkable 200,000 fruit and ornamental trees for sale. In the late 1870s, Boynton experienced financial difficulties and lost his business. The nurseries continued under other ownership until an 1881 fire consumed several buildings on the site. (Williams County atlas of 1874.)

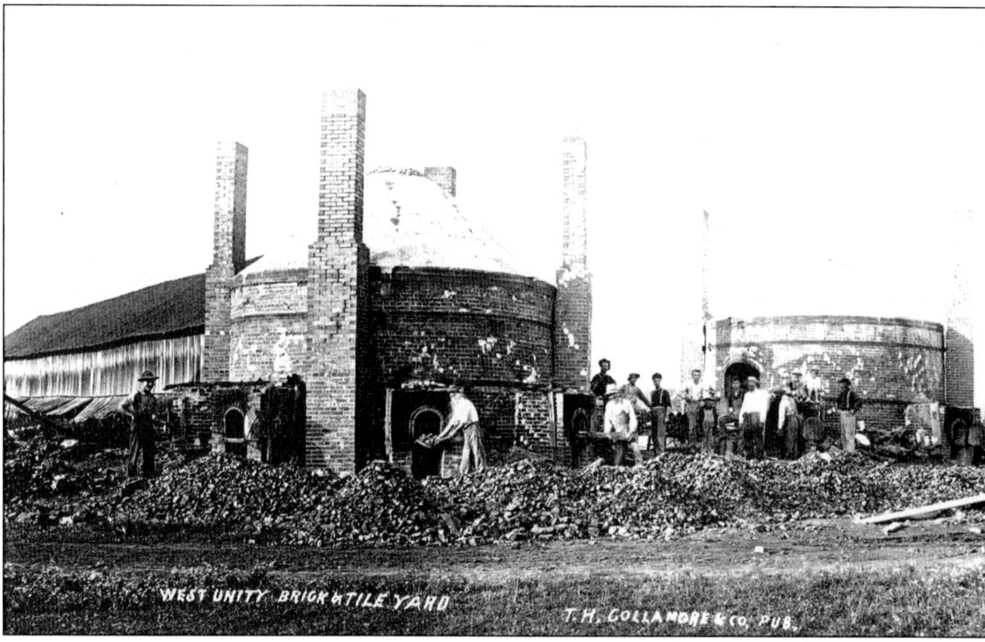

Draining and tiling allowed local pioneers to convert heavily forested, swampy acreage into productive farms. Williams County is blessed with abundant clay, providing raw material for numerous brick and tile factories established in the 1800s. Clay was formed into brick or tile, dried, and baked or fired in kilns like those above to create finished products. Local brick and tile production continued well into the 1900s. (WCPL Photographic Archives.)

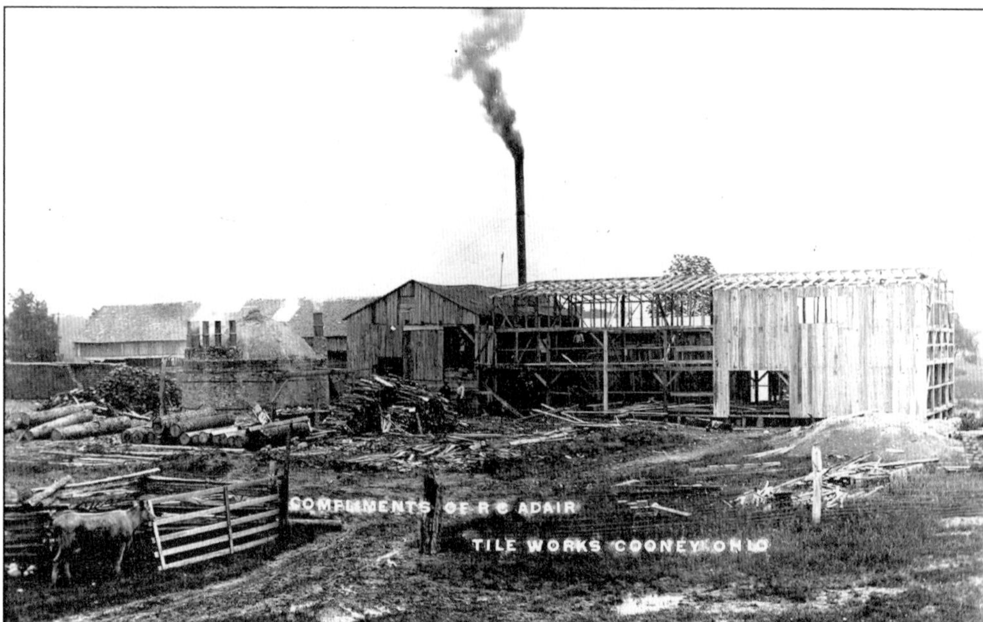

About 1880, Cornelius P. Taylor established a brick and tile mill on the west side of Ohio 49 one-half mile north of Cooney that provided part-time employment for many area laborers. In 1906, R. Clarence Adair purchased the industry and operated it until competition and dwindling markets forced abandonment of the once thriving enterprise about 1915.

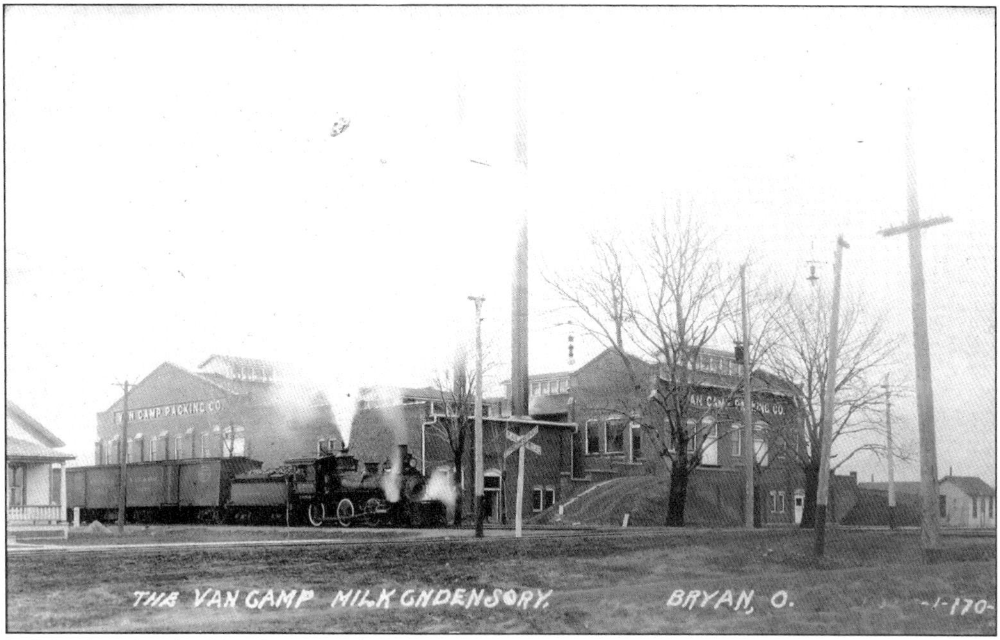

In March 1909, the Van Camp Packing Company began production at this milk evaporating plant (or condensery) on East High Street in Bryan where the Cincinnati Northern Railroad and the Toledo and Indiana interurban railway intersected. The condensery was the largest building in town at the time and was reportedly "the most modern, best-equipped milk evaporating plant in the United States."

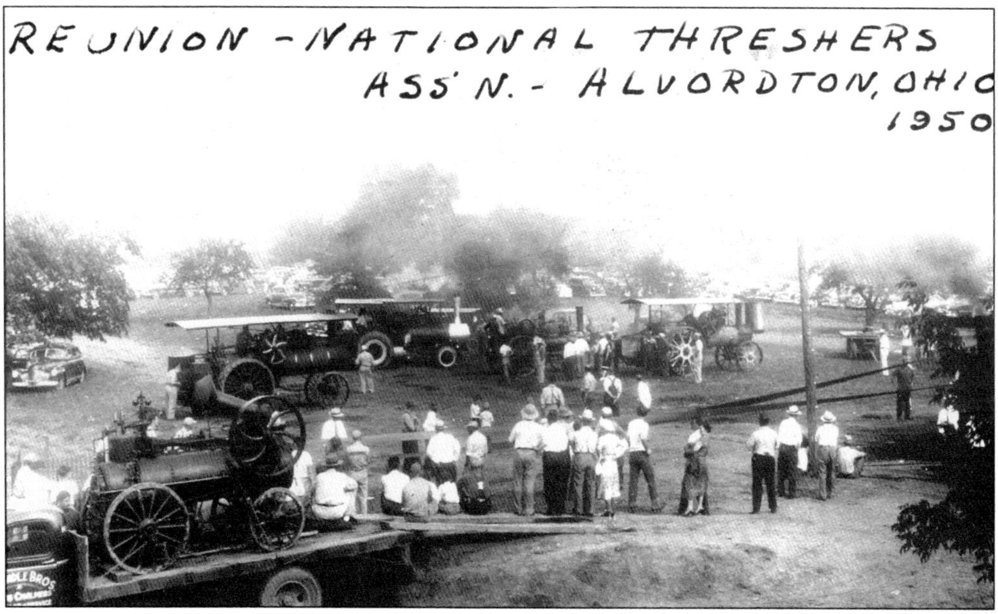

The National Threshers Association was founded by LeRoy and Lucile Blaker of rural Alvordton. The steam engine enthusiasts' first annual reunions were held on the Blaker farm, but growing attendance forced a move to the Williams County Fairgrounds in 1952. Since 1965 the reunion has been held at the Fulton County Fairgrounds in Wauseon.

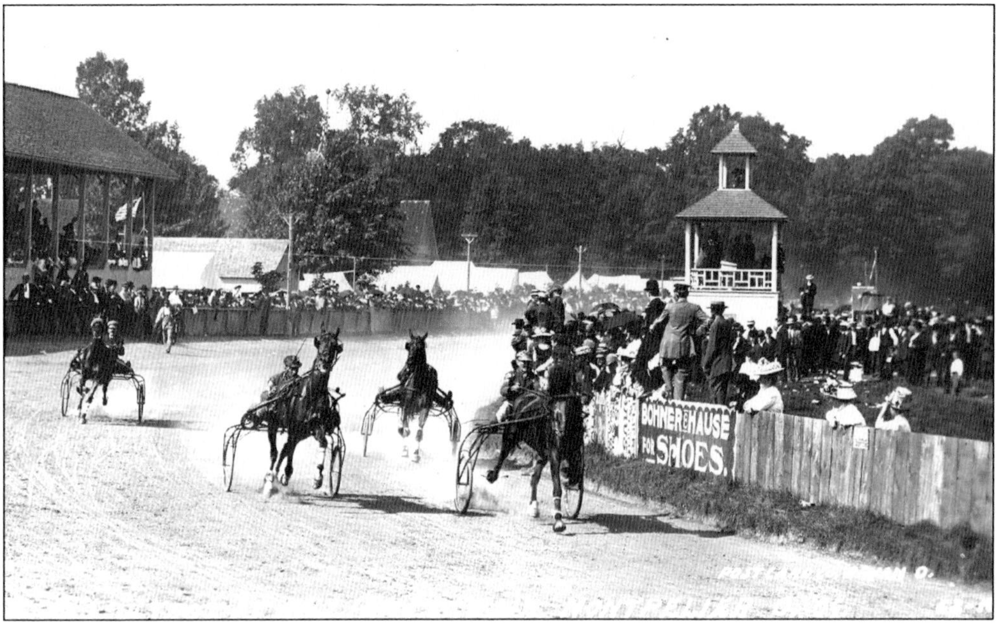

On June 14, 1856, the Williams County Agricultural Society was organized. On October 7–8, 1856, the first Williams County Fair was held on the courthouse square in Bryan. The fair was held at various Bryan locations for 30 years. In 1885, the Montpelier Union Agriculture Company was organized and developed a fairgrounds on Montpelier's east side. In 1886, two local fairs were held—the Williams County Fair in Bryan and the Montpelier Fair. The Montpelier Fair prospered for 15 years, and the Williams County Fair was discontinued. By 1899, the Montpelier Fair was a bust. In 1900, the Williams County Agricultural Society purchased the Montpelier fairgrounds and has held the Williams County Fair there ever since. These 1909 photographs show a harness race (above) while below, finely dressed men and women crowd the fair's midway. (Above, WCPL Photographic Archives.)

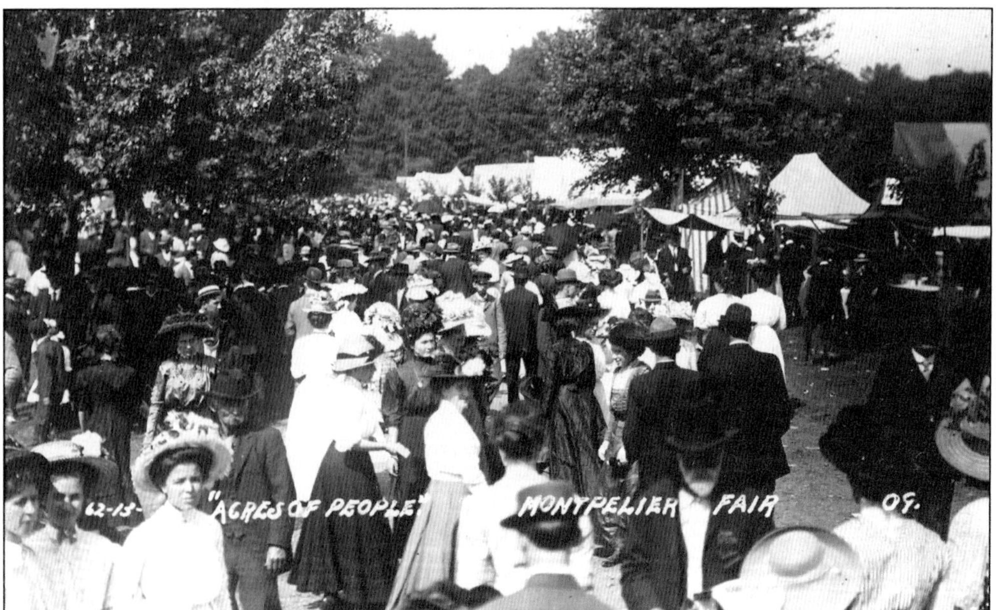

Three

Business and Industry

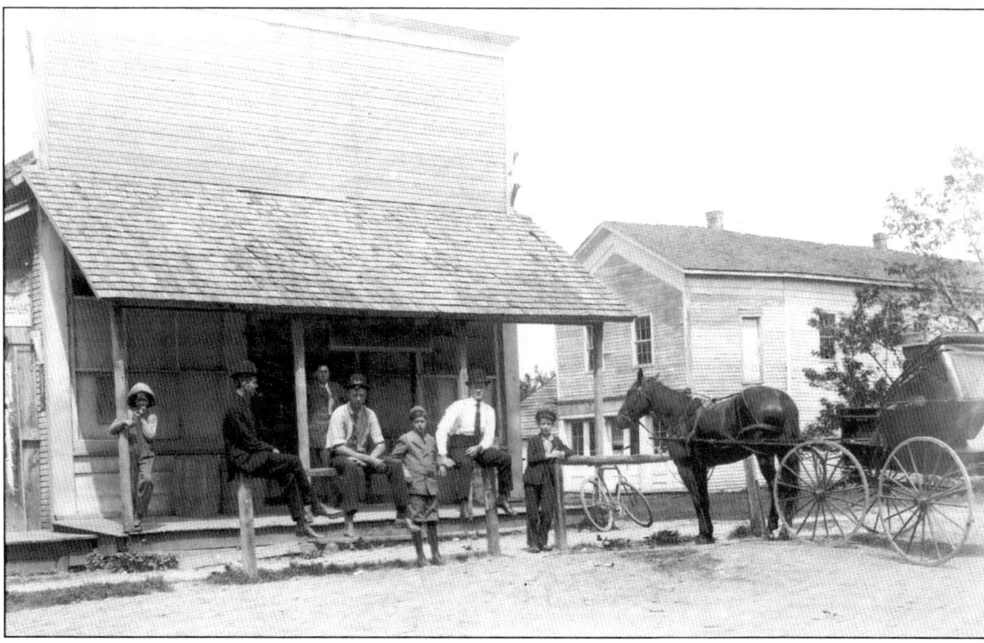

The general store on the southwest corner of North and High (U.S. 127) Streets in Pulaski was one of Williams County's first businesses. The store is believed to have been opened prior to 1837 by Pulaski's founder, John Perkins. In 1890, the store was destroyed by fire and was replaced by the frame building above. When the store closed in April 1985, it ended a string of nearly 150 years in business at the same location. W. J. Carroll's former Farmers Grocery building is on the right. (WCPL Photographic Archives.)

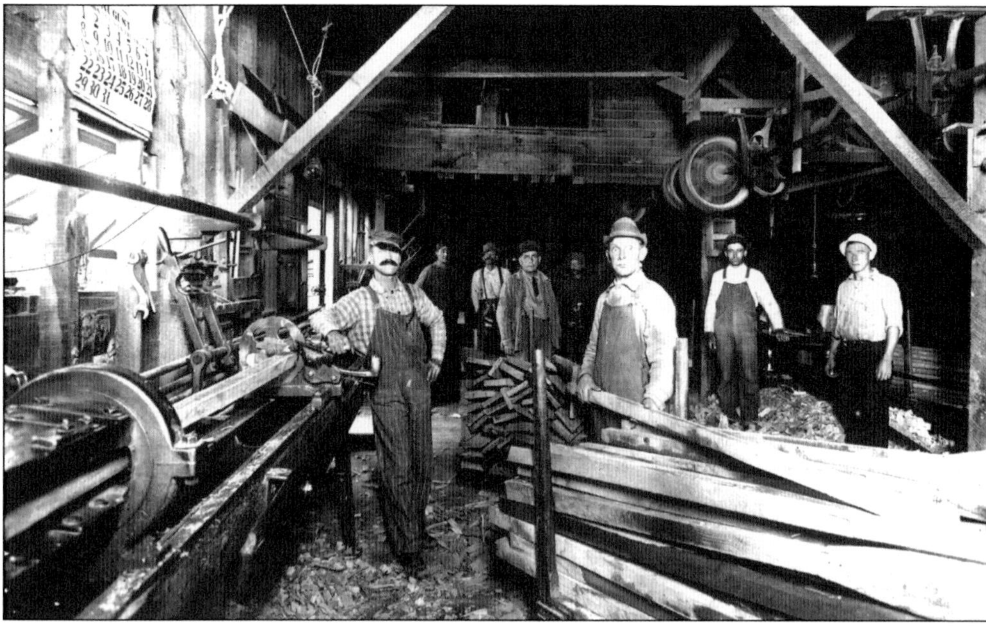

Stryker's most prominent manufacturing concern from the Civil War to the 1920s was the Stryker Boat Oar and Lumber Company, a homegrown industry that grew to worldwide recognition. In 1861, Frederick Von Behren started a tannery at the northeast corner of Defiance and Mulberry Streets. In 1867, the company began manufacturing oars, spokes, and other wooden products. In July 1926, fire destroyed the facility, and the business relocated to Archbold. (WCPL Photographic Archives.)

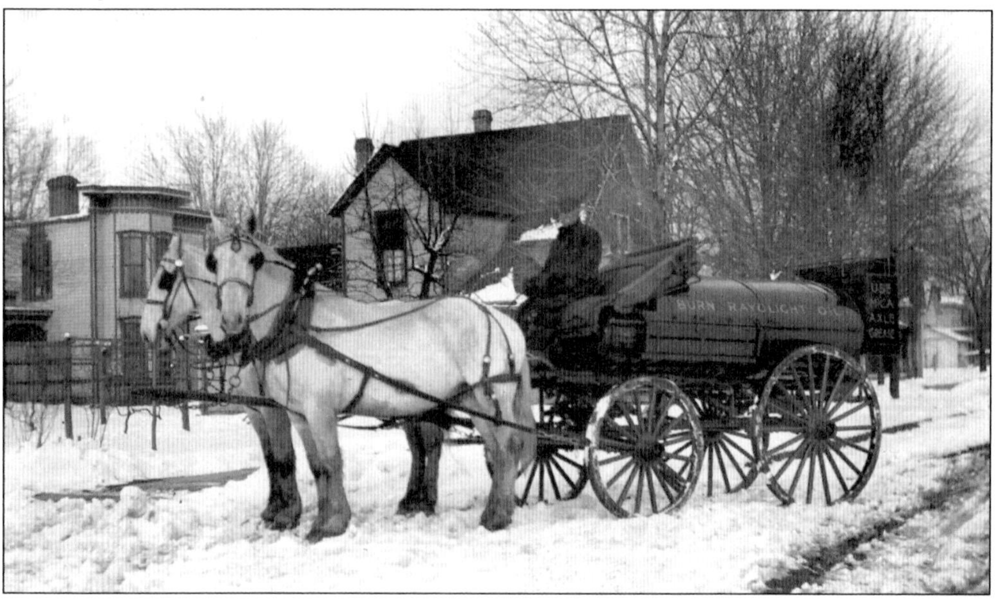

Home heating oil has long been a necessity in cold weather. Before large tank trucks delivered fuel oil, customers relied on true horsepower to supply their needs. Alex Connin of Bryan was a Standard Oil distributor from 1892 to 1920 and sold Ray-O-Light Oil and Mica Axle Grease. Connin's rig is shown in front of his home at the northwest corner of Mulberry and Lynn Streets. (WCPL Photographic Archives.)

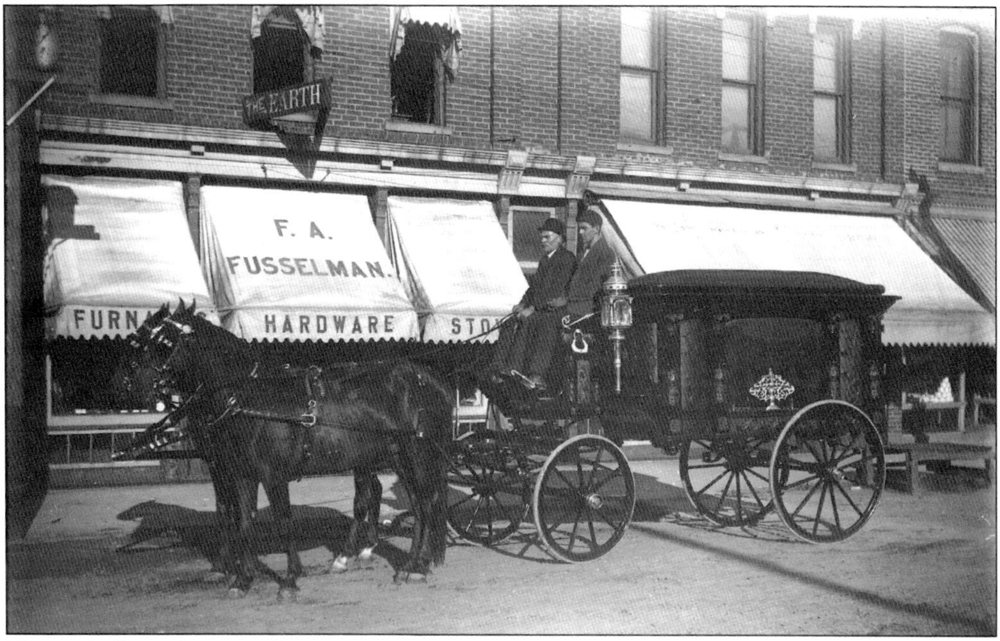

Henry Krill was born in Germany in 1859 and immigrated to this country when he was 10. In 1875, Krill began working for J. H. Miller's Edgerton furniture and undertaking firm. Around 1885, he became Miller's partner and assumed full ownership a few years later. He claimed to have arranged funerals for more than 2,000 people. Krill's horse-drawn hearse is shown on North Michigan Avenue. (WCPL Photographic Archives.)

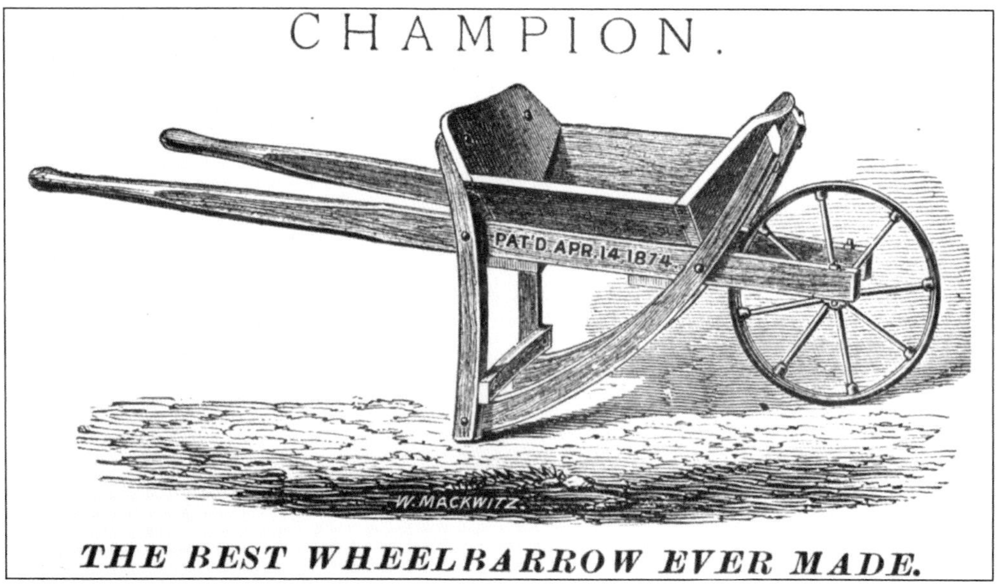

The Bryan Manufacturing Company was organized around 1870 and manufactured patented wheelbarrows—including the Champion Wheelbarrow—for about 50 years on North Portland Street. In 1925, the *Bryan Press* reported, "In the half-century of its existence, the Bryan Manufacturing Company has sold many thousands of wheelbarrows, which have gone into every state in the union and into every civilized country in the world, and into some not so civilized."

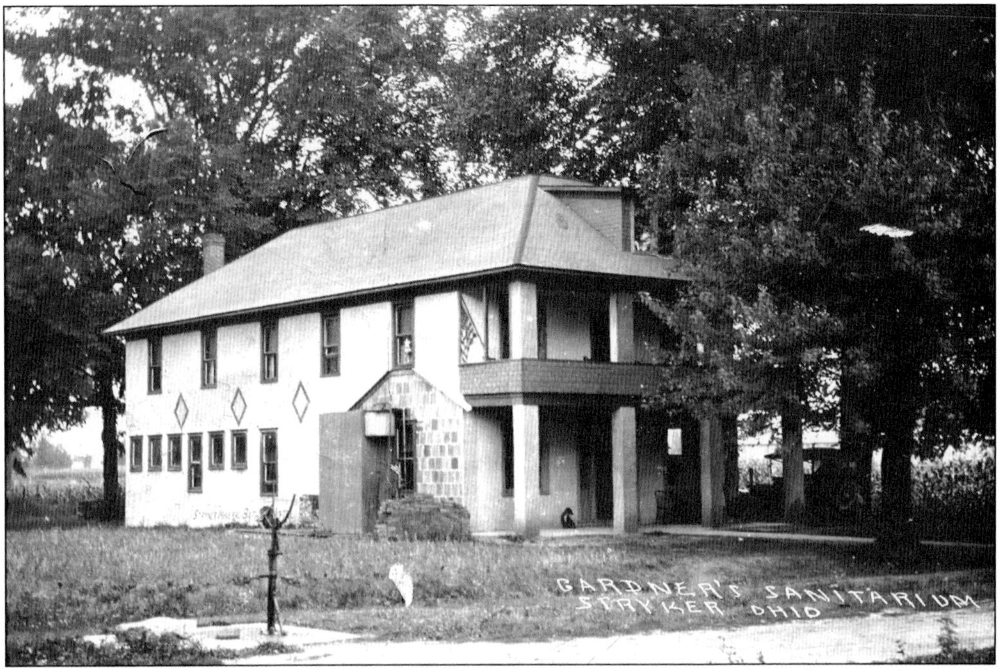

In 1861, a company was organized at Stryker to search for oil. After drilling about 70 feet, work ceased due to inadequate equipment and the Civil War's outbreak. In 1864–1865, the Stryker Oil Company was organized at Boston. After drilling two years to a depth of 860 feet, the well was abandoned due to insufficient gas and oil. Mineralized water began regularly spouting from the well, and in 1884, the Stryker Mineral Springs Company built a two-story bathhouse at Center and Curtis Streets. In 1900, the bathhouse burned down; about 15 years later John A. Gardner erected the two-story bathhouse above on the site. In 1953, the bathhouse became a nursing home. This business closed in the late 1960s, and the building was razed in 1977. People gather around the mineral well in the *c.* 1915 photograph below. (Below, WCPL Photographic Archives.)

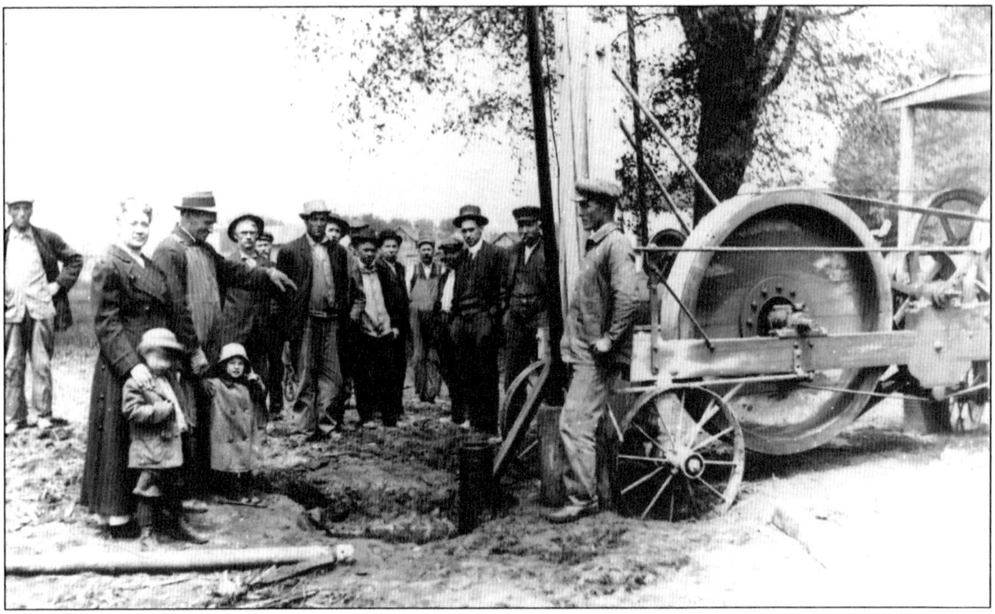

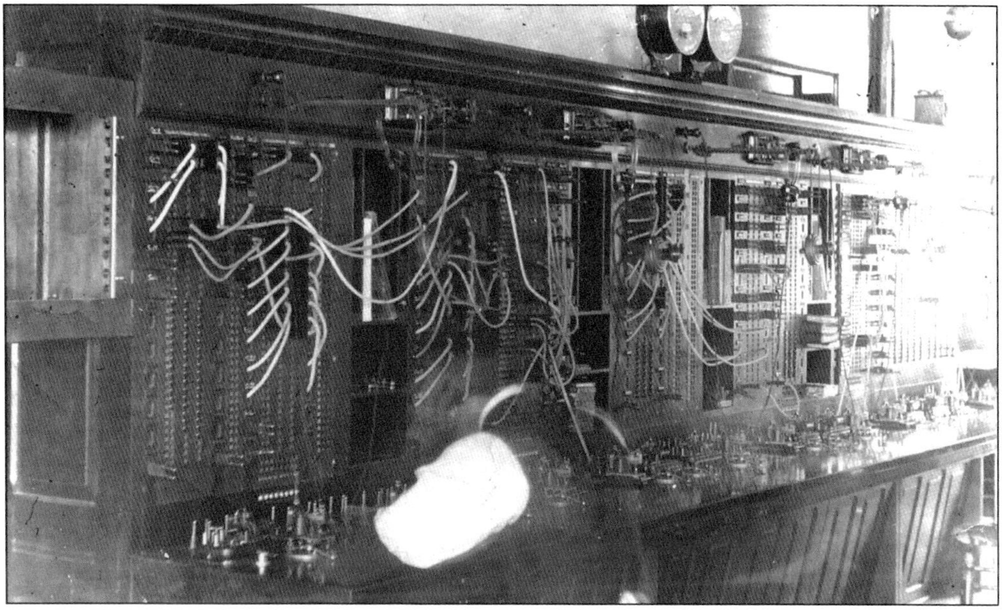

Area residents first received telephone service in the 1880s through small local exchanges. Patrons rang an operator who connected parties using a switchboard like the one above, believed to be Bryan's switchboard on the First National Bank's third floor. In 1915, many local exchanges were merged into the Williams County Telephone Company with further consolidations over time. Dial telephones appeared in the 1950s, eliminating the need for local operators. (WCPL Photographic Archives.)

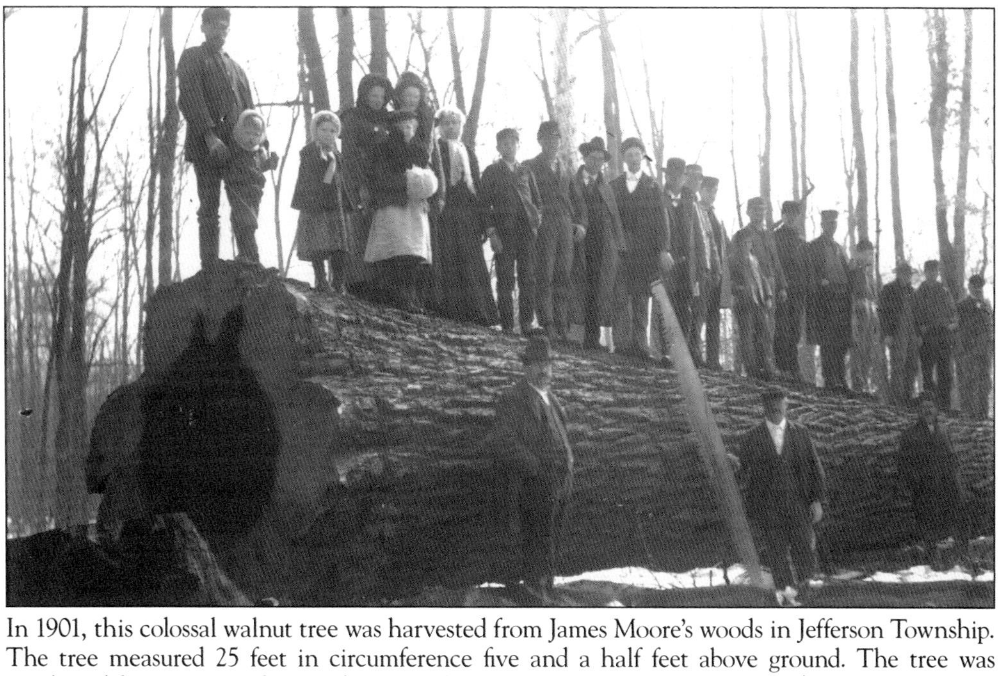

In 1901, this colossal walnut tree was harvested from James Moore's woods in Jefferson Township. The tree measured 25 feet in circumference five and a half feet above ground. The tree was purchased for a German firm, and prior to shipping a Boston company offered $3,300 for it. When the massive walnut arrived in Europe, no one would match the stateside offer, so it returned across the Atlantic Ocean to Boston. (WCPL Photographic Archives.)

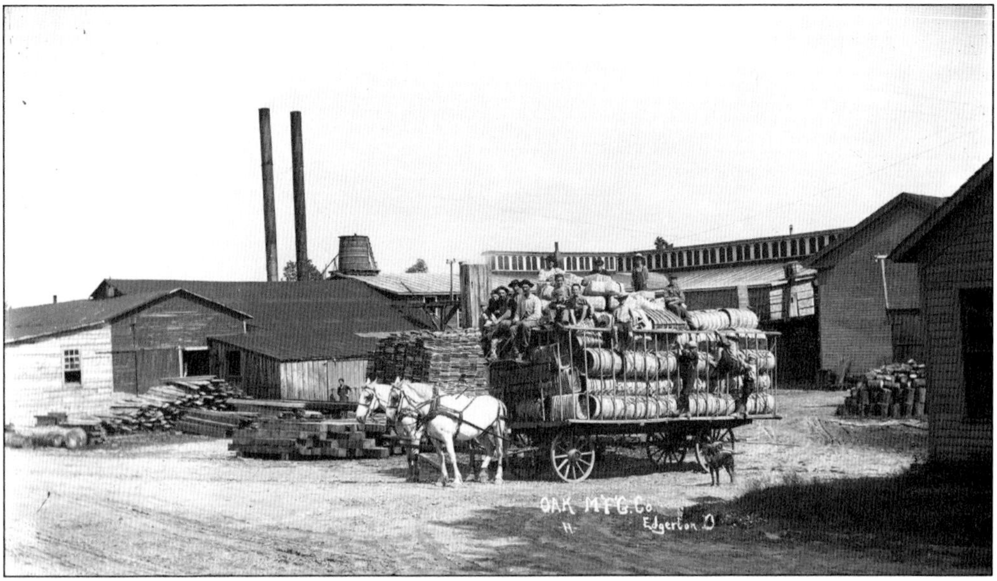

Edgerton's Oak Manufacturing Company was organized in 1902 and built a plant on East Bement Street near the St. Joseph River that produced oak stave baskets, quart berry boxes, fruit and vegetable containers, bushel shipping packages, clothes baskets, picking baskets, grain baskets for farmers, and peach baskets. In 1936, the *Bryan Democrat* stated, "The products of this company are of fine quality, shippers and growers everywhere acknowledging their superiority." (WCPL Photographic Archives.)

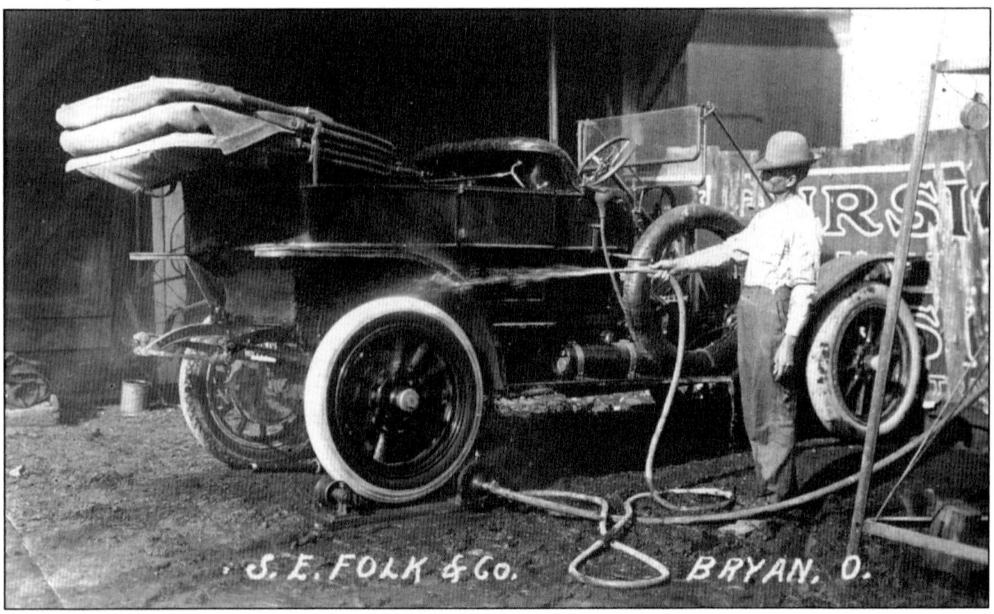

In the 1800s, Samuel Folk and his father, William, manufactured firearms in Bryan. Samuel also patented an oil stove, built a steam automobile, manufactured bicycles, was superintendent of Bryan's municipal utilities, and invented a pump that automatically kept tanks full of soft water using municipal water system pressure. The pumps were manufactured on Butler Street east of the Cincinnati Northern Railroad. Here an automobile powers one of Folk's pumps. (WCPL Photographic Archives.)

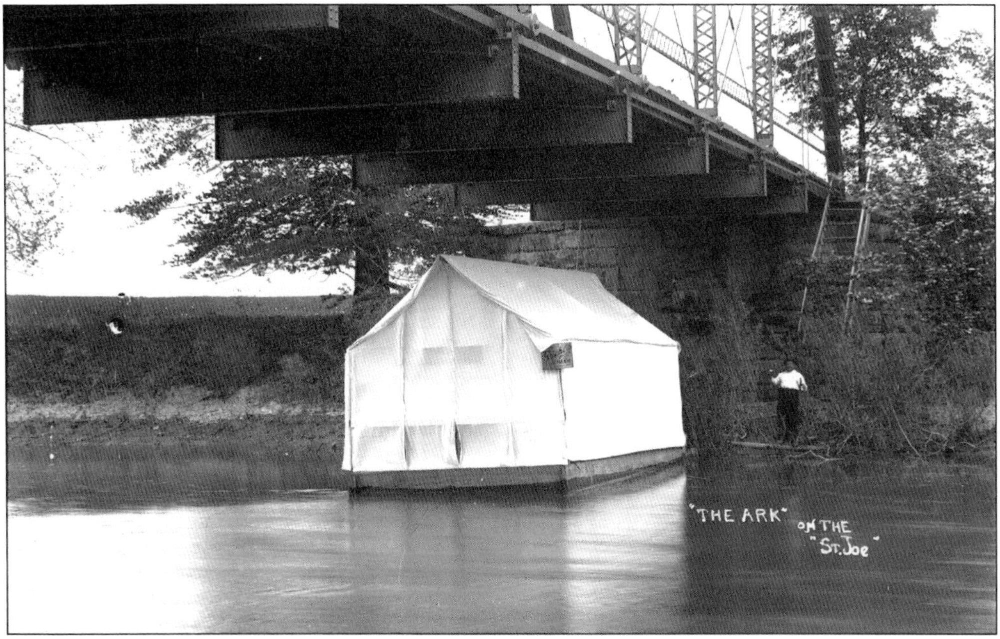

In 1908, Williams County was voted dry while Defiance County remained wet. In May 1909, Jacob Lahrman and William Cape launched this floating tavern, christened "the Ark," from Edgerton, floating it down the St. Joseph River to the county line. The Ark anchored under the Clarksville Bridge on the Defiance County side of the river. Local residents labeled it a nuisance, claiming noise and lights reflected from the river frightened horses crossing the bridge at night. After several days the river rose due to heavy rains, threatening to crush the Ark under the bridge. The proprietors cast off and floated to safety, but when they anchored on adjacent land, property owners set in with injunctions. Petitions were quickly circulated, and on June 18, 1909, Milford Township, Defiance County, was voted dry, ending the Ark's hopes of success. (WCPL Photographic Archives.)

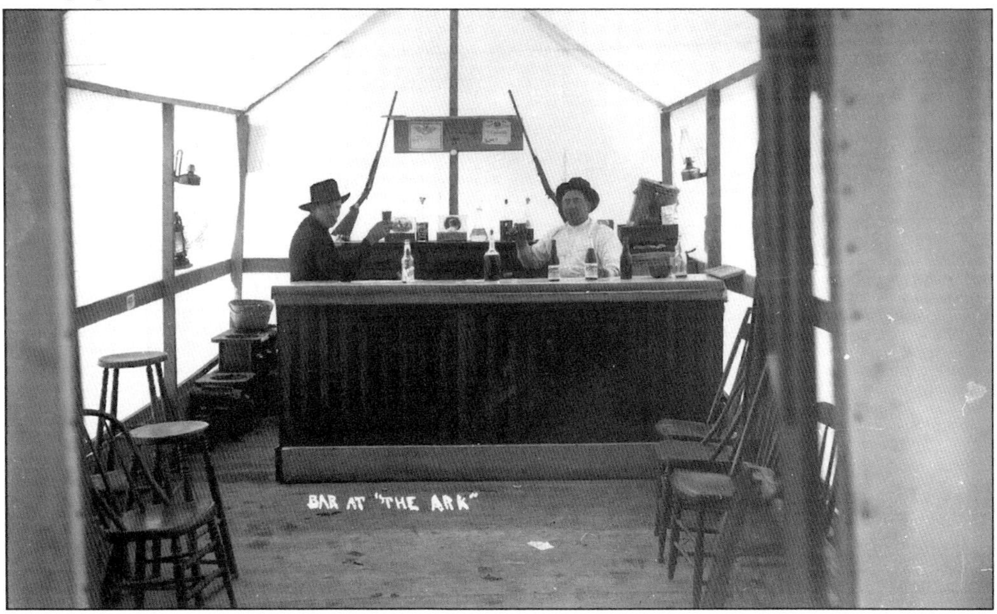

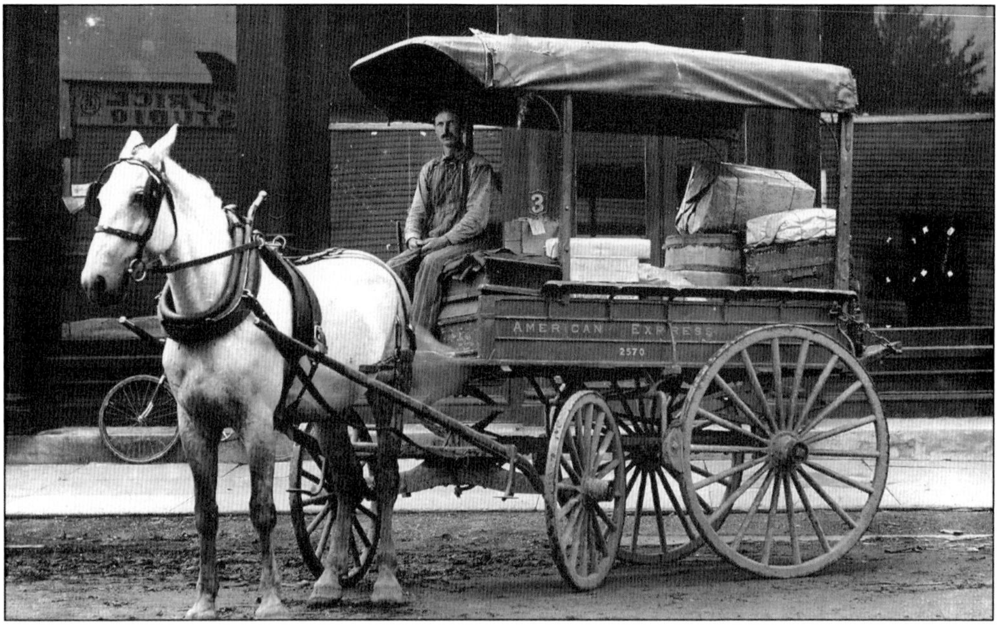

Established in 1850 in New York, the American Express Company originally provided express delivery of parcels and freight at a time when nothing larger than a letter-sized envelope could be sent via U.S. Mail. This *c.* 1910 photograph shows an American Express wagon loaded with parcels on the southwest corner of Bryan's courthouse square. (WCPL Photographic Archives.)

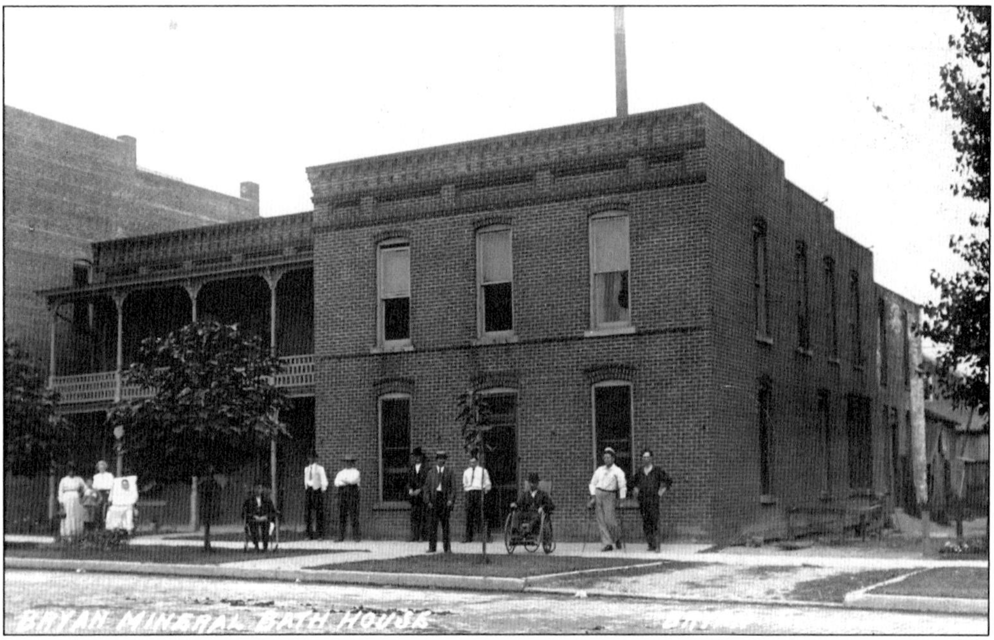

In 1908, W. J. Fulghum opened this mineral bathhouse for treatment of rheumatism, nervous troubles, skin diseases, and paralysis in the Park Hotel on Bryan's South Main Street. Patients bathed in heated mineral water (from an oil and gas well) "together with a rubbing process" and were then taken to a warm room, wrapped in blankets, and subjected to thorough sweating. In 1917, Fulghum moved his business to Sherwood.

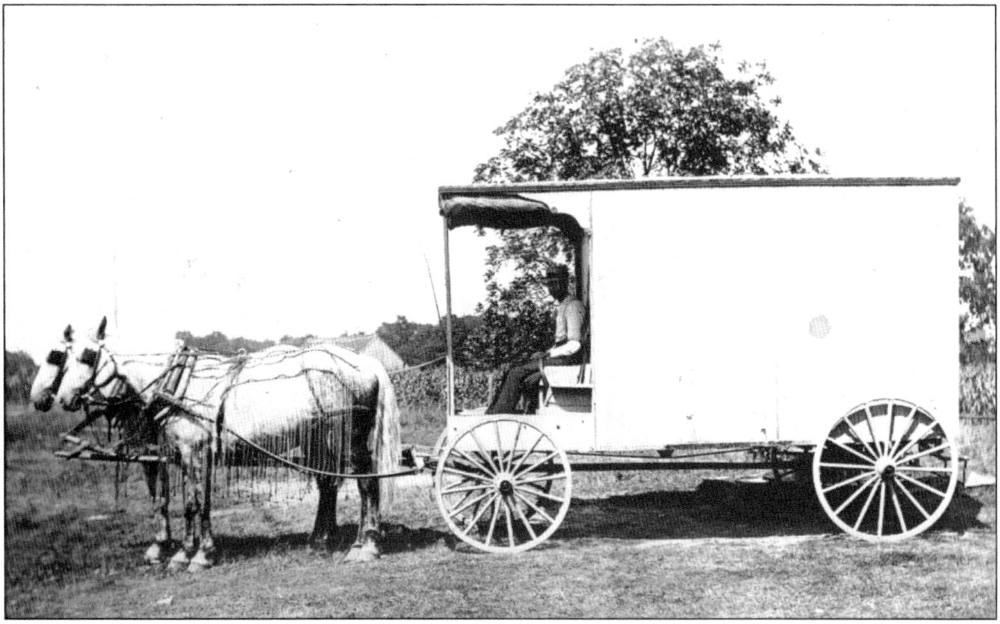

This photograph shows James Daniels and the Cooney peddling wagon. Daniels worked for Frank Malcolm, longtime owner of the Cooney general store. When Malcolm's store closed in 1920, the *Montpelier Enterprise* opined, "This is a demonstration of what the automobile and good roads do in the way of ease of transportation of the rural citizen to the more populous centers of trade." (WCPL Photographic Archives.)

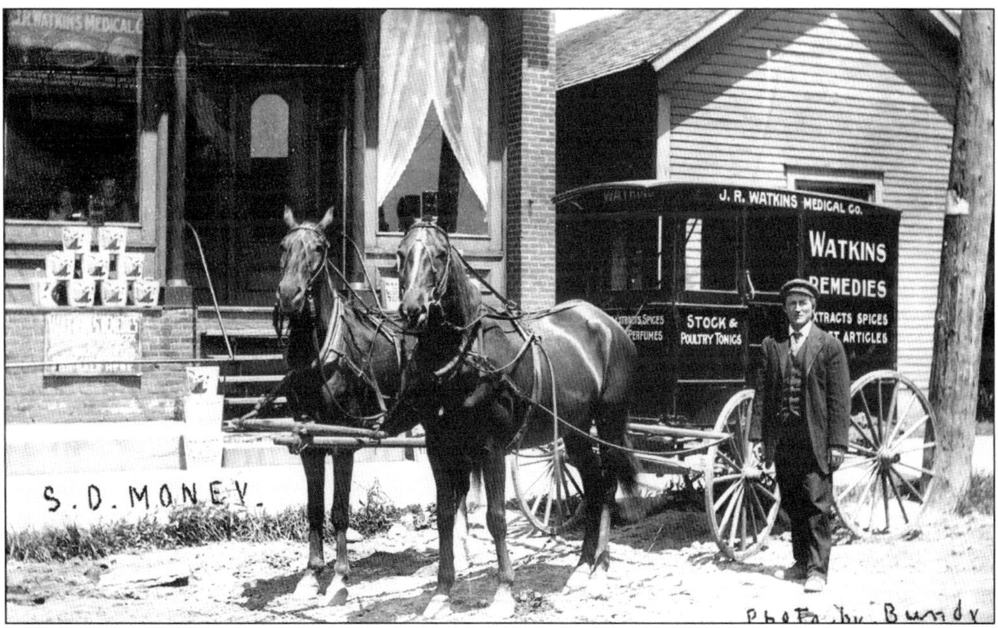

J. R. Watkins Medical Company representative S. D. Money is shown in this c. 1910 photograph taken by Montpelier professional photographer Miles Bundy. By 1914, Money was associated with the Montpelier Machine Shop. The J. R. Watkins Medical Company of Winona, Minnesota, sold spices, extracts, and patent medicines such as Dr. Ward's Liniment, Petro-Carbo Salve, and cathartic pills. (WCPL Photographic Archives.)

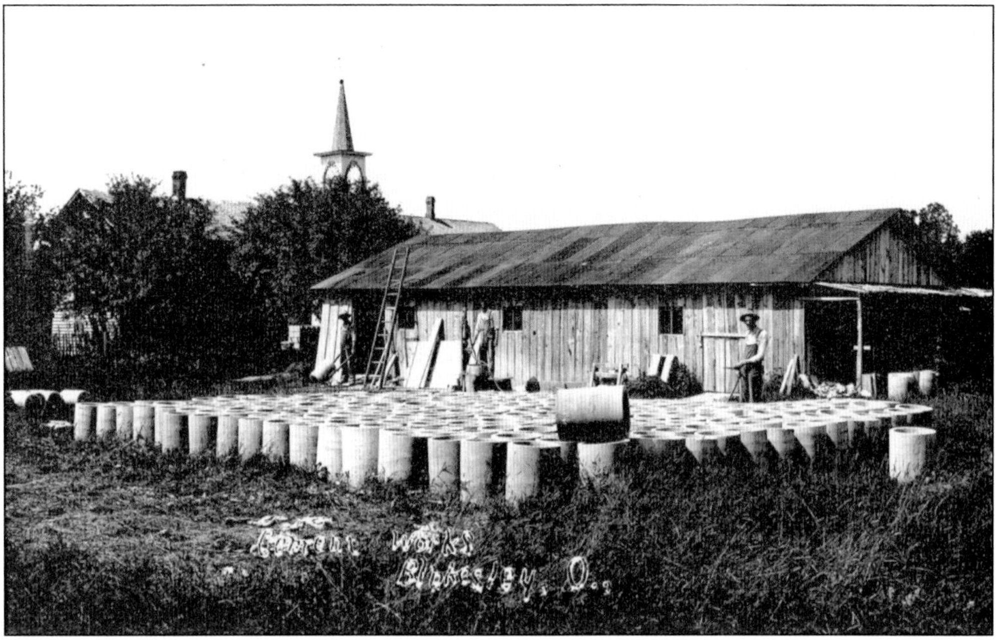

Around 1910, Alva "Skip" Nichols and his brother or brothers operated a brick, tile, and cement block factory northeast of Madison and Dearborn Streets in Blakeslee. In 1913, the *Edgerton Earth* reported, "The Nichols brothers are behind with orders for cement blocks. Can't make them fast enough. The masons say they are the best cured blocks in northwestern Ohio." The Blakeslee United Brethren Church is visible in the background.

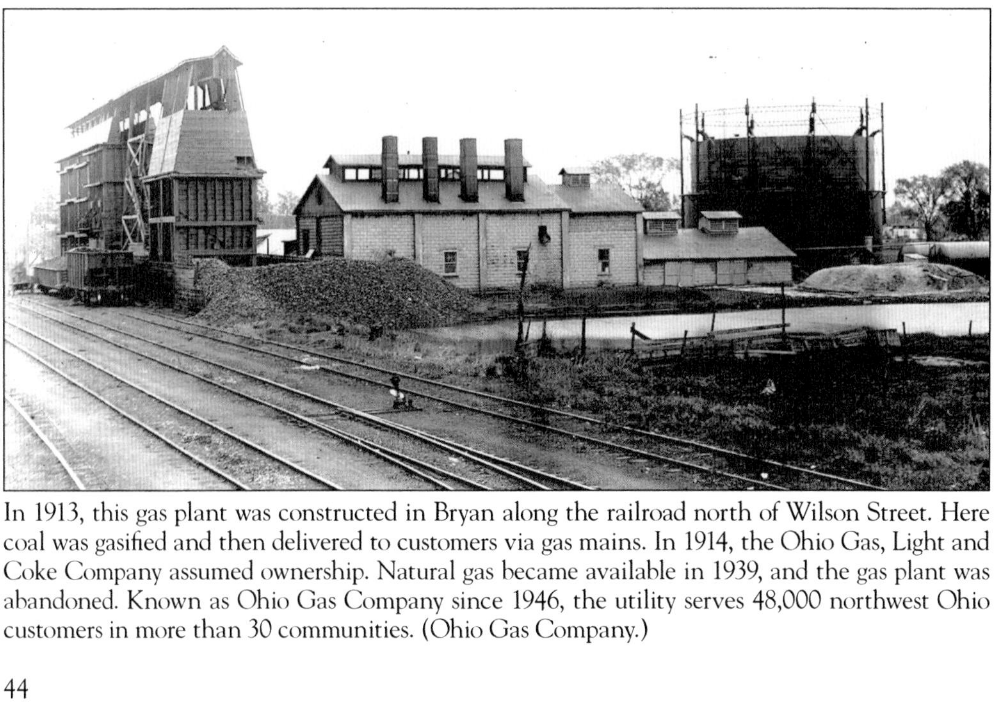

In 1913, this gas plant was constructed in Bryan along the railroad north of Wilson Street. Here coal was gasified and then delivered to customers via gas mains. In 1914, the Ohio Gas, Light and Coke Company assumed ownership. Natural gas became available in 1939, and the gas plant was abandoned. Known as Ohio Gas Company since 1946, the utility serves 48,000 northwest Ohio customers in more than 30 communities. (Ohio Gas Company.)

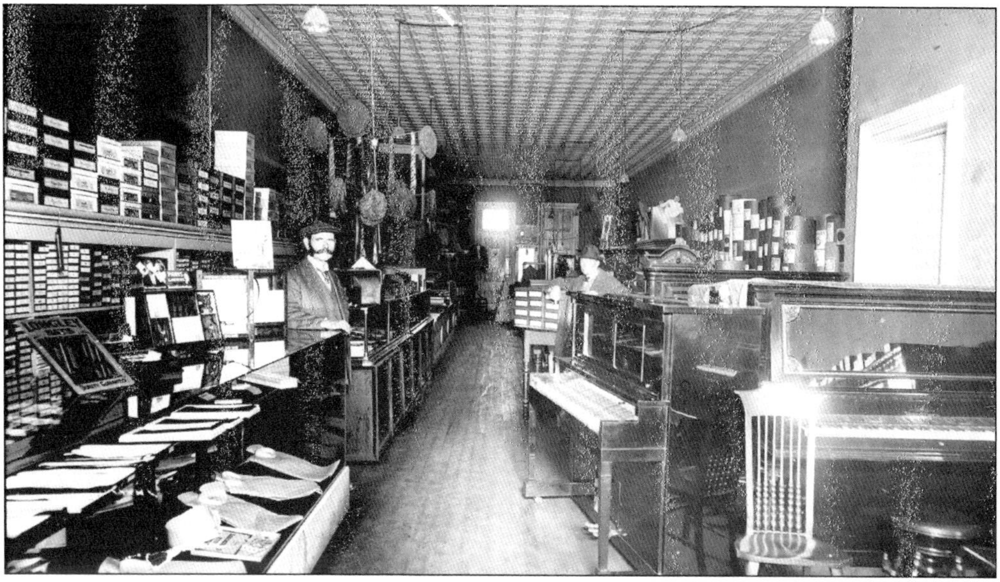

This 1915 photograph shows Hugh MacPhail (left) in his clothing shop on West High Street in Bryan. The music store on the right side of the shop was operated by Don Tubbs, son of Forrest A. Tubbs, who directed the Bryan City Band for 30 years. Behind the piano stands Eugene C. Thomas who, with Roswell Russell, started Russell and Thomas' clothing store on Main Street, later known as Russell's. (WCPL Photographic Archives.)

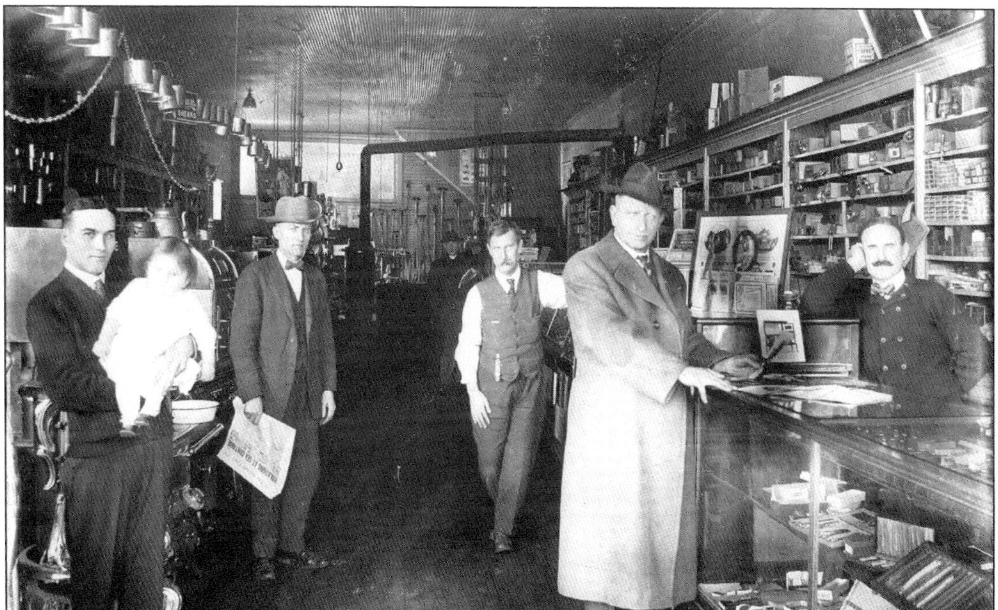

In 1858, Peter Charpiot emigrated from France and opened a hardware store in Stryker. In 1897, Charpiot constructed the brick building at the northwest corner of Defiance and Lynn Streets. Shown in the hardware store in this c. 1916 photograph are, from left to right, undertaker Sylvanus Rupp holding an unidentified baby, shoe store owner Nevin Huffman, clothing store owner G. D. Wiederkehr, owner Ed Charpiot, unidentified, and owner Babe Charpiot. (Sue Buehrer.)

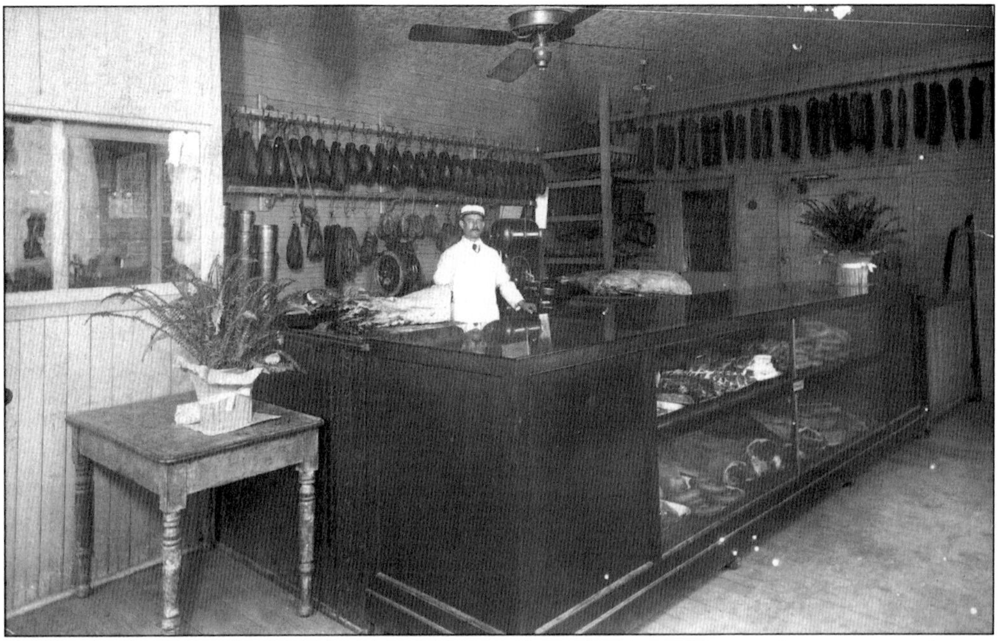

Before supermarkets carried fresh meats, local residents slaughtered livestock or patronized meat markets. This undated photograph shows the Dewees Meat Market that operated on Bryan's North Main Street from the 1880s to the 1930s. An 1890s account states Dewees was equipped with "the very best appliances and devices for carrying on this trade. He utilizes one of the finest refrigerators in northwestern Ohio and employs three assistants." (WCPL Photographic Archives.)

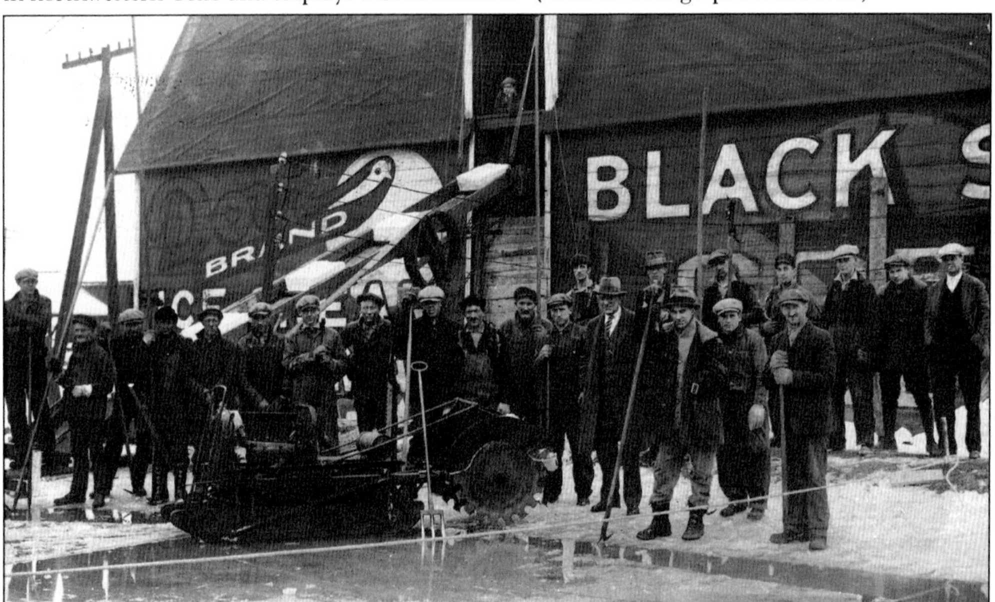

In 1917, Ed Frappier and Olin Gleason founded the Bryan Ice and Ice Cream Company, occupying the former Bryan Steel Grave Vault Company facility at Edgerton Street and the Cincinnati Northern Railroad. The firm sold Dove brand ice cream and ice that they manufactured or harvested from a pond west of their facility. This *c.* 1927 photograph shows ice being harvested and moved by conveyor into the company's icehouse. (WCPL Photographic Archives.)

In 1919, the Delite Manufacturing Company began producing electric washing machines at the northeast corner of Bryan's High and Beech Streets. By 1923, the plant was producing 250 washing machines per month, and assembly was moved to the third floor of the former Bryan Plow Company building at 119 South Beech Street. A new factory was constructed on West High Street in 1930. Washing machine production ceased in 1940.

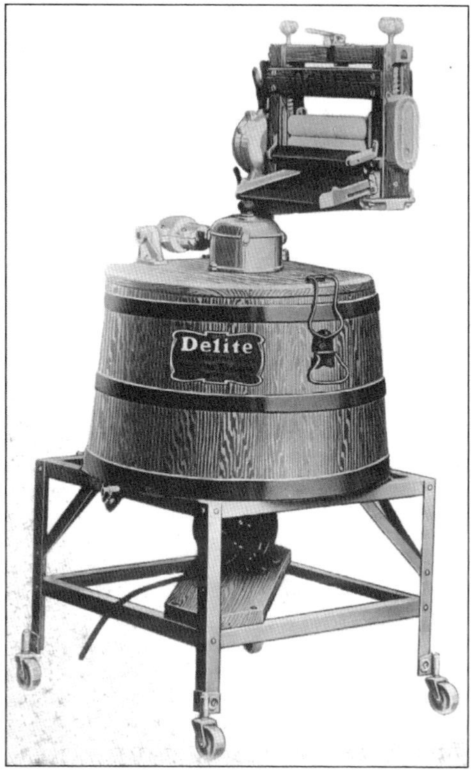

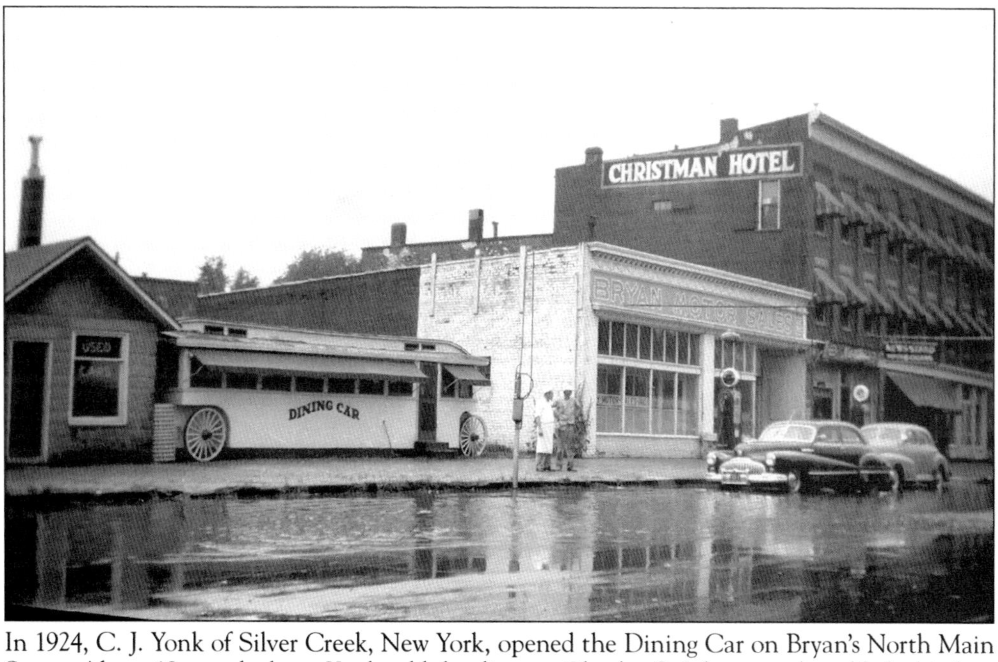

In 1924, C. J. Yonk of Silver Creek, New York, opened the Dining Car on Bryan's North Main Street. About 18 months later, Yonk sold the diner to Charles O. Johnson, who added a kitchen in the rear. William H. "Herb" Saltzman Sr. managed the restaurant as early as 1933 and retired in May 1960 when Lindsey Motor Sales razed the Dining Car to expand its car lot. (WCPL Photographic Archives.)

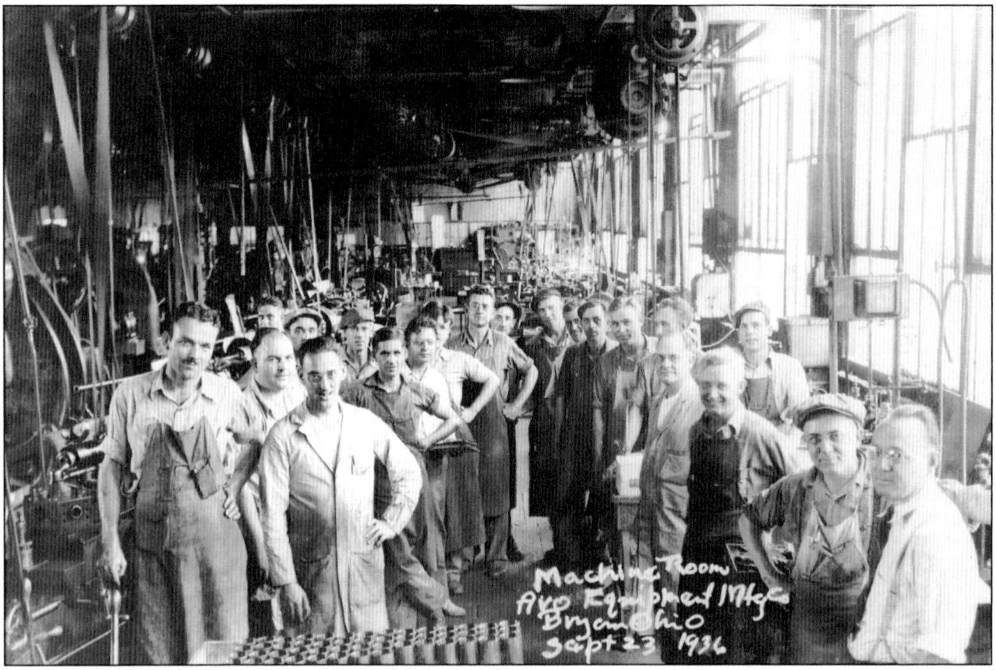

In 1930, John Markey founded the Aro Equipment Corporation in Bryan. The company manufactured air-powered tools, pumps, hoists, valves, controls, and aeronautical life support products. Aro became Williams County's industrial powerhouse with seven manufacturing facilities and nearly 2,000 employees worldwide. In 2005, the former Aro assets in Bryan were acquired by New Era Ohio. Aro staff poses in the company's machine room in this 1936 photograph.

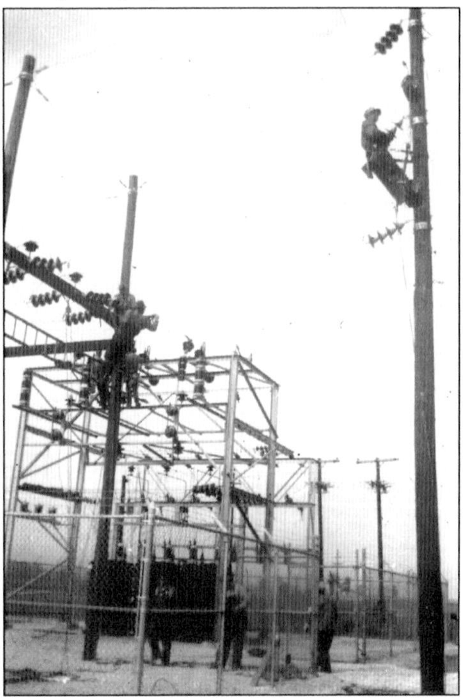

In 1936, North Western Electric Cooperative was organized by Williams and Defiance County farmers to provide reliable, affordable electric service to 1,000 rural families. Electric distribution lines were first energized in January 1938. North Western currently serves nearly 6,000 consumers through 836 miles of distribution lines. A 34,500-volt bypass structure is added to North Western's Montpelier substation in this October 1951 photograph. (North Western Electric.)

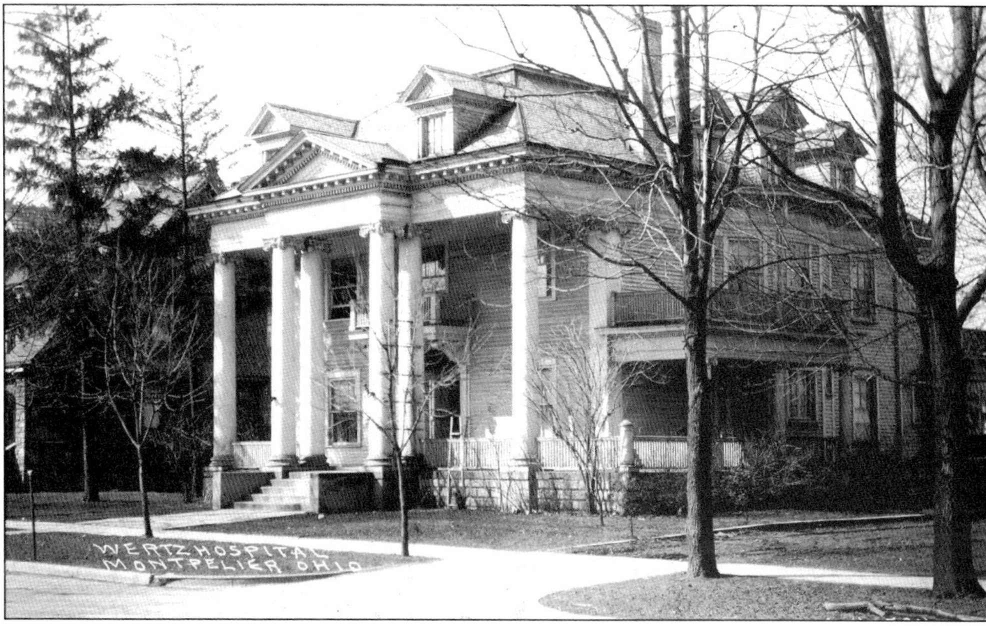

In 1909, George and Julia Kollar completed this Greek Ionic neoclassical home at 315 Empire Street, Montpelier, which the *Montpelier Leader* newspaper called one of the "most noble, magnificent residence structures in Williams County." About the same time, Dr. Harry Wertz constructed a combined hospital and residence at 314 North Pleasant Street. When the Pleasant Street structure burned in 1915, Wertz reestablished his hospital and home in the former Kollar residence.

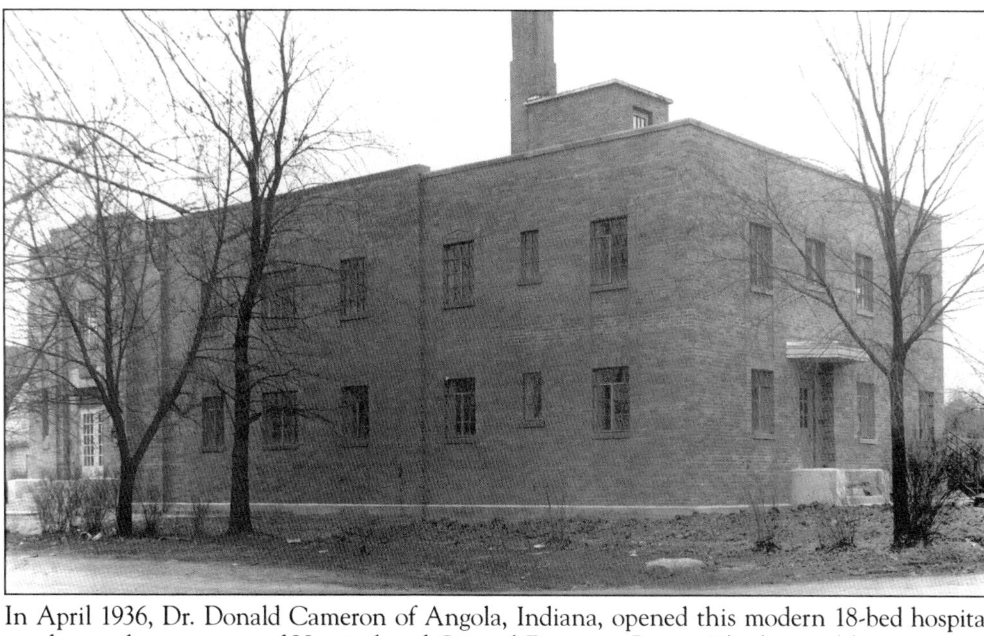

In April 1936, Dr. Donald Cameron of Angola, Indiana, opened this modern 18-bed hospital on the northeast corner of Hospital and Central Drives in Bryan. The hospital has witnessed numerous expansions in its facilities and services and is today known as Community Hospitals and Wellness Centers with facilities in Bryan, Montpelier (the former Williams County General Hospital), and Archbold. (WCPL Photographic Archives.)

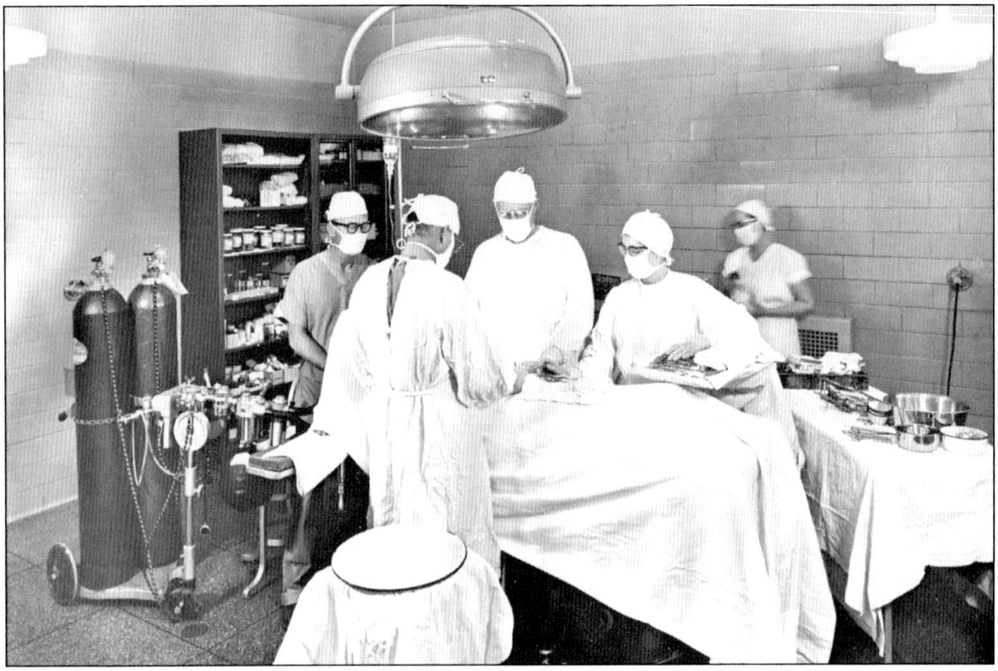

Williams County General Hospital, 909 East Snyder Avenue, Montpelier, was formally dedicated on June 22, 1952. The facility cost $750,000 and housed 43 beds in its four wings. In 1978, the hospital began sharing administration, services, purchasing, and equipment with Bryan Community Hospital to reduce costs and improve services. The two hospitals formally merged on January 1, 1986, as Community Hospitals of Williams County.

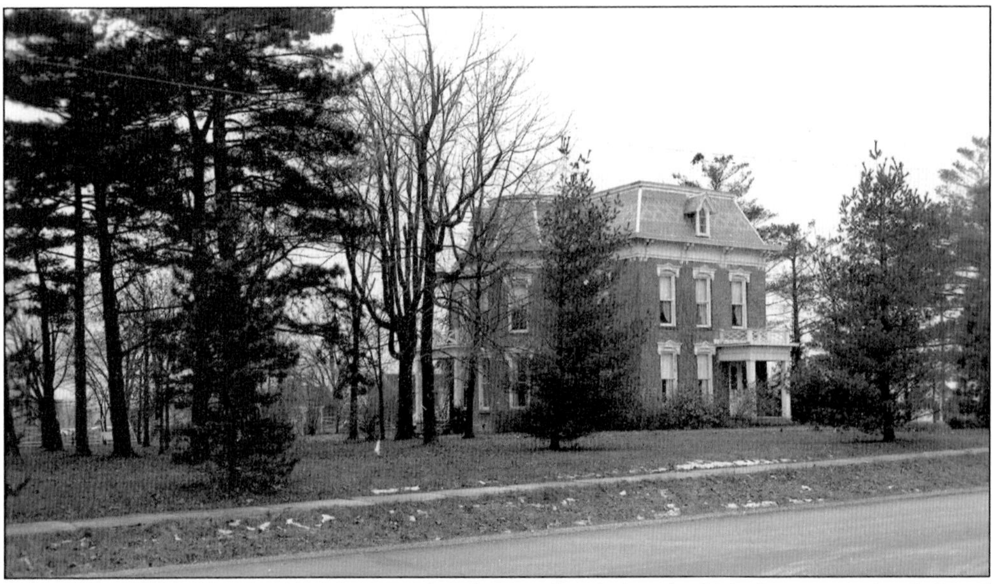

In 1885, Alvordton's founder, Henry Alvord, completed this $8,000 three-story brick hotel on West Main Street. In 1947, James Masters opened a rest home in the building with accommodations for 24 persons. The *Bryan Democrat* reported Masters would have "a registered nurse in attendance, and he will have an adequate staff to care for the home. Mrs. Masters, who is a teacher, will plan the menus."

Four

EDUCATION

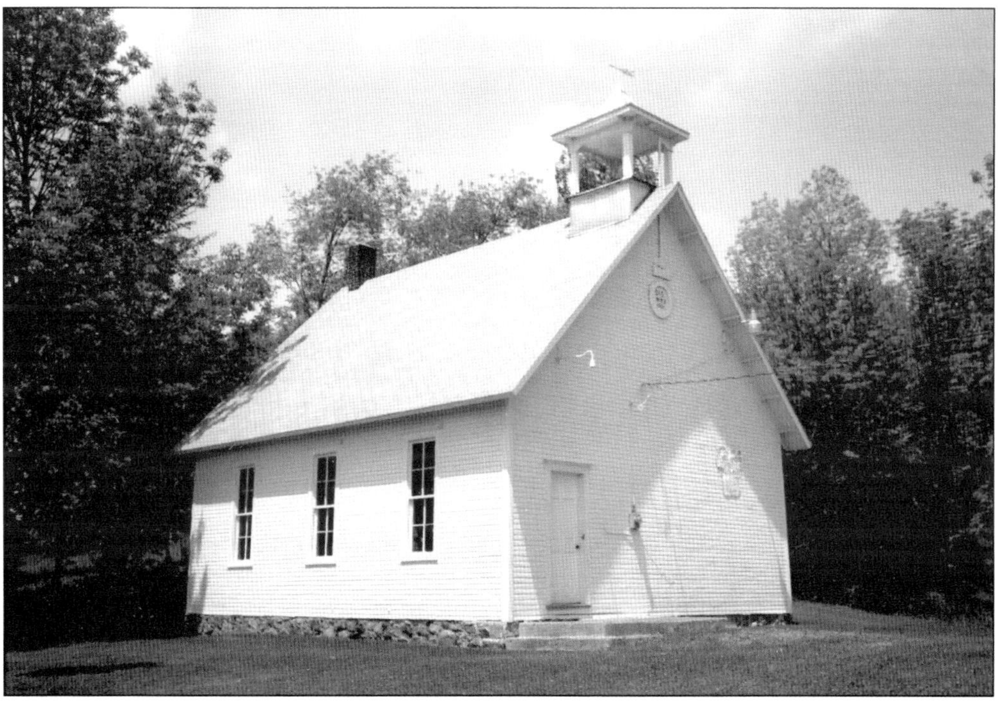

Before Williams County's large school districts were established, townships were divided into districts of about four square miles with each district served by a one-room schoolhouse. Pupils generally did not have to walk more than a mile to school. One teacher provided instruction for all students in grades one through eight. Bridgewater Township's Hay Jay one-room schoolhouse above was built in 1901, replacing a wooden frame building north of it. The school closed in 1957 when Bridgewater Township became part of the new North Central School District.

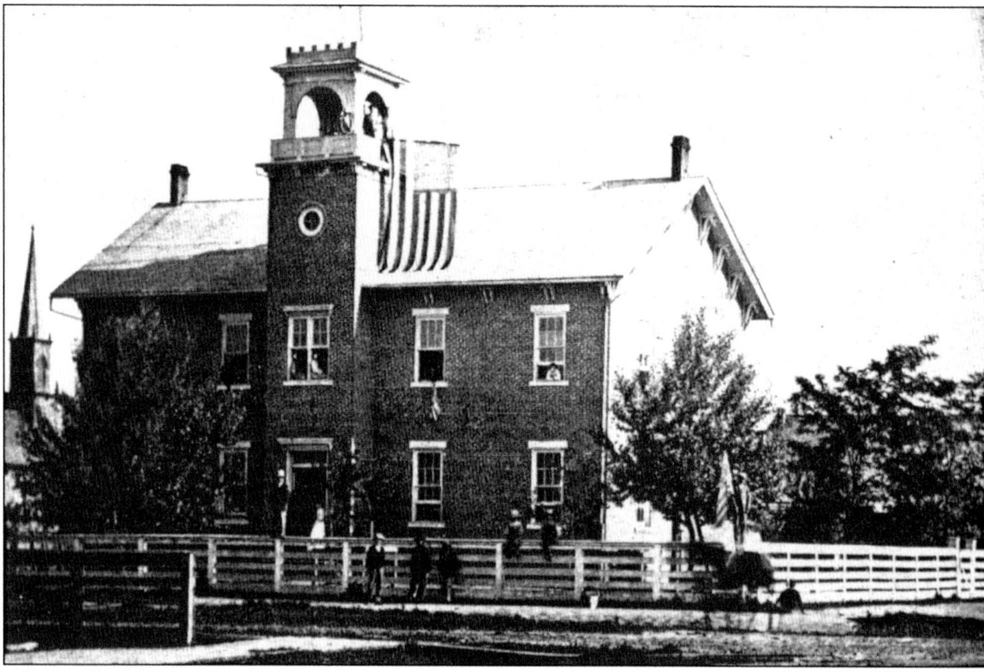

The Butler Street School, Bryan's first brick schoolhouse, opened in 1858 on the northwest corner of Butler and Beech Streets. The first floor was divided into primary and intermediate classrooms; the upper floor contained a high school classroom, library, and recitation rooms. The building was torn down in 1904 following construction of a new high school north of it. The Baptist church's steeple is visible on the left.

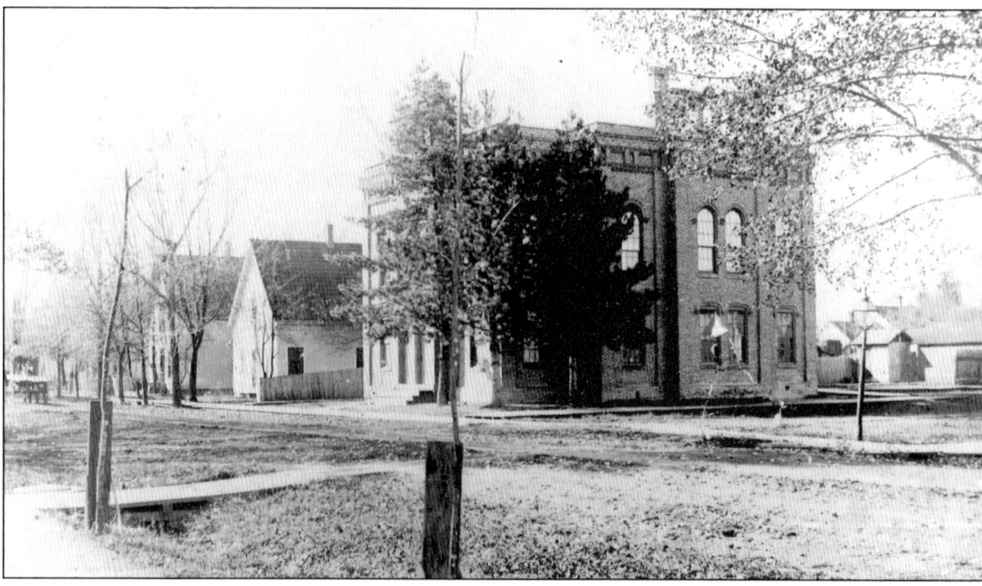

In 1867, C. W. Mykrantz erected the Bryan Normal College—where many local residents pursued higher education—at the southwest corner of Lynn and Mulberry Streets. The first floor of the 47-by-52-foot academy contained a public hall and classrooms with living quarters for male students on the second floor. The building was later converted into Bryan's first duplex residence and was torn down in 1980. (WCPL Photographic Archives.)

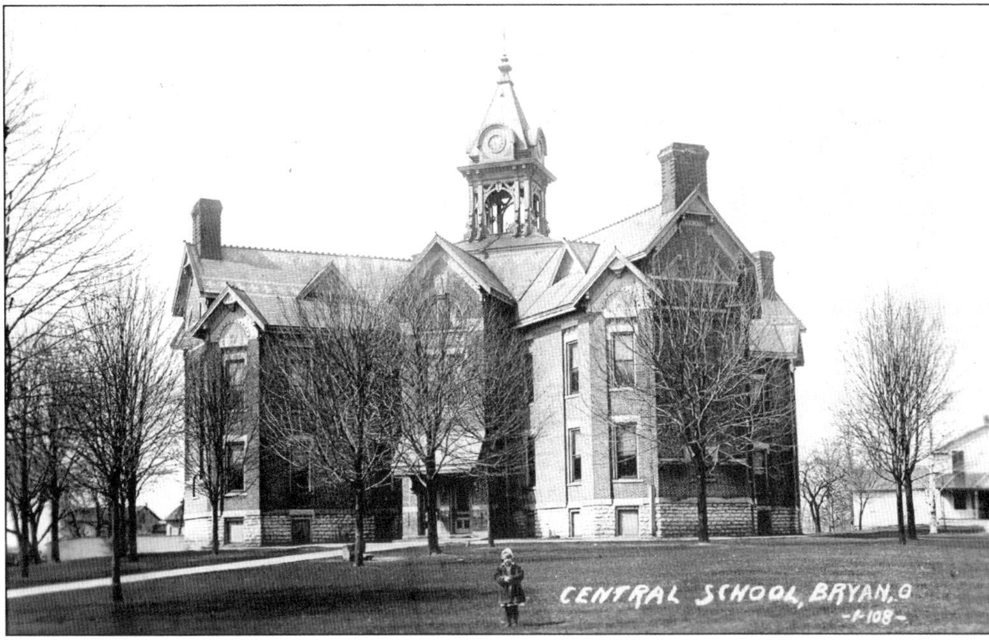

Bryan's Central or Park School opened on South Portland Street in September 1885 with grammar school students on its first floor and high school scholars on its second floor. The Greek cross-shaped building featured four wings extending from a central hall containing offices and storerooms. This design provided excellent lighting, ventilation, and classroom access. The school was razed in 1956 to make room for the current high school.

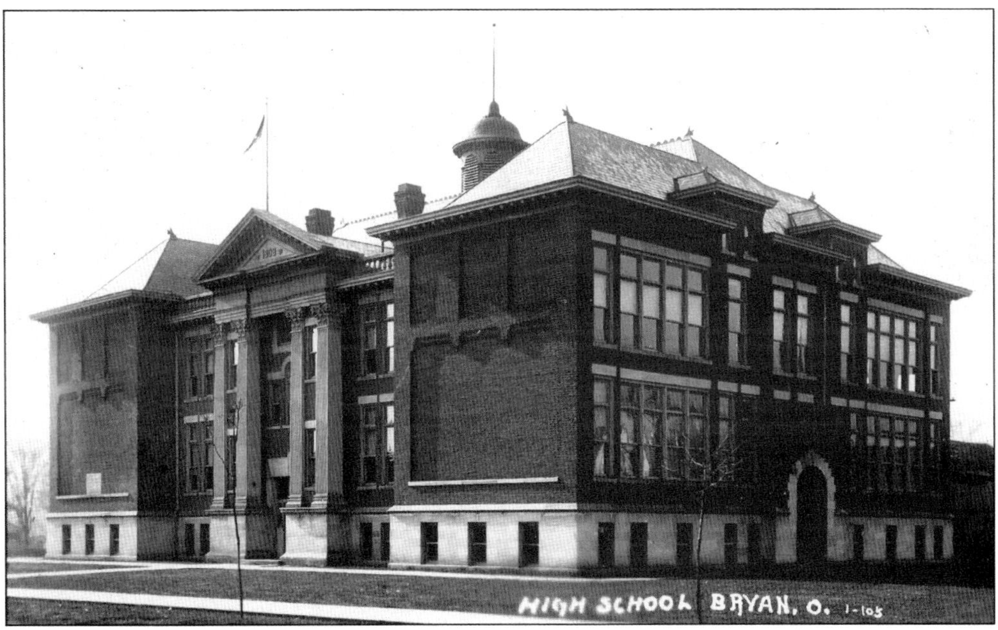

This Bryan High School was constructed on South Beech Street at a cost of $28,000 and opened for classes on September 5, 1904. After the current high school was completed in 1958, this building became the Bryan Middle School. The school building served the community 83 years before it was razed in 1987.

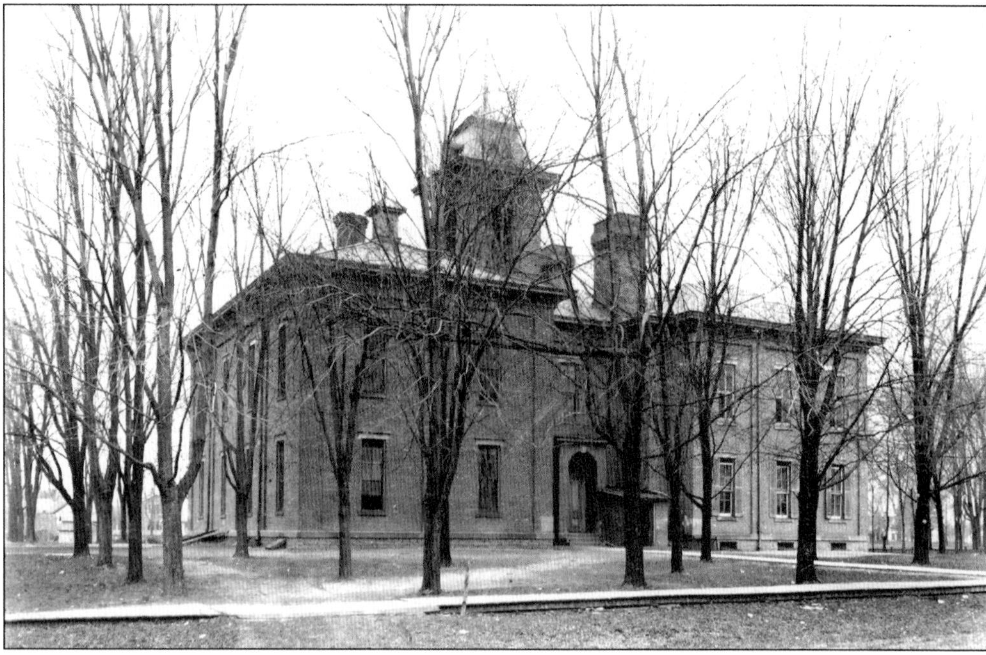

Stryker's first school was a one-room log building near the northeast corner of Defiance and Curtis Streets and was replaced in 1857 with a two-story, two-room frame schoolhouse. In 1869, the east (left) portion of this brick school was completed on the site of the present elementary school. In 1886, a two-story addition was built on the school's west side that virtually mirrored the 1869 building with the large bell tower in between. (WCPL Photographic Archives.)

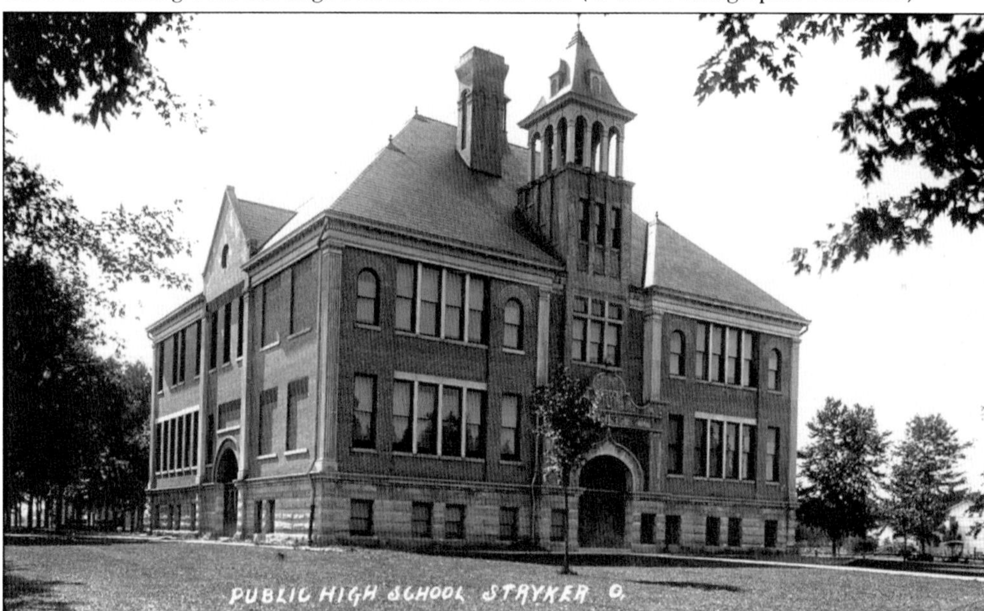

In 1902, Stryker's school was destroyed by an arsonist. It was replaced by this $28,000 facility on Defiance Street in 1904. The school was designed by W. H. Powers and constructed by Monroe Snyder of Fort Wayne. It housed all 12 grades until completion of the 1922 high school building. In February 1979, the structure was razed to make room for the present elementary school.

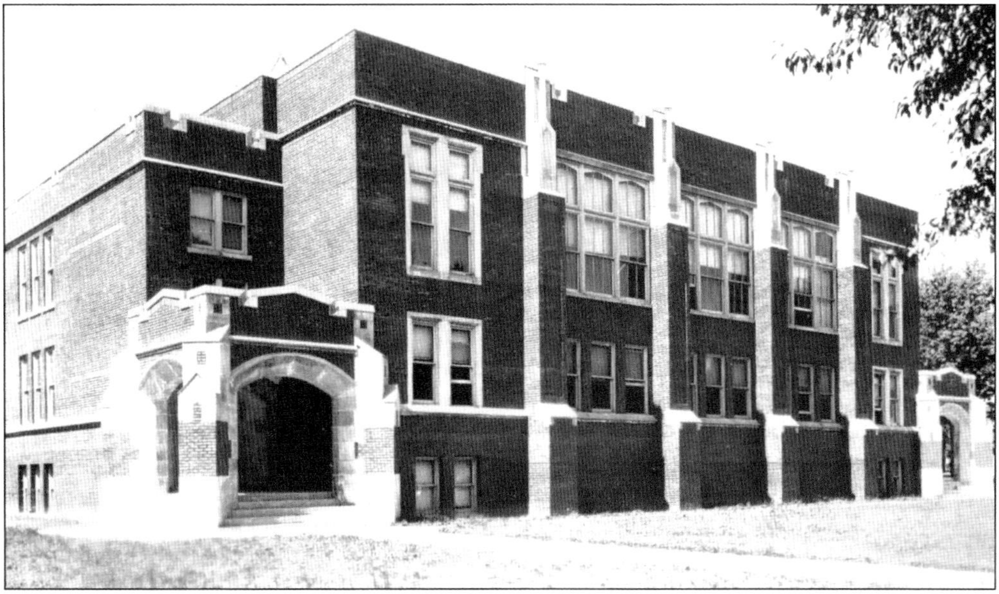

In January 1919, Stryker voters approved a $120,000 bond issue to construct this high school building. Toledo architect M. M. Stophlet designed the building, constructed northwest of the intersection of Defiance and Curtis Streets. In May 1919, the school board awarded the construction contract to V. M. Gettins of Toledo for $87,771.96. The new high school opened in the spring of 1922.

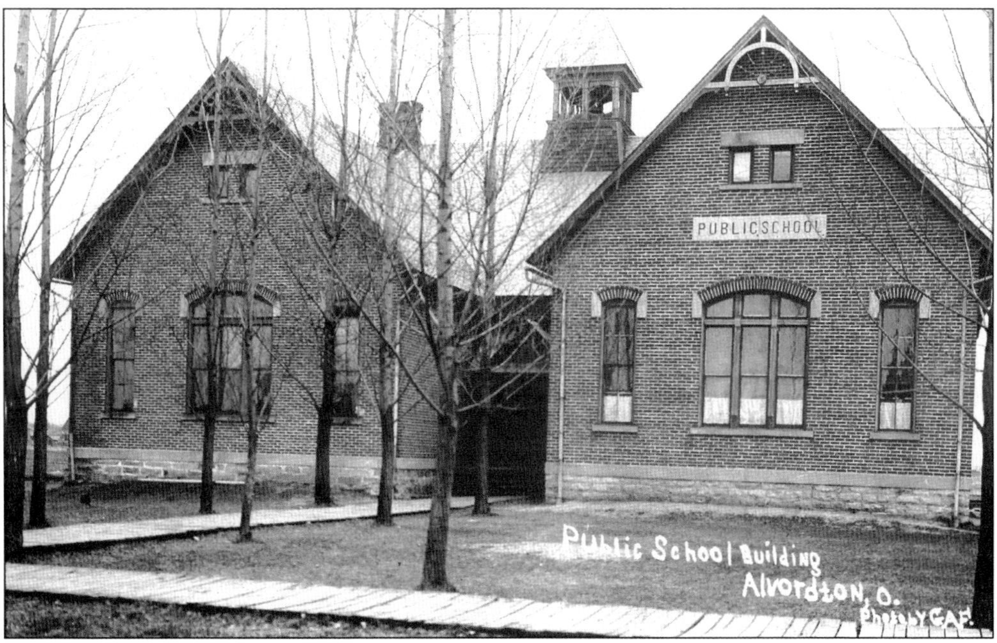

Alvordton's first school was a log building at Main and Michigan Streets. In 1894, the two southern (right) rooms of this brick school were constructed, with two identical rooms added in 1898. Several additions were made, including a gymnasium in 1929. In 1956, the Millcreek and West Unity school districts merged. In 1980, part of the school was razed with the remaining structure turned over to the village.

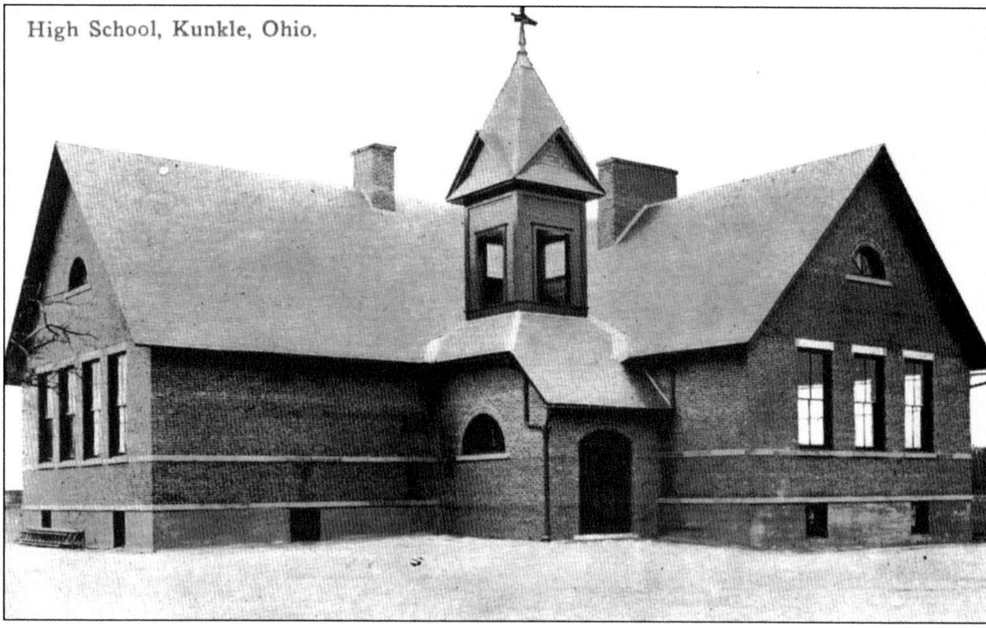

In 1912, this brick school was constructed in Kunkle to replace a frame building south of town that was destroyed by fire. An addition was built in 1919–1920 when neighboring one-room schools were consolidated with Kunkle. In 1956, the Kunkle, Bridgewater Township, and Pioneer school districts merged to become the North Central School District. The last classes were held at the Kunkle School in 1993.

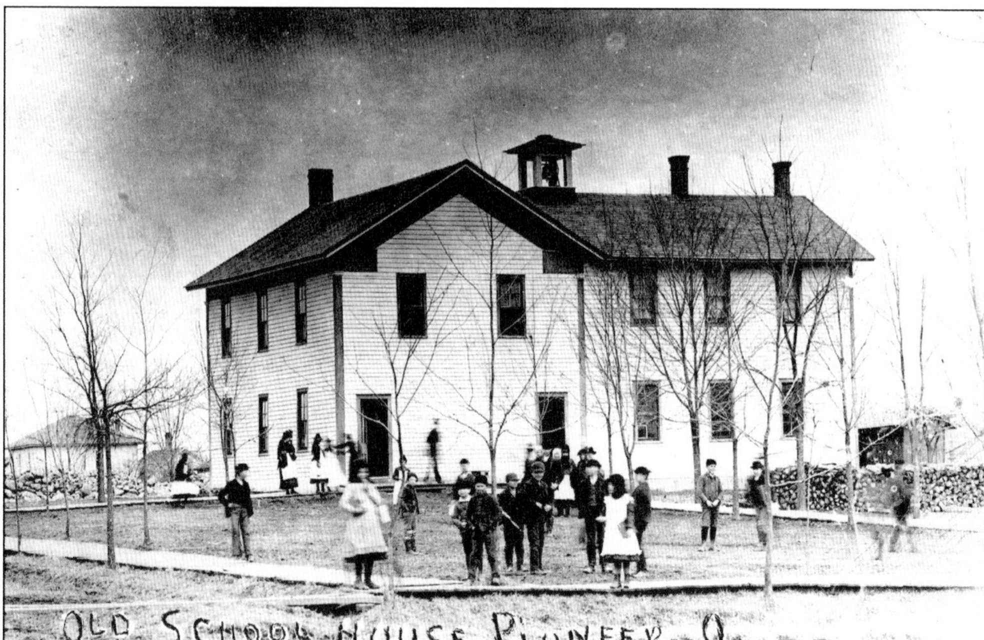

The Pioneer area's first classes were held in a log structure as early as 1844. In 1847, a frame schoolhouse was built on the east side of South State Street. Just prior to the Civil War, the frame school above was erected southwest of Cedar and Church Streets. An addition was constructed in 1875, making four classrooms in the schoolhouse. (WCPL Photographic Archives.)

In 1889, this brick school was completed west of Pioneer's frame school building on the southeast corner of North State and Church Streets. It served the community until a new high school was built in 1922–1923 on Baubice Street. After they were no longer needed for educational purposes, the old frame schoolhouse and this brick school building housed local industries. The two historic education buildings were razed in 1974.

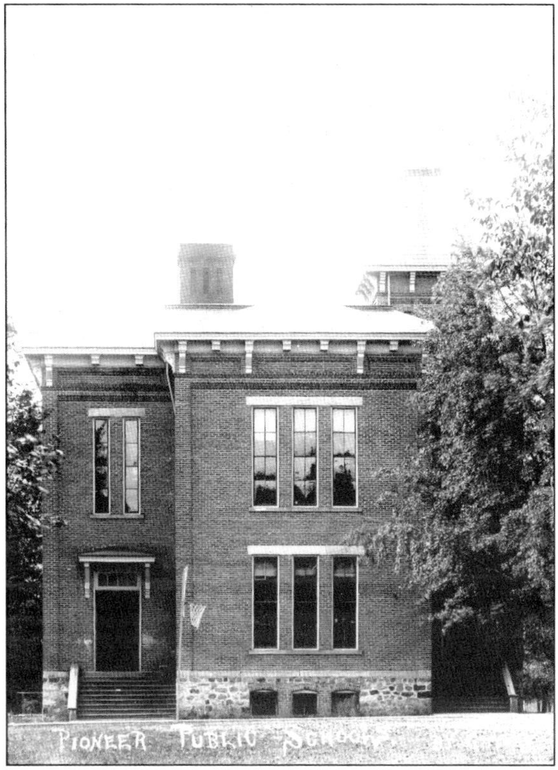

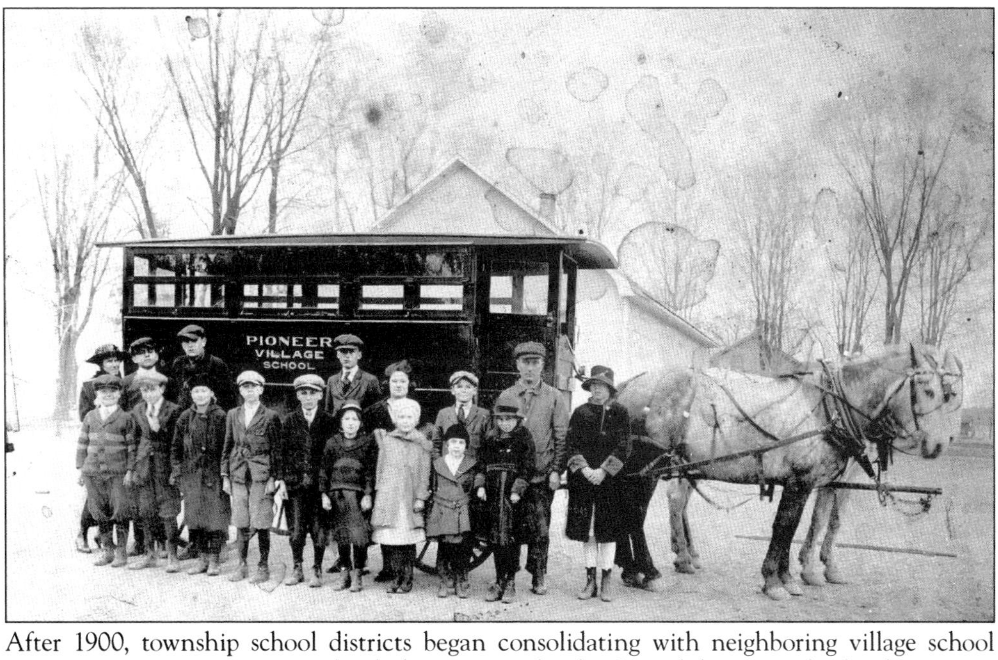

After 1900, township school districts began consolidating with neighboring village school systems or constructing centralized elementary schools. Consolidation made the distance to school too great for most rural students to walk, so transportation was provided. This 1919 photograph shows a horse-drawn school bus used by the Pioneer School prior to motorized buses. (WCPL Photographic Archives.)

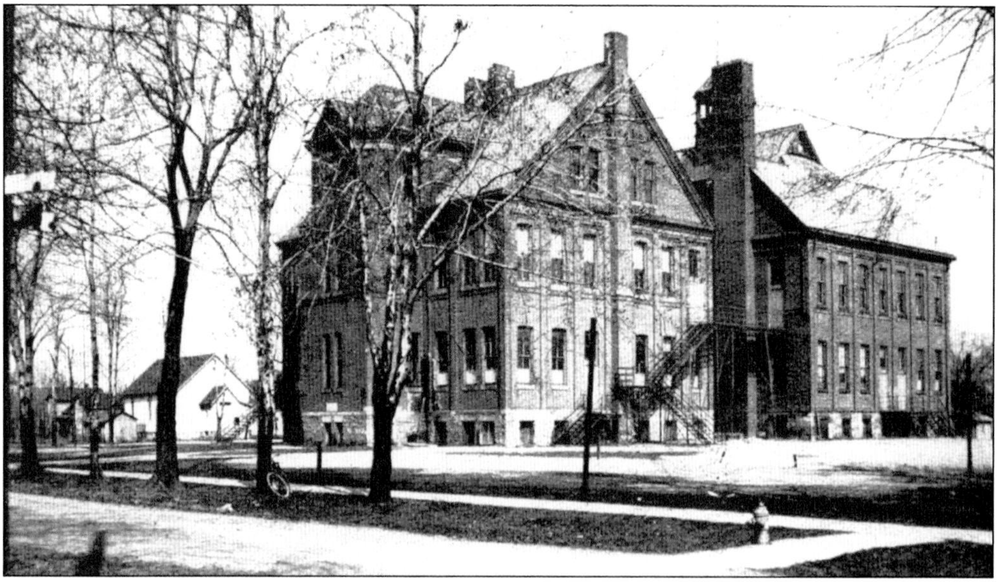

In the 1840s, a log house served as Montpelier's first school. By 1863, a frame school was constructed on Monroe Street south of Jefferson Street. The frame building was replaced by new schools on the site in 1874 and 1881. In 1887, this large brick Union School was built at the southeast corner of Platt and Jefferson Streets. The building was razed in 1939 and replaced by Storrer Elementary School.

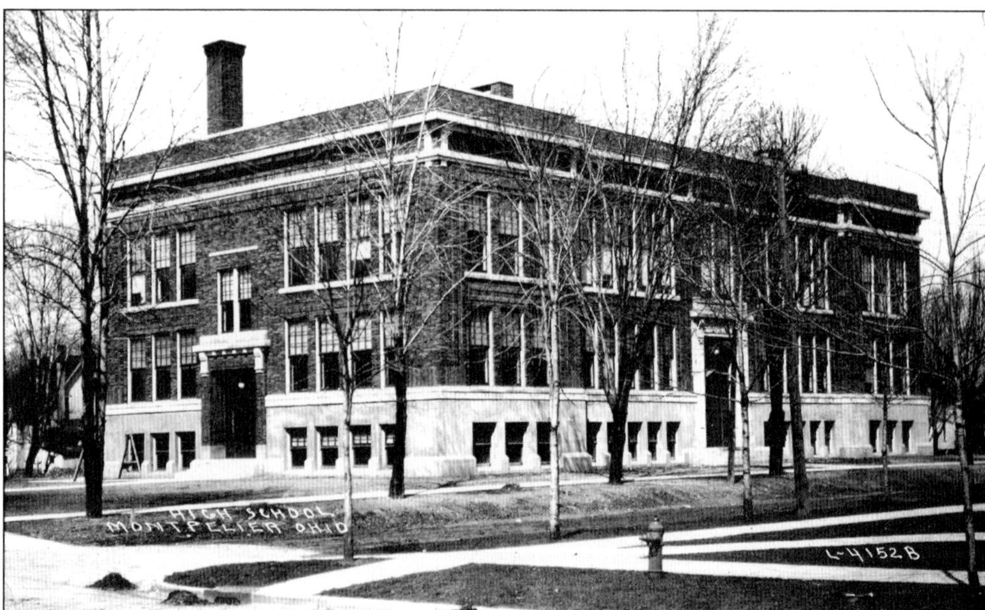

In 1915, this Montpelier High School was built on East Main Street at a cost of $75,000. In 1939, an auditorium was constructed, followed by an addition on the north side in 1959. In May 2006, this building and Storrer Elementary School were razed following completion of the new $28 million, 173,000-square-foot prekindergarten through grade 12 facility on Brown Road.

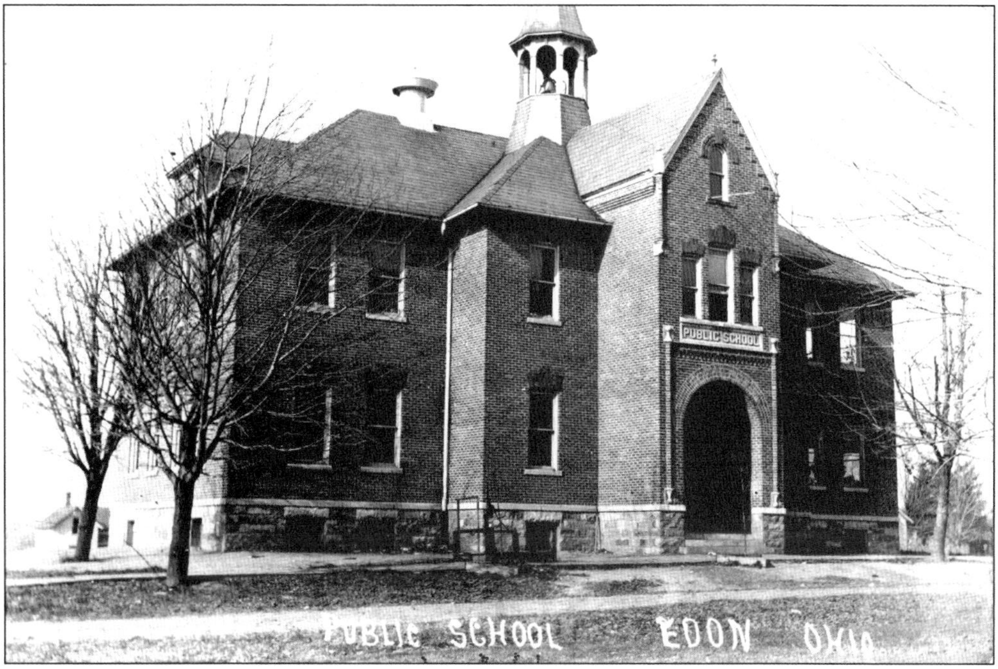

In 1874–1875, Solomon Metzler taught Edon's first school on the third floor of Sheline's Hotel. The following year Edon's first school building was erected on the northwest corner of Franklin and Porter Streets. A new school constructed in 1899 was destroyed by fire in January 1904. This building, completed in 1905, served the community until 1957 when it was demolished to make room for an elementary school addition. (WCPL Photographic Archives.)

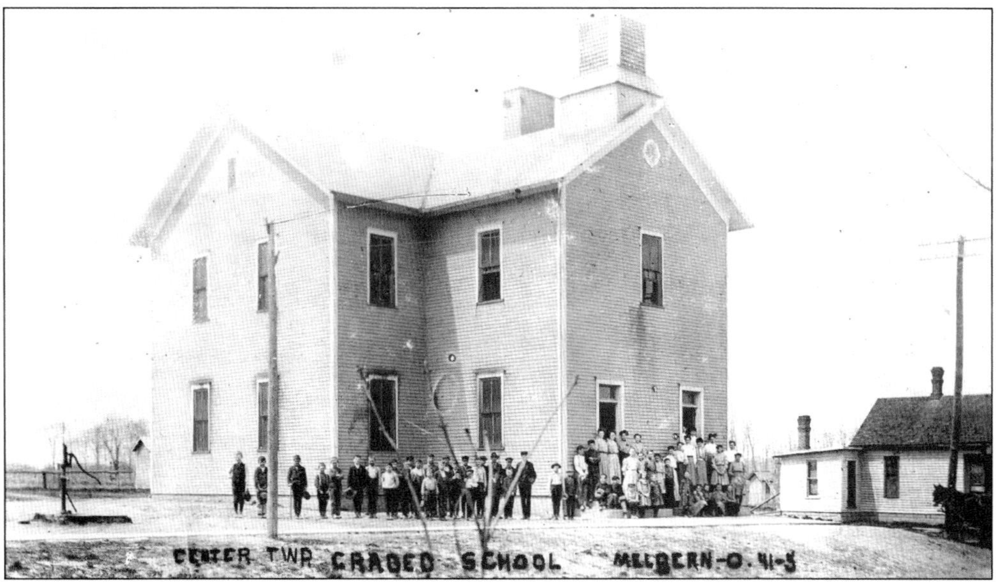

In 1905, the Center Township Board of Education erected this two-story frame school on Melbern's Main Street and offered a two-year high school program for a number of years. In 1944, following consolidation of Center Township schools with neighboring districts, the Center Township trustees purchased the Melbern School for use as a community center. The building was razed in 1987. (WCPL Photographic Archives.)

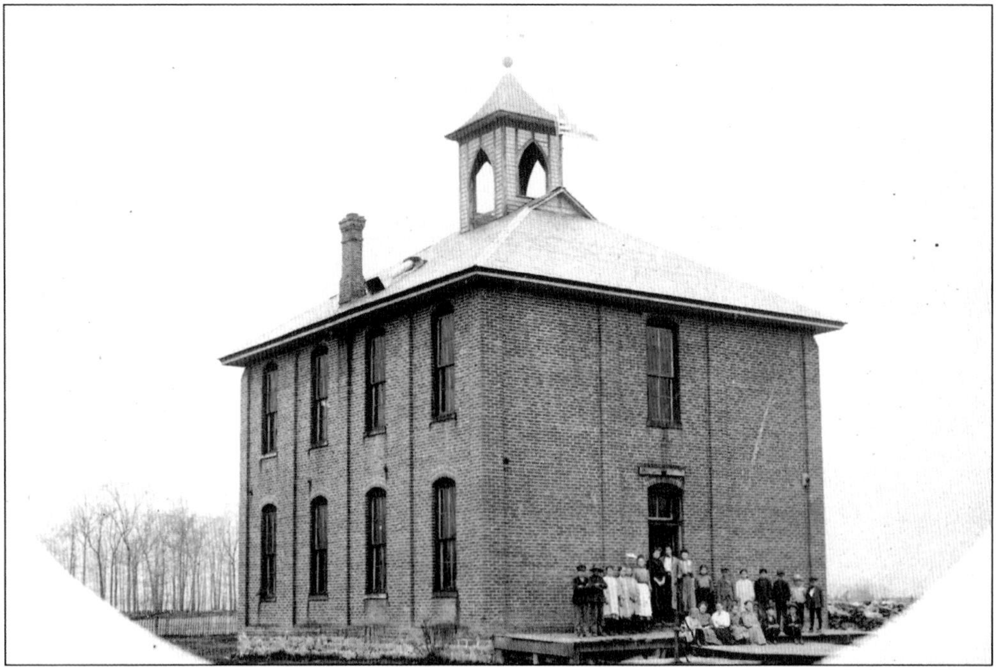

In 1887, Blakeslee's two-story brick school was constructed on the west side of Madison Street south of Dearborn Street. Prior to this, local children attended classes in store buildings. The brick school was used until the 1930s, and the building was razed in 1966. (WCPL Photographic Archives.)

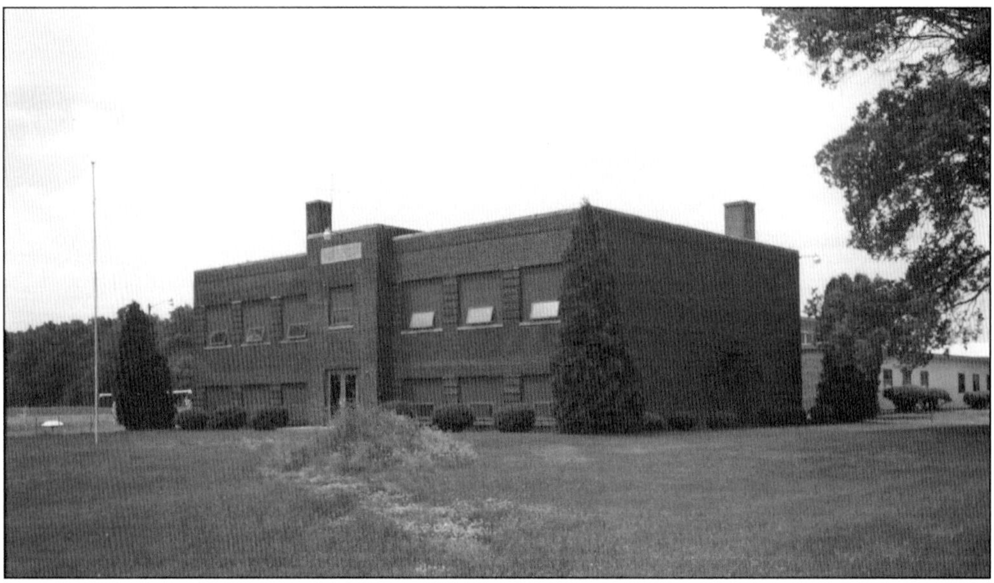

In 1940, this $25,000 centralized grade school was completed at Cooney to replace five Northwest Township rural schoolhouses. The Edon and Northwest Township school districts merged in 1956, prompting an addition to the Cooney School containing three classrooms, general purpose room, cafeteria, kitchen, and boiler room. Following completion of the new prekindergarten through grade 12 facility in Edon in 2004, Northwest Township acquired the Cooney School and demolished the 1940 section.

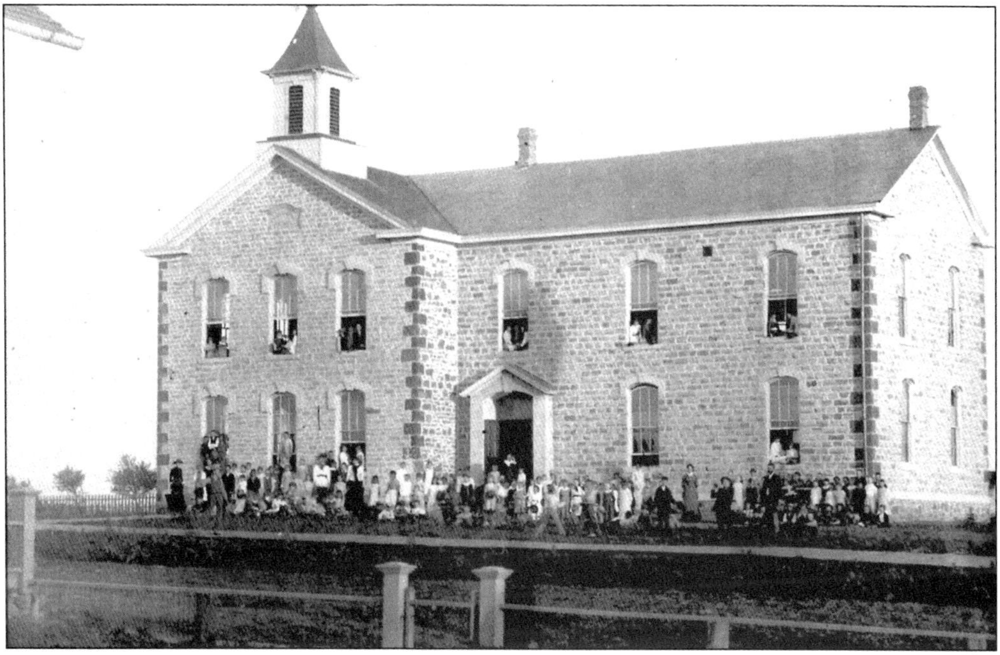

Available information indicates Edgerton's first schoolhouse stood on North Michigan Avenue at the site of the 1906 school building. The next school was erected near the intersection of Michigan Avenue and Indiana Street. A third building was constructed prior to 1864 west of the Methodist church on Hull Street and later served as a Masonic hall. In 1867, the brick school above was built at the southeast corner of Elm and Bement Streets. This two-story, 40-by-70-foot school contained four rooms. The brick school below was completed on North Michigan Avenue in 1906. The building saw several additions and was used until the 2004 high school building was completed. (Above, Edgerton Historical Society; below, WCPL Photographic Archives.)

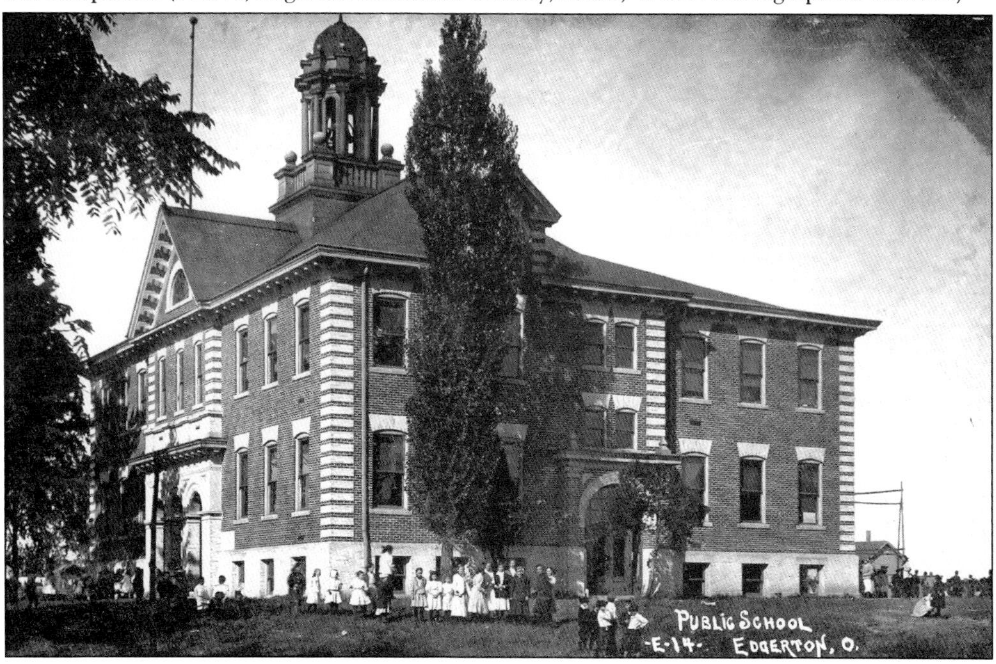

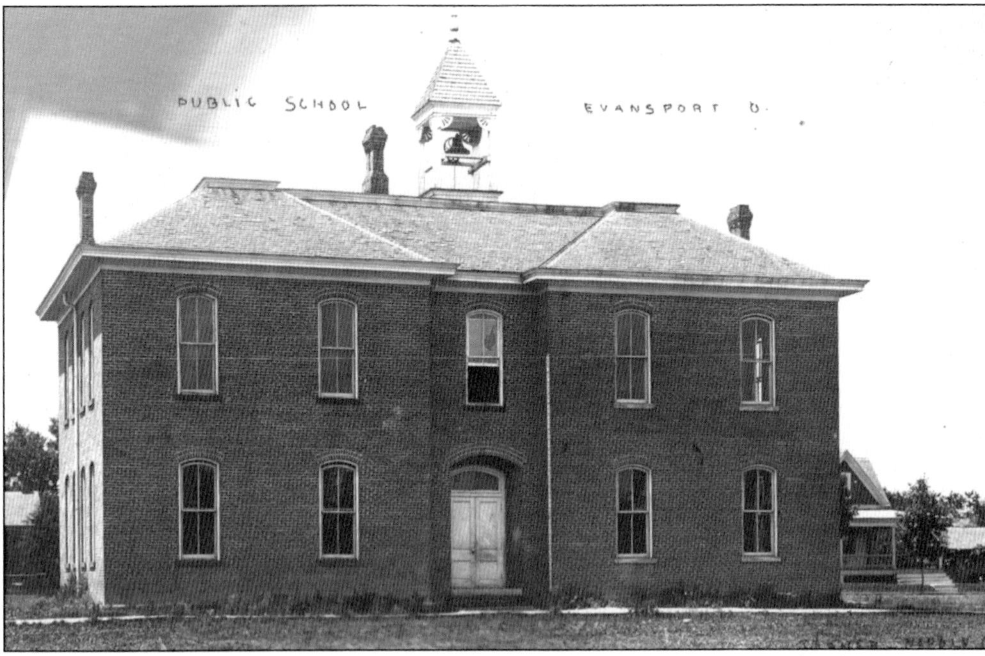

The date Evansport's first school was established is unknown. Directors of School District No. 1 Tiffin Township purchased Lot 104 for $30 on March 13, 1843. A schoolhouse was probably erected around that time. This two-story brick school was built about 1890 east of the Methodist church. The building's second floor was removed around 1920. It was used for classes until around 1930 and was razed in November 2004. (Sue Buehrer.)

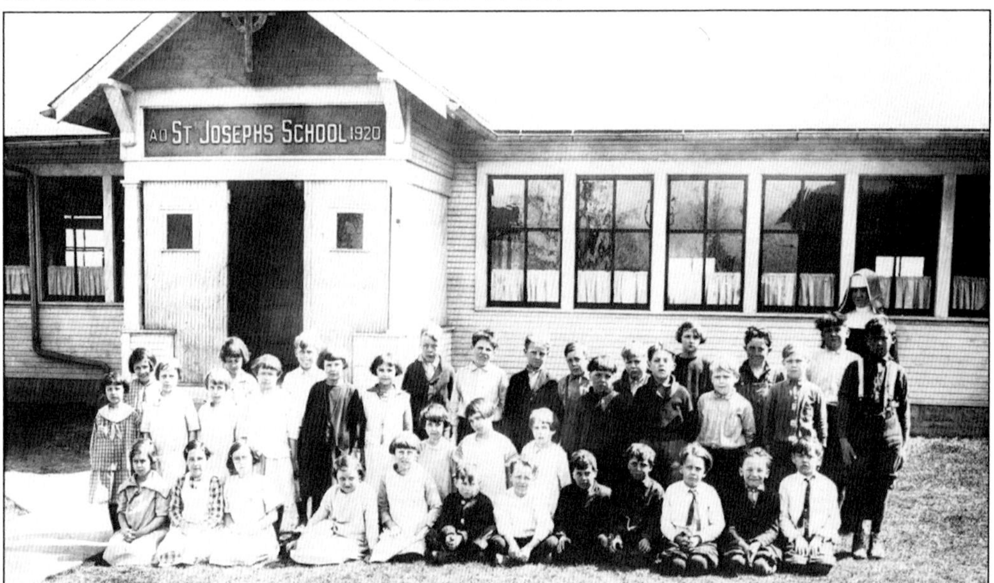

In 1920, the frame St. Joseph's Parochial School shown in this c. 1926 photograph was constructed in Blakeslee. Nearly 60 students in grades 1–8 occupied its two classrooms. In 1960, a $170,000 four-room brick facility with a basement and cafeteria was dedicated. Enrollment peaked at about 150 students in the 1960s; with a final enrollment of only 24 pupils, the school closed in 2007. (WCPL Photographic Archives.)

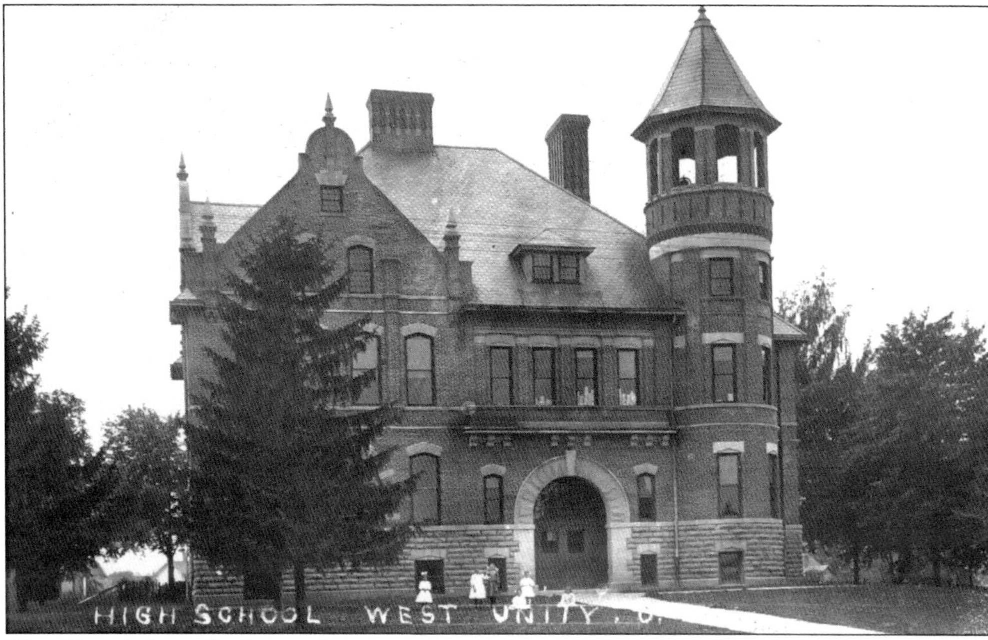

West Unity's first school was a log structure near Rings Cemetery replaced by a frame building on the southwest corner of Jackson and Main Streets. In 1854, a frame schoolhouse was constructed at School and Church Streets. In 1878, West Unity's first brick school was completed on a hill west of South High Street at a cost of about $10,000. This facility was destroyed by fire in November 1897. In September 1900, the imposing $19,000 brick and limestone building above opened for classes. The high school below was completed in 1921 next to the 1900 building. In 1980, the 1900 school building was razed.

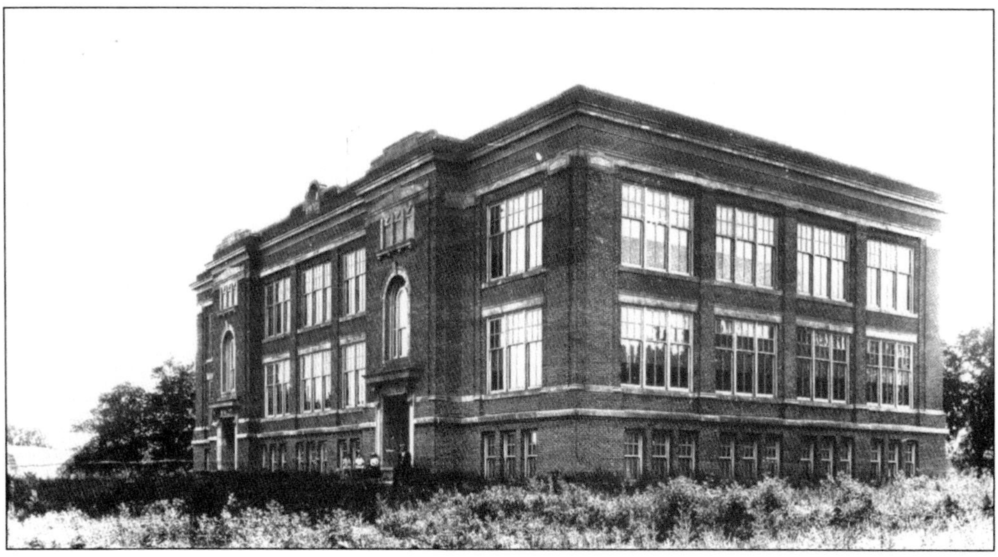

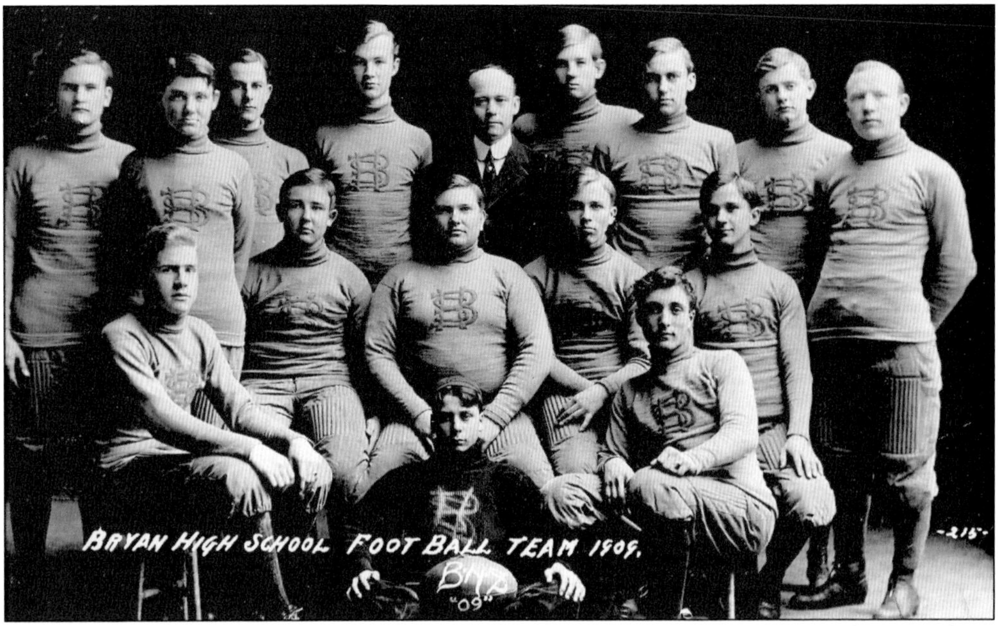

The 1909 Bryan High School football team won five of its nine games. Team members are, from left to right, (first row) mascot Red Waffle and D. O. Stewart; (second row) George Mignin, Earl Stripe, Doc Kittredge, Carl Neblung, and Harry Culbertson; (third row) Charles E. Arnold, Charles Ensign, Arthur Neff, James Schrider, Principal Alstetter, Ralph Diehl, Wendel Greiser, Don Squires, and Ed Murray. (WCPL Photographic Archives.)

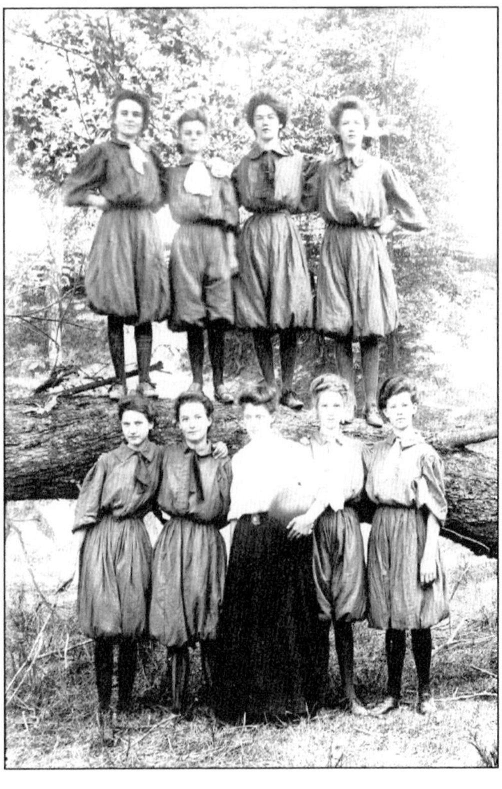

Girls' basketball has long been enjoyed in Edgerton. Members of the 1908 Edgerton High School girls' basketball team are, from left to right, (first row) Esther Sharp, Alice Lahrman, Helen Sharp, Florence Frager, and Gertie Fisher; (second row) Minnie Krill, Berneice Smith, Marian Fusselman, and LaRue Gabriel. (Edgerton Historical Society.)

Five

PUBLIC SERVICE

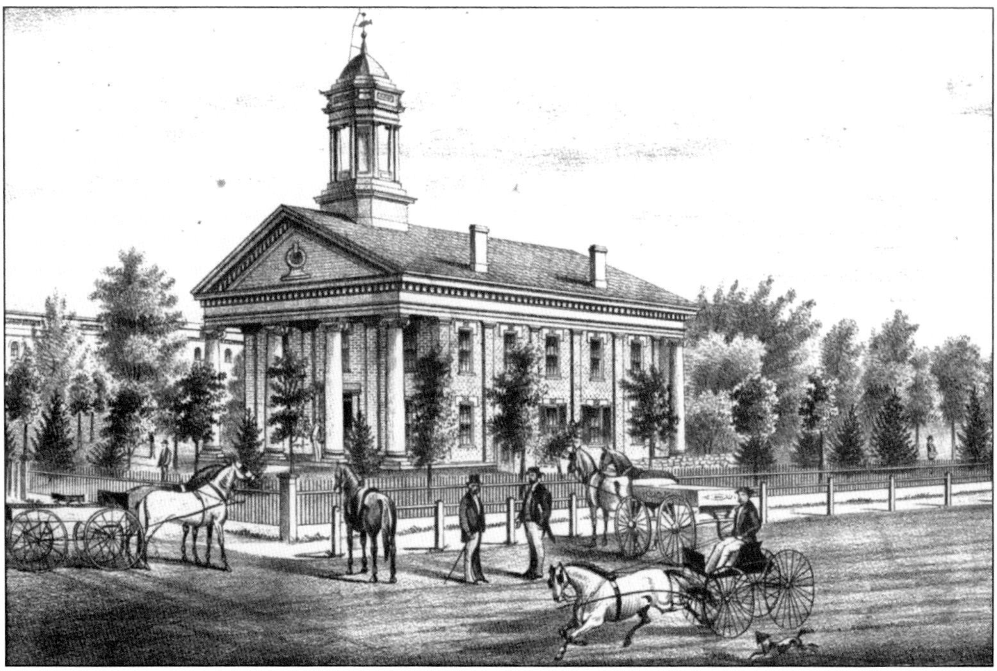

When the county offices were moved from Defiance to Bryan in 1841, court was held in a log building at the southeast corner of Main and Mulberry Streets. Construction of the courthouse above began on Bryan's public square in 1843, and the building was occupied in late 1845 or early 1846. The courthouse fell victim to the dispute between Montpelier and Bryan over location of the county seat. The courthouse was razed in 1888 and was replaced by the existing county courthouse. (Williams County atlas of 1874.)

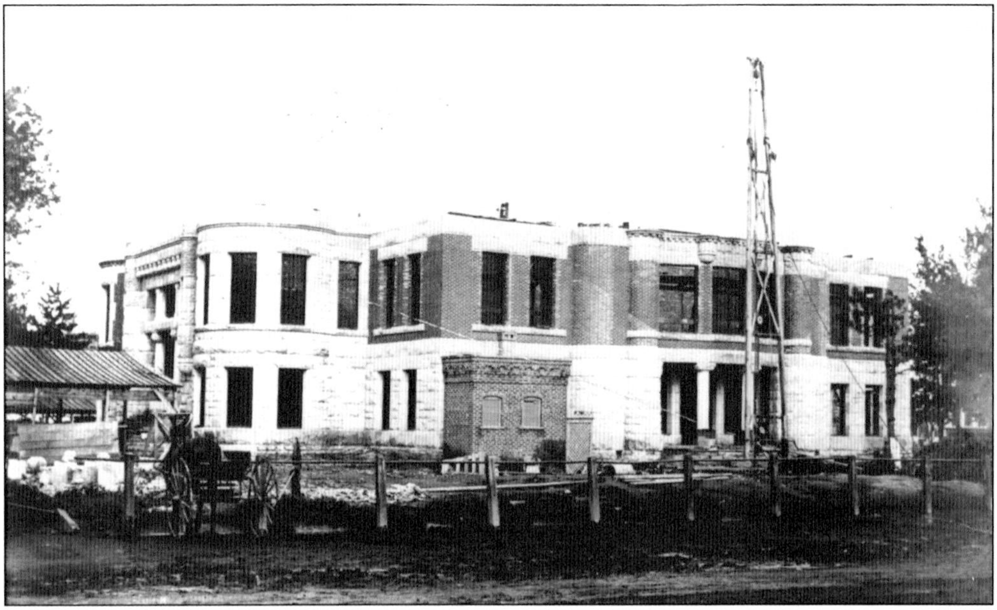

Construction of the present Williams County Courthouse began in 1888. Pressed brick used in its construction came from Chicago, and its Berea and Amherst stone were dressed by Scottish stonecutters who amazed onlookers by working from narrow scaffolds 125 feet in the air. The courthouse tower walls are three feet thick. Its distinctive windows are quality American plate glass with a curve designed to allow more light into its offices. (WCPL Photographic Archives.)

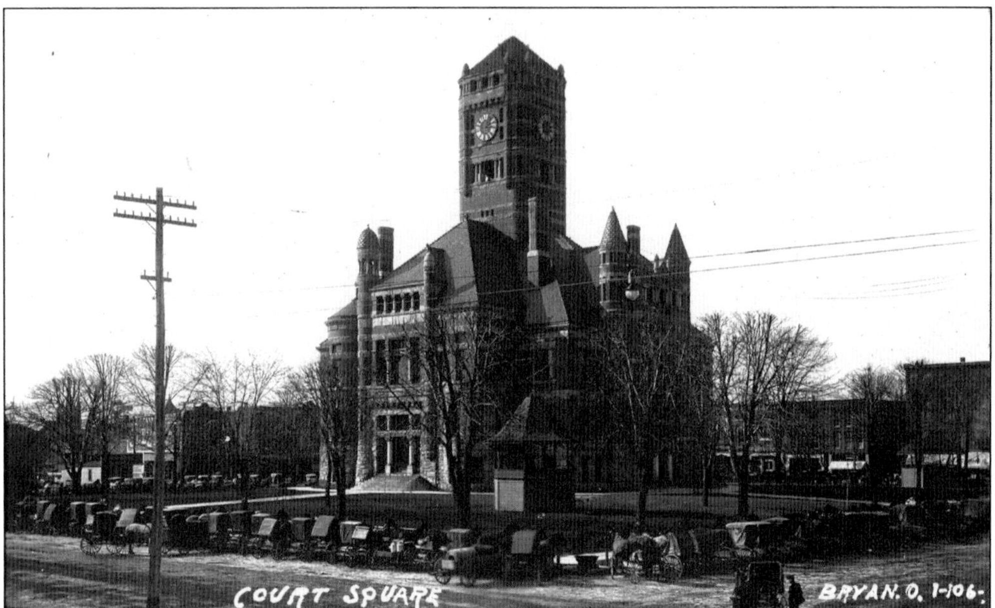

The Williams County Courthouse was designed by Edward O. Fallis and built by Malone Brothers and Earhart—both from Toledo. It took three years to complete the massive 160-foot structure, which was first occupied on July 2, 1891. The building cost about $185,000, including furniture purchased from Conant Brothers of Toledo. This photograph was taken from the southeast corner of the square between 1902 and 1908.

Williams County's first sheriff was William Preston, who defeated James Shirley 48–14 in the county's first election in April 1824. This photograph shows Deputy Sheriff Mick Fletcher (left) with Williams County sheriff Leroy Siders, who served from 1932 to 1940. (WCPL Photographic Archives.)

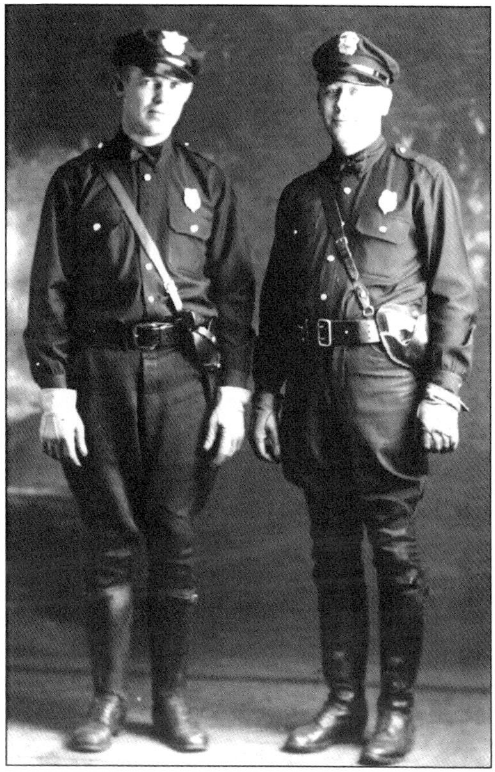

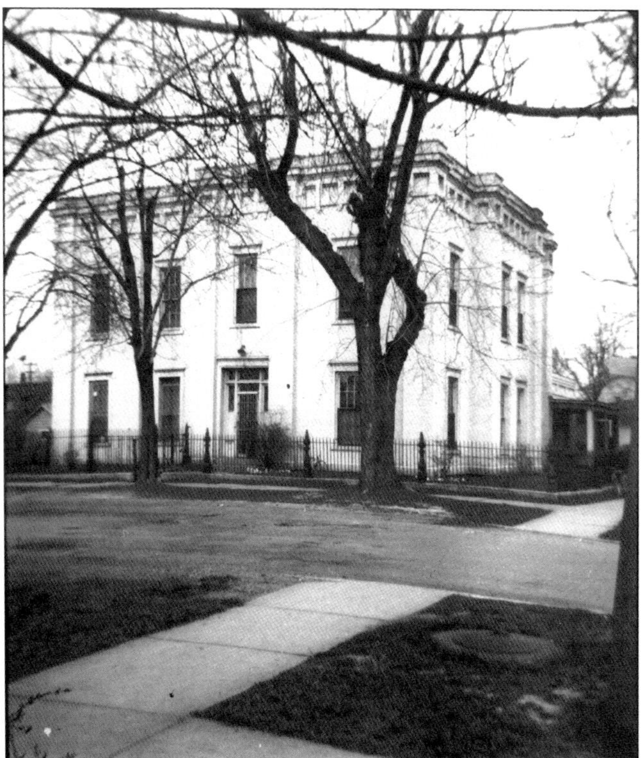

The brick Williams County Jail was completed on the northeast corner of Bryan's Beech and Bryan Streets in 1868, replacing two earlier log structures. This early-1930s photograph was taken before the jail was extensively remodeled, including a tan brick exterior veneer. Following the 1990 completion of the Corrections Center of Northwest Ohio, southeast of Stryker, the old jail became the Williams County Safety Building. (WCPL Photographic Archives.)

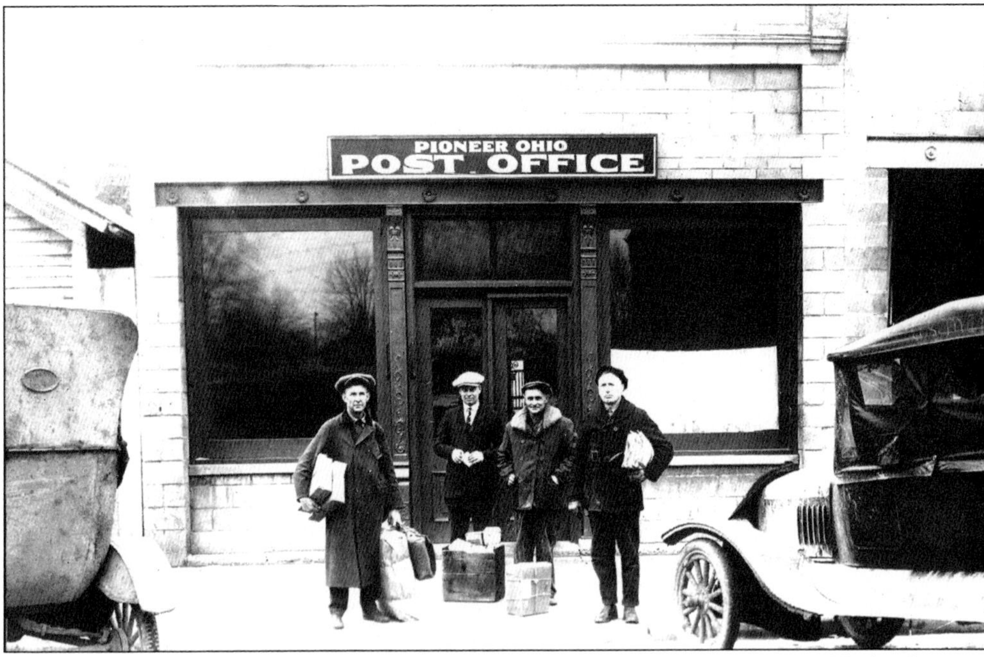

Post offices were among the area's first governmental institutions. On May 1, 1837, the first post office in current Williams County was established at Pulaski with town founder John Perkins the first postmaster. This photograph shows, from left to right, Fred Blount, Al Ritchley, Charley Wiley, and an unidentified man in front of the Pioneer Post Office. Note the automobile on the right with "U.S. Mail" scrawled along its top. (WCPL Photographic Archives.)

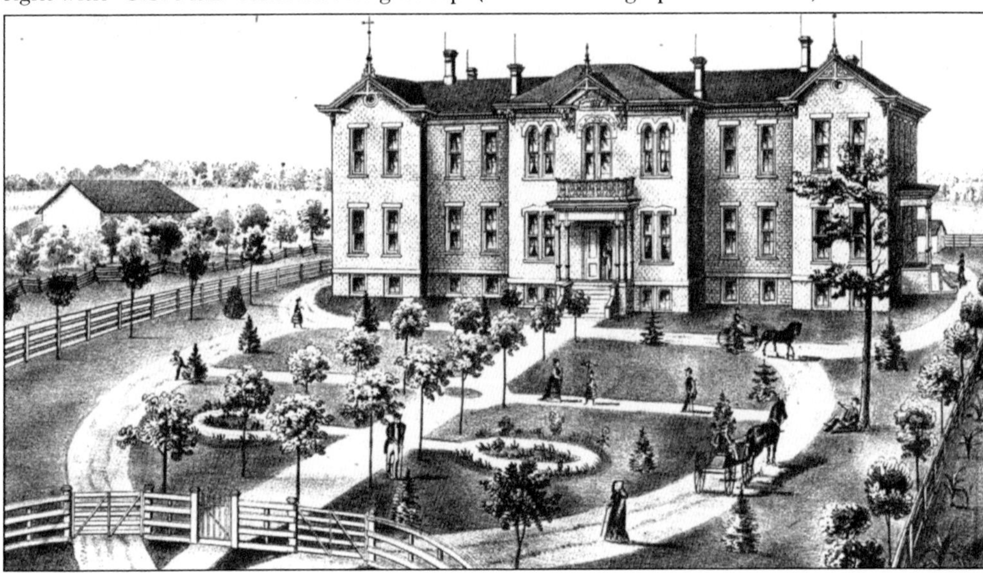

In 1874, Williams County constructed this two-story, 104-by-45-foot brick infirmary or "poorhouse" on a 200-plus-acre Jefferson Township site along County Road 16 north of County Road I.50. Cultivating crops and raising livestock on the surrounding farm helped offset the infirmary's operating costs. In 1966, Hillside Nursing Home (now part of Hillside Country Living) was built to replace the infirmary; the 103-year-old structure was razed in 1977. (Williams County atlas of 1874.)

In 1841, Daniel Wyatt dug a well behind his home on Bryan's square. He stopped work after reaching hardpan. When Wyatt returned, water had burst through the hardpan and was running from the well. The number of fountains grew with Bryan until there were more than 500 flowing wells in the Fountain City. This c. 1910 photograph shows a 10-inch municipal well along the Cincinnati Northern Railroad. (WCPL Photographic Archives.)

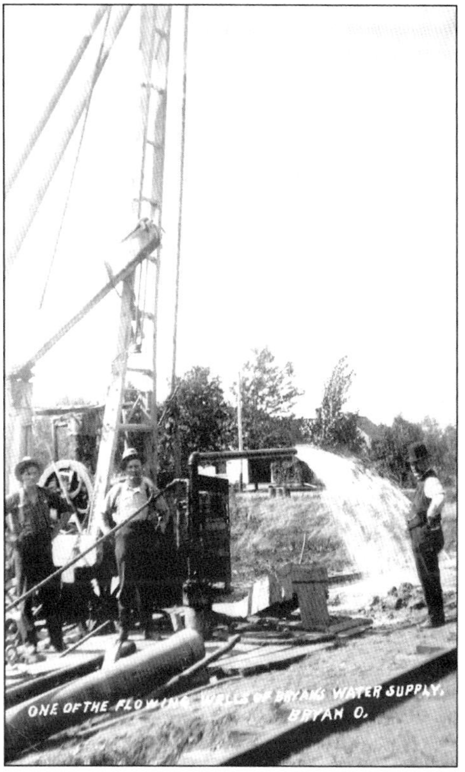

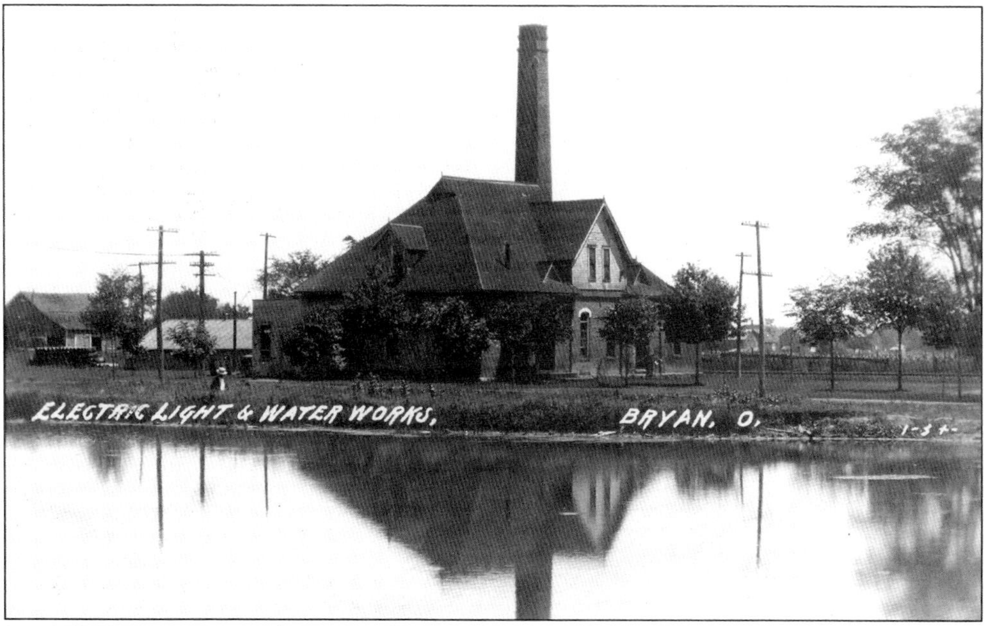

In 1892, Bryan's municipal waterworks was constructed next to the Cincinnati, Jackson and Mackinaw Railroad north of Wilson Street. The building was expanded to accommodate generators when the municipal electric system was created in 1896. In 1919, the present brick power plant was erected around this building, which was then torn down. This photograph was taken looking across Garlow's Ice Pond at Emmett and Maple Streets.

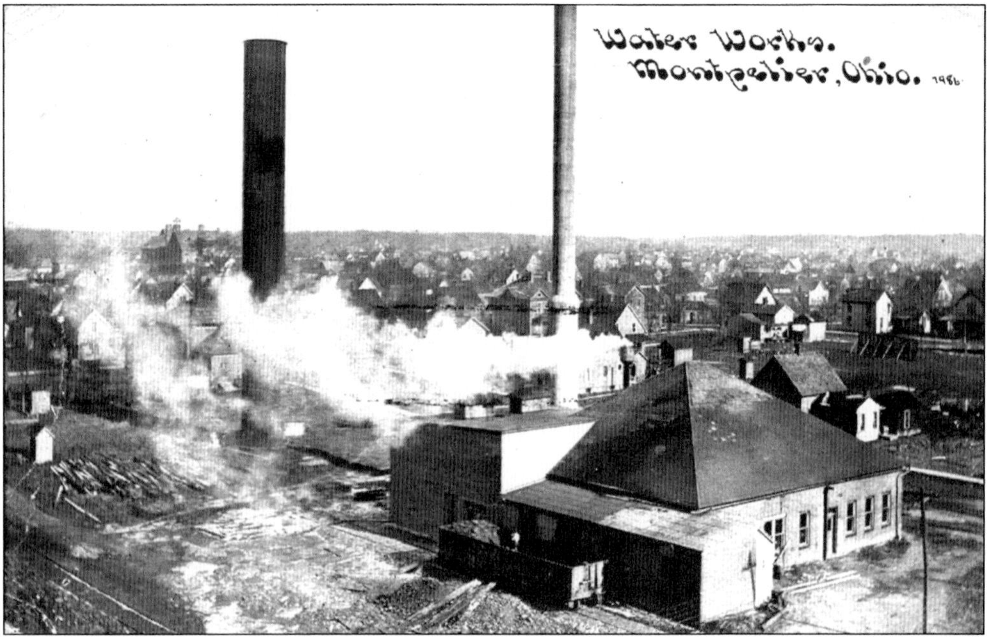

In August 1895, Montpelier awarded contracts for this power plant and waterworks pumping station at Depot and Bryant Streets. The brick building housed two coal-fired boilers to power electric generators. Three wells supplied water to nearly five miles of water mains and 63 fire hydrants. The 110-foot steel standpipe on the left provided water storage and stabilized pressure. On December 14, 1895, streetlights were switched on for the first time.

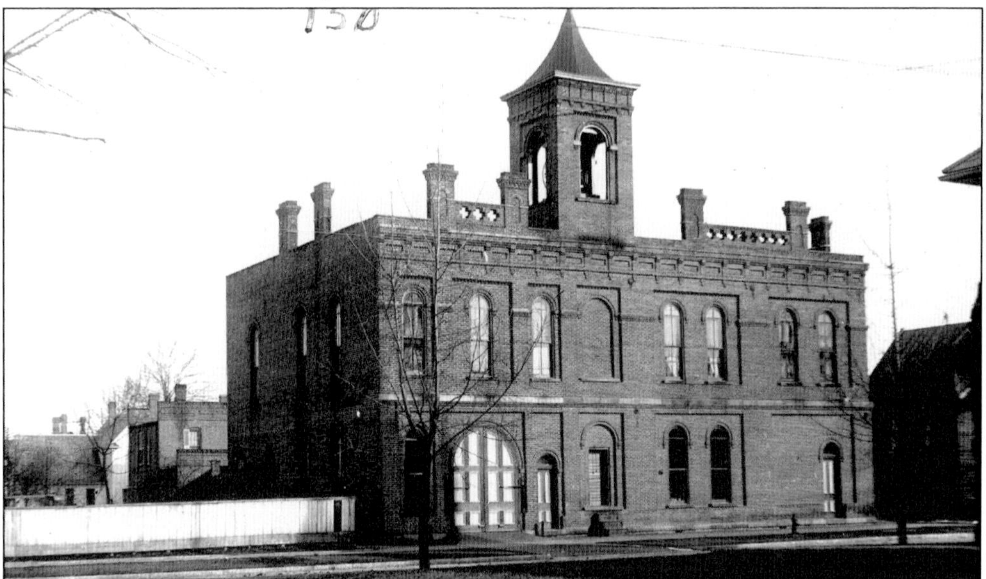

Bryan City Hall has undergone many additions and alterations. The building was constructed by Henry Clay of West Unity and formally dedicated on November 25, 1874. The first floor housed firefighting equipment, a large water tank, and a coal bin. The second floor was divided into rooms for the fire department and council. A rope dangled from the fire alarm bell in the tower to allow people to summon volunteer firefighters. (WCPL Photographic Archives.)

This $8,000 town hall was erected jointly by Edgerton and St. Joseph Township. On August 15, 1884, the building's cornerstone was laid with imposing ceremonies. It was probably first occupied in late 1884 or early 1885. The structure's second floor featured a public hall or "opera house" that hosted speakers, entertainment, and high school commencement exercises. Iron hitching rails on the building's north and west sides were removed in 1946.

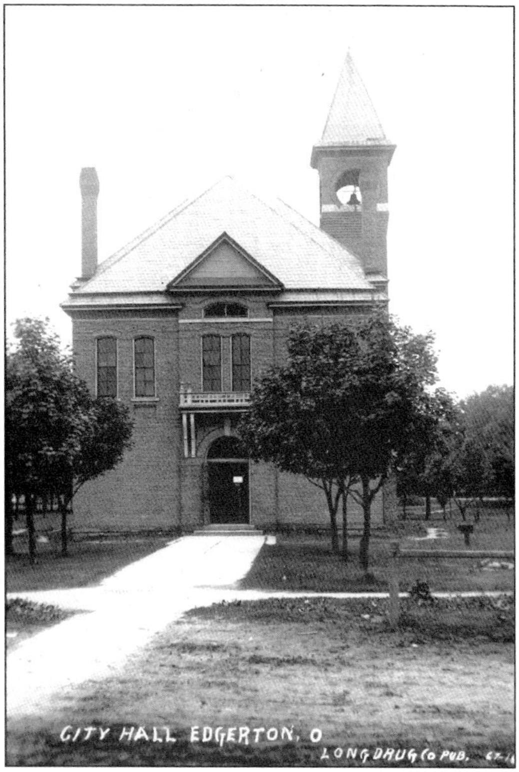

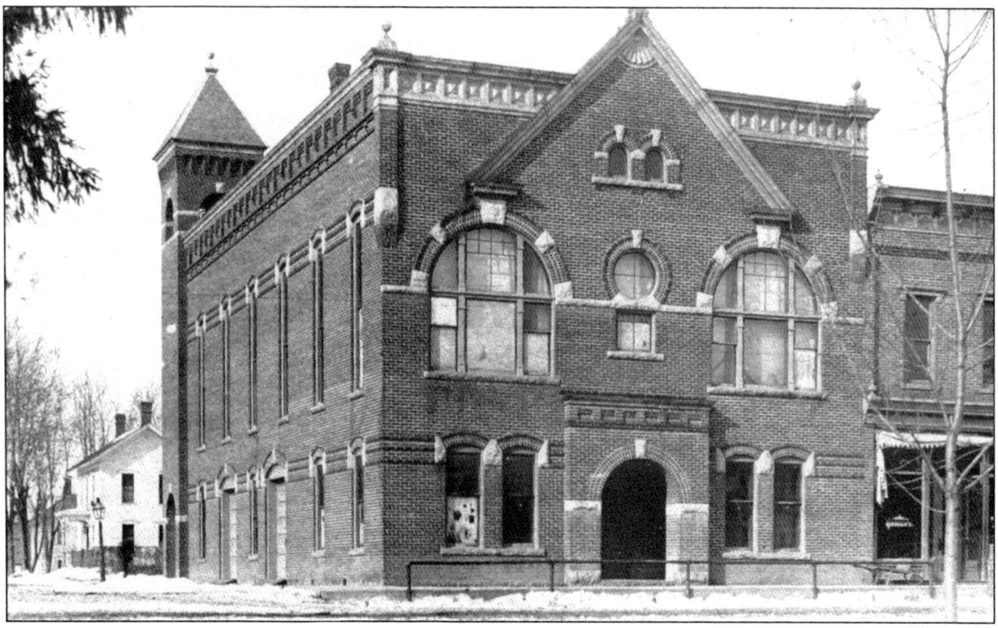

West Unity's town hall was constructed in 1894–1895 at the northeast corner of Jackson and High Streets. Council chambers, a community band room, the fire department, and the village jail occupied the first floor. The second floor housed an auditorium and theater for many years. Note the iron hitching rail in front. The building still serves as West Unity's municipal headquarters following extensive alterations, including removal of its second floor.

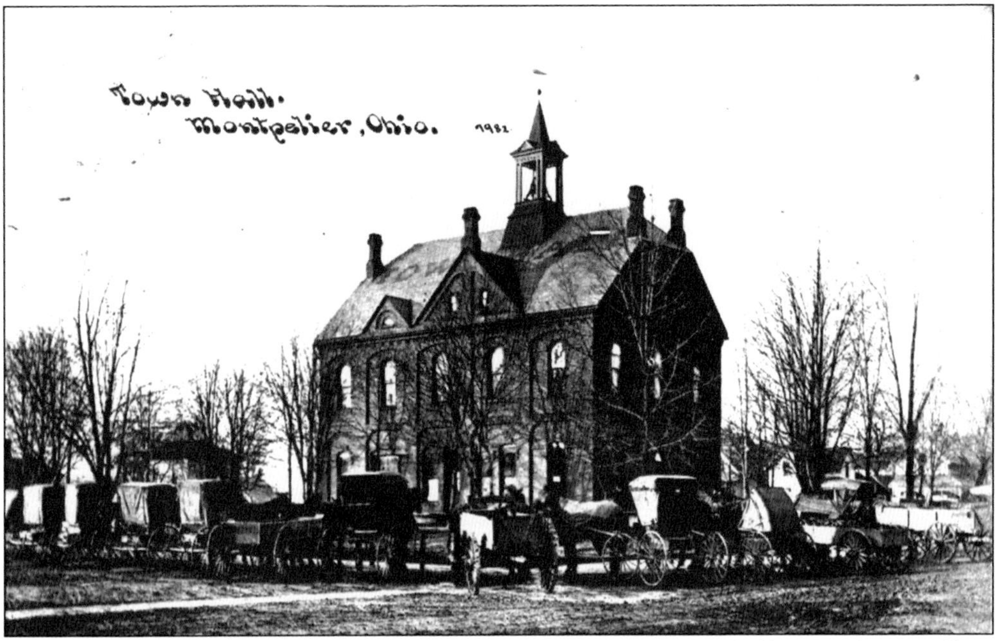

Montpelier was incorporated in 1874, and its first municipal election was held in April 1875. Village council met in Allen's Drugstore until an old schoolhouse was moved to the public square to serve as a municipal building. In 1892, this town hall was constructed jointly by Montpelier and Superior Township. Sam Martin was awarded the construction contract for $4,190.85, and the building was first occupied in January 1893.

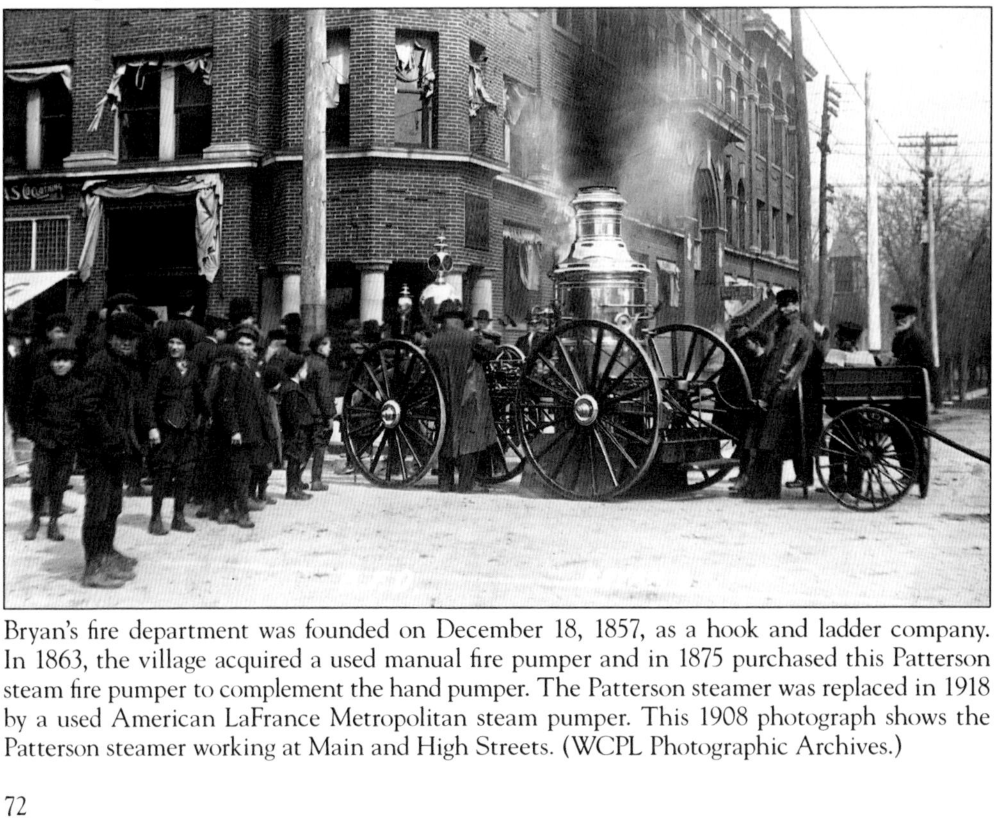

Bryan's fire department was founded on December 18, 1857, as a hook and ladder company. In 1863, the village acquired a used manual fire pumper and in 1875 purchased this Patterson steam fire pumper to complement the hand pumper. The Patterson steamer was replaced in 1918 by a used American LaFrance Metropolitan steam pumper. This 1908 photograph shows the Patterson steamer working at Main and High Streets. (WCPL Photographic Archives.)

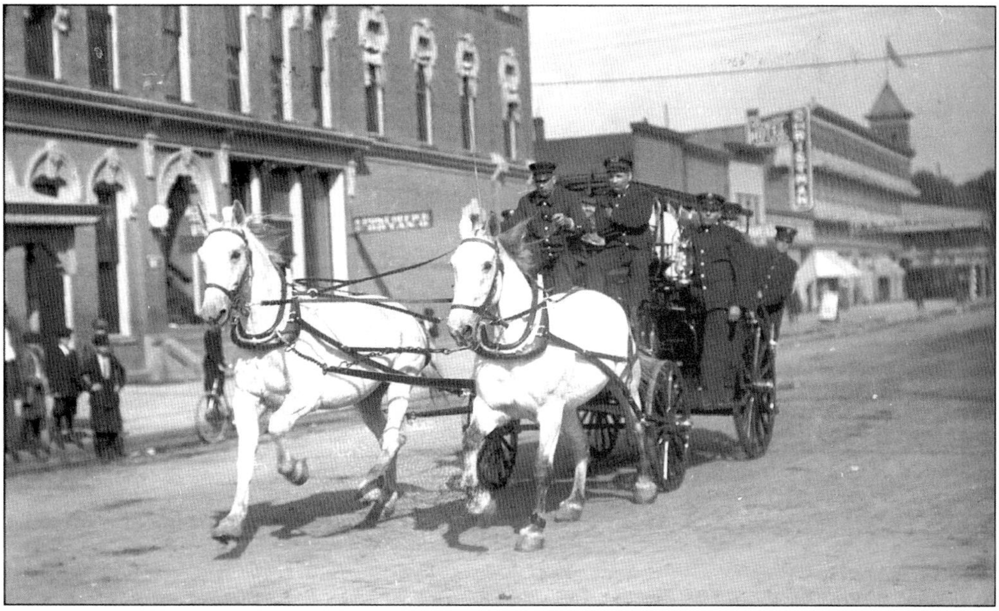

Bryan firefighters pulled their equipment to fires until the American House Hotel blaze in July 1878. The steamer and hand pumper became mired in muddy streets, and people scurried past the stranded equipment to watch the fire. Afterward the village purchased horses to transport fire department apparatus. In this c. 1910 image, firefighters Alex Partee and Wilson Connin drive the department's hose wagon south on North Main Street. (WCPL Photographic Archives.)

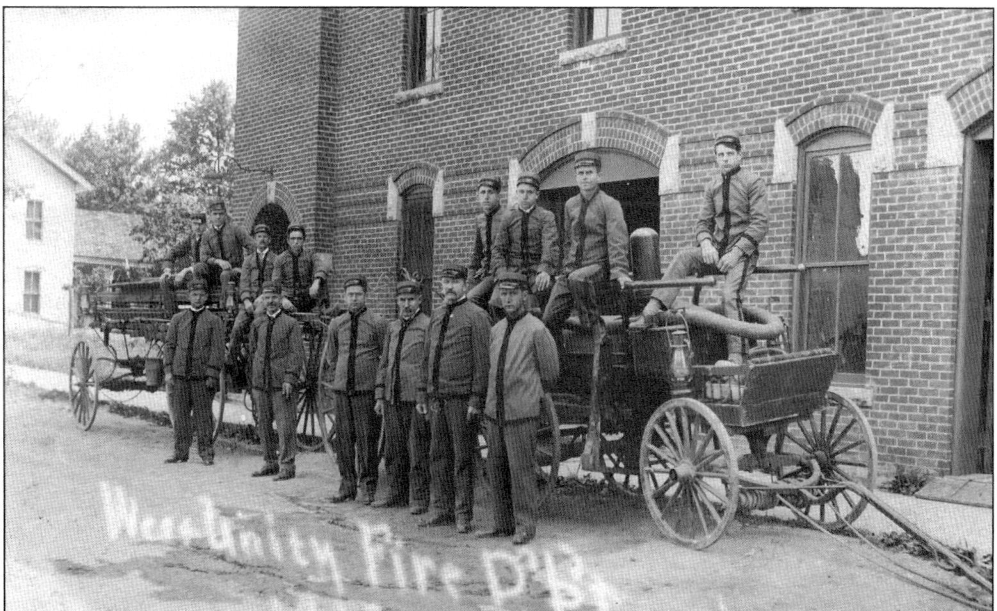

The West Unity Fire Department was created around 1892 in the wake of an August 2, 1888, blaze that destroyed everything but David Holtzberg's residence in the block bounded by Main, High, Jackson, and North Streets. In this 1912 photograph, uniformed firefighters pose with the department's equipment next to the West Unity Town Hall, where the apparatus was stored.

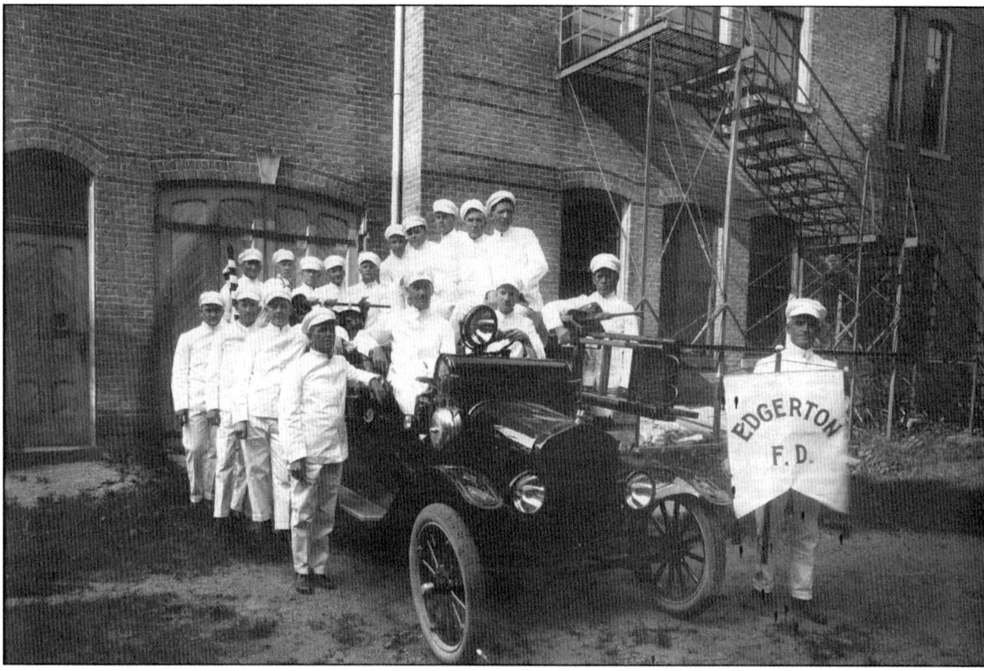

In the 1870s, Edgerton purchased a "Little Giant" fire engine but experienced difficulty maintaining an organized fire department to operate it. In July 1893, fire destroyed the block northeast of Indiana Street and Michigan Avenue. The following year, Edgerton purchased Bryan's used hand-pumped fire engine and organized a fire department. This undated photograph shows Edgerton firefighters in dress uniform at the firehouse next to Edgerton's town hall. (Edgerton Historical Society.)

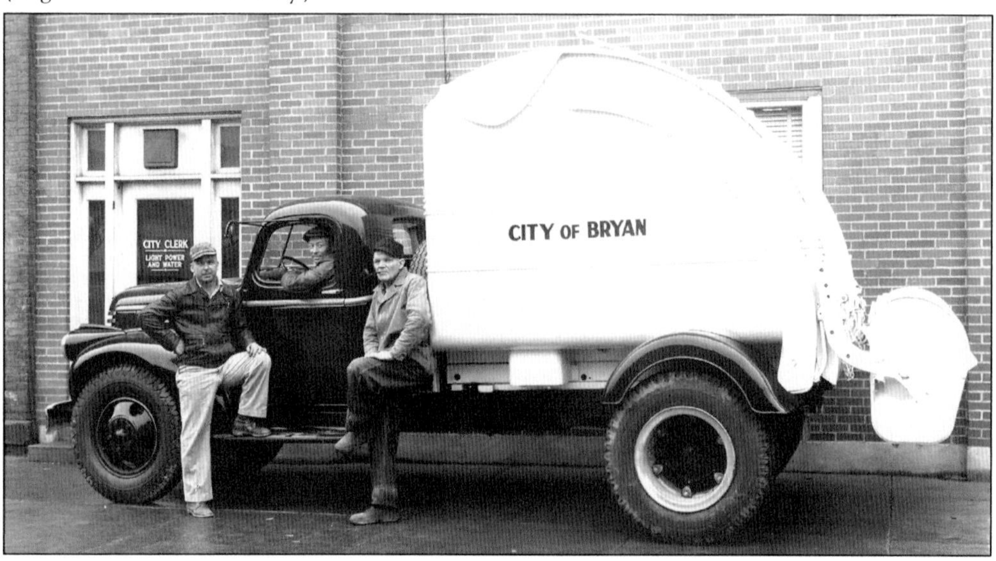

In 1946, the City of Bryan purchased this "Refuse-Getter" to replace an uncovered garbage truck. Collectors placed refuse in the rear hopper, and as the truck moved forward, the hopper rose to the top of the truck and dumped refuse into the enclosed box. Shown with the Refuse-Getter are, from left to right, assistant street commissioner Vernon Coil, city fire truck driver Guy Eager, and street commissioner Burt Rosendaul. (Eldon Smith.)

Six

Religious Life

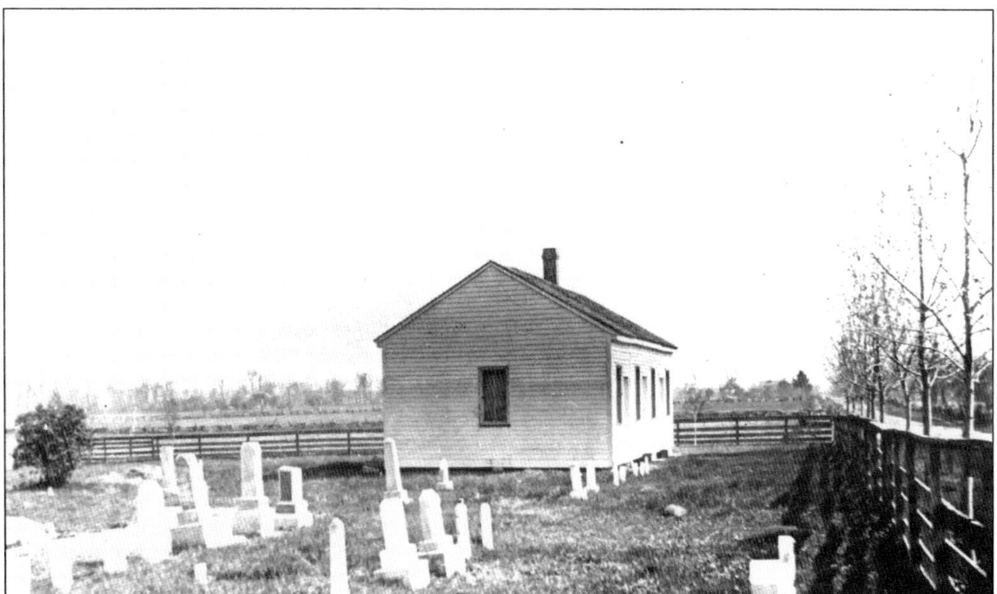

Establishment of the local Society of Friends or Quakers is connected with the Borton family's arrival from New Jersey in the 1830s. Quaker religious meetings were held as early as 1840–1841. In 1850, this meetinghouse was erected on the east side of County Road 22 northeast of West Unity by William Ely Sr. for $250. The Borton brothers—Benjamin, Nathan, Betheul, John, and Job—paid for and helped construct the facility. The Quaker congregation dwindled as older members passed away, and services ceased around 1895. (WCPL Photographic Archives.)

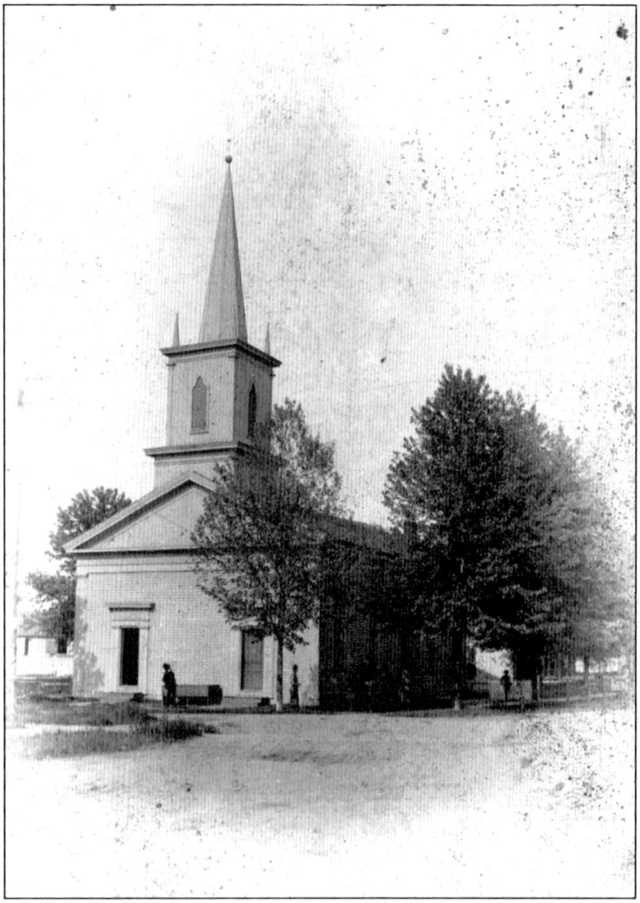

The sweeping changes in church architecture and services are readily visible in these photographs of the buildings that have served Bryan's Wesley United Methodist congregation. In 1855, the simple 40-by-60-foot frame structure at left was dedicated on the southwest corner of Butler and Beech Streets and is believed to be Bryan's first church building. In 1895, this frame house of worship was replaced by the severely Gothic brick church below designed by R. C. Loos of Philadelphia. The Methodist congregation met in this building until the new Wesley United Methodist Church on Center Street (opposite page, top) was completed in 1969. (Above, WCPL Photographic Archives.)

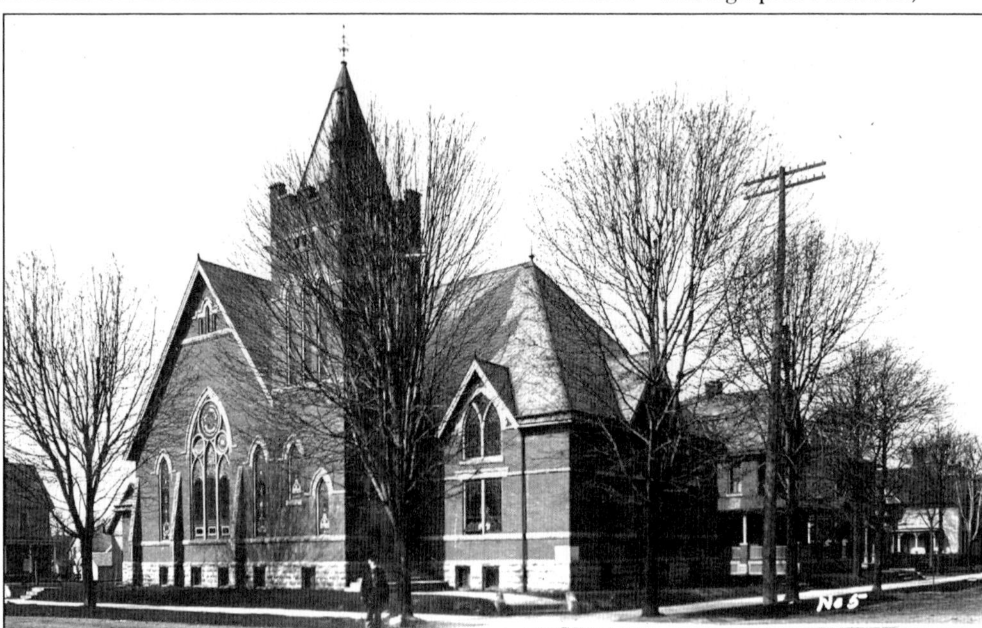

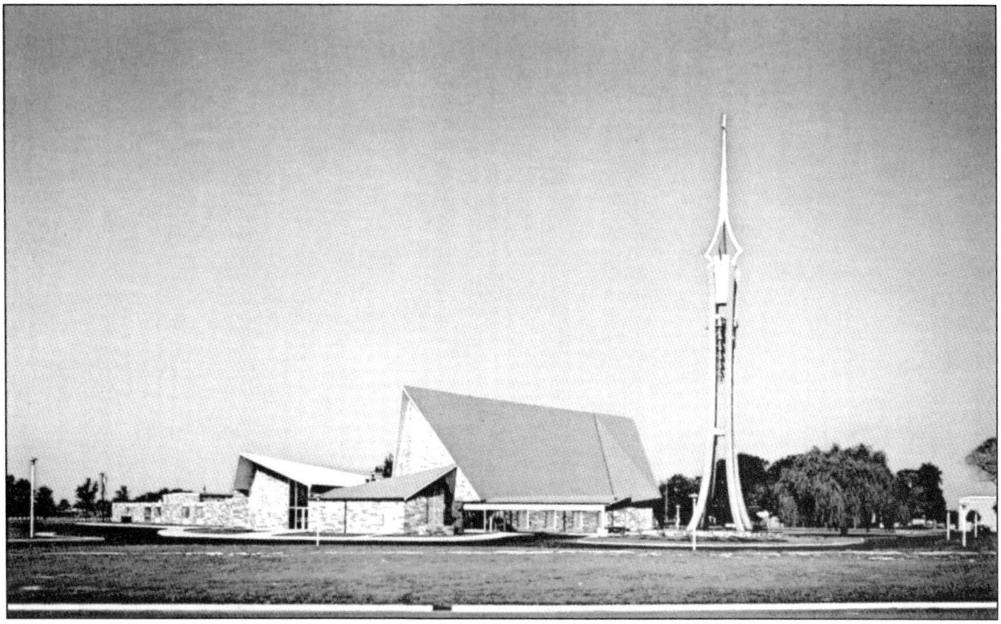

Shown here is the Wesley United Methodist Church completed in 1969.

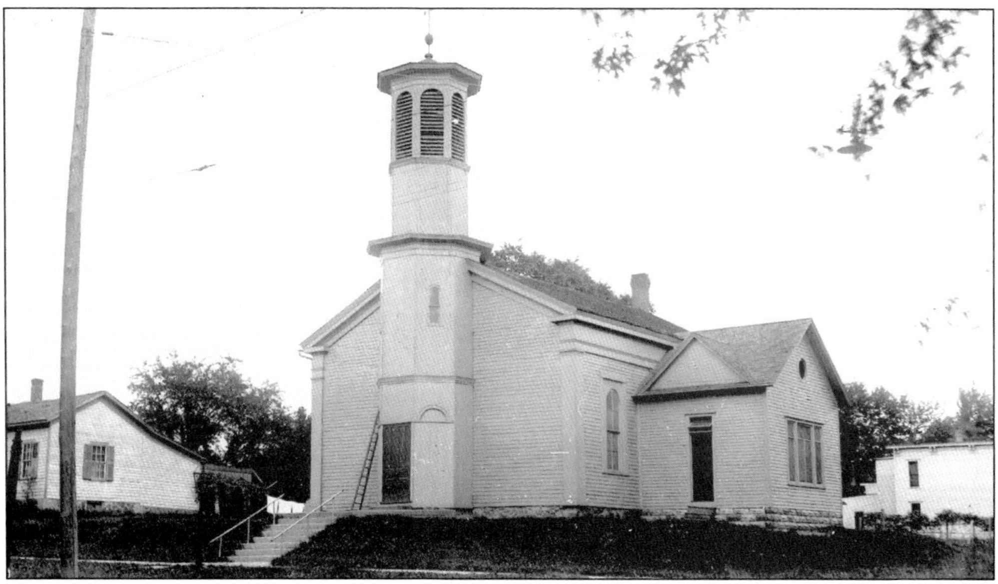

The Pioneer United Brethren in Christ was organized in the 1850s and dedicated this frame church at the northeast corner of North State and Church Streets in 1860. In 1891, the United Brethren denomination split nationally into "Liberal" and "Radical" factions with Pioneer's Liberal congregation continuing to worship in this building. In 1936, Pioneer Grange No. 1992 purchased the church and used it as a Grange hall for many years. (WCPL Photographic Archives.)

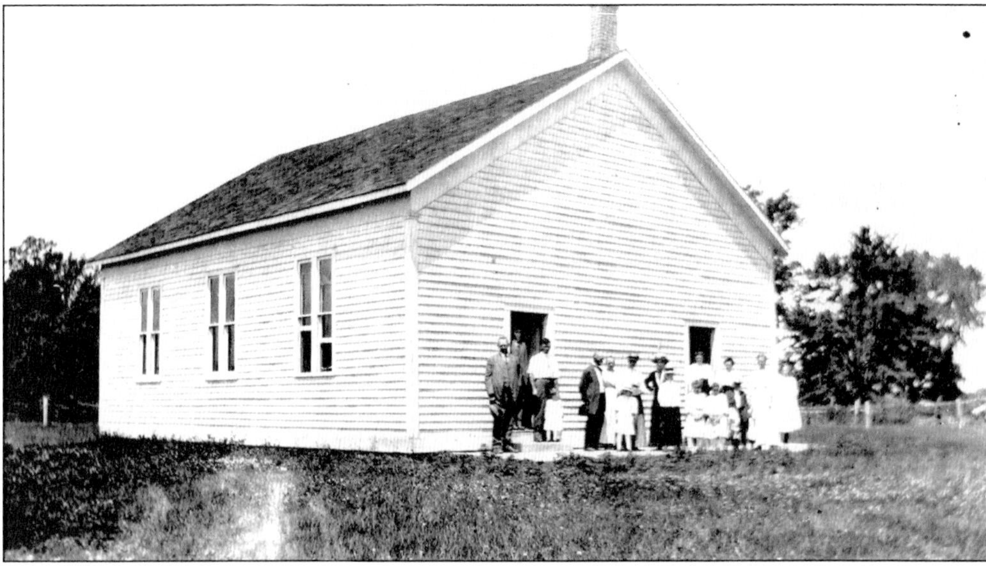

Fountain Chapel Methodist Episcopal Church at the northwest corner of County Roads H.50 and 19.50 in Brady Township was dedicated on February 18, 1862. A divider split the sanctuary, separating men and women during services. Lighting was provided by kerosene lanterns with reflectors on the walls. Fountain Chapel closed around 1931 due to declining membership. The church was converted into a farm machinery storage building and burned down in 1986. (WCPL Photographic Archives.)

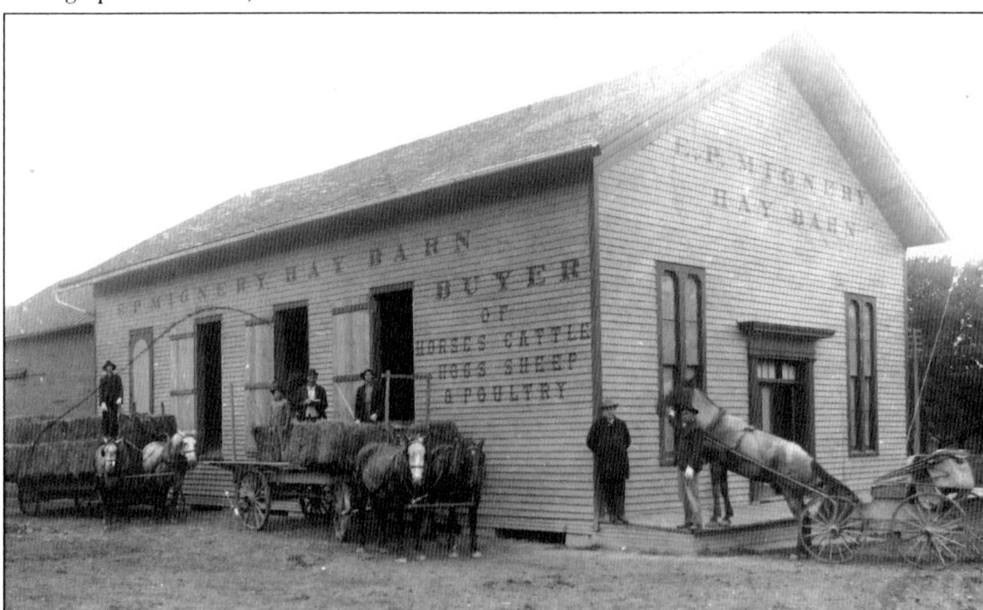

In 1862–1863, Stryker Methodists erected this building on Church Street east of Center Street. The structure served the congregation until a new church was dedicated on the northwest corner of Defiance and Short Streets in January 1902. E. P. Mignerey purchased the old church in 1905, moved it to South Depot Street, and used it for hay storage until fire destroyed the building in July 1909. (WCPL Photographic Archives.)

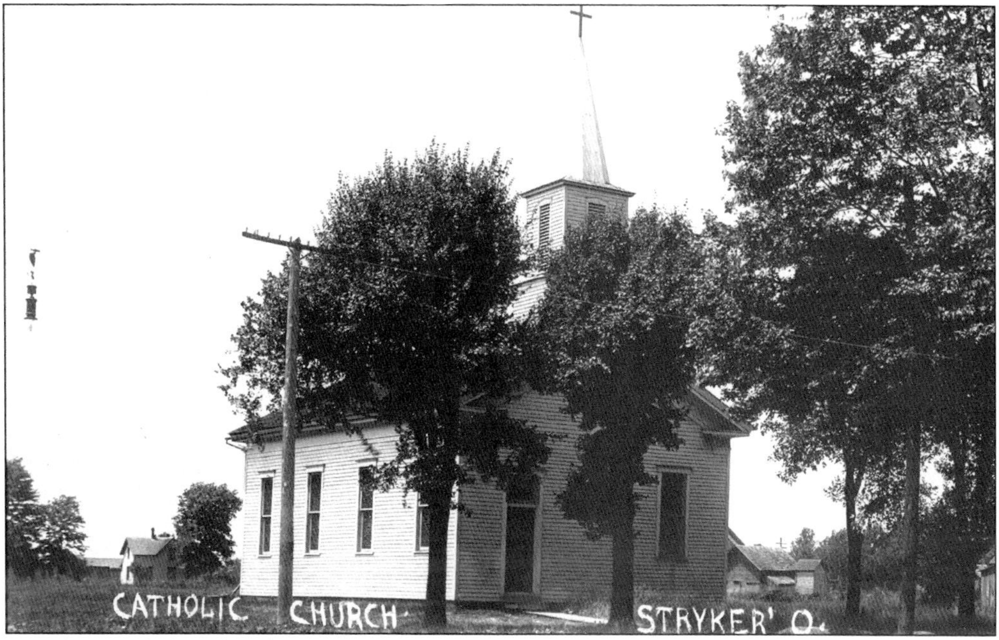

St. John's Catholic Church erected this frame church—Stryker's first house of worship—in 1861–1862 at the northwest corner of Church and Center Streets. It was replaced with a brick structure dedicated on June 16, 1957. In 2004, the Toledo Diocese closed St. John's, and the brick church was razed soon afterward.

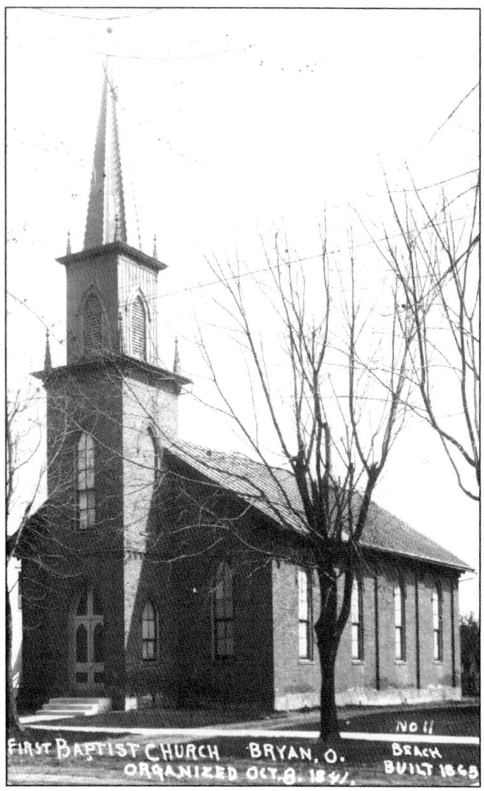

The First Regular Baptist Church in Bryan was organized in October 1841. The congregation began construction of this church in 1863 on the south side of High Street east of Portland. The structure (Bryan's first brick church) was built by Philetus S. Gleason and dedicated on April 2, 1865. The congregation dwindled, and the building was torn down in late 1932 by Olin W. Gleason, the builder's grandson. (WCPL Photographic Archives.)

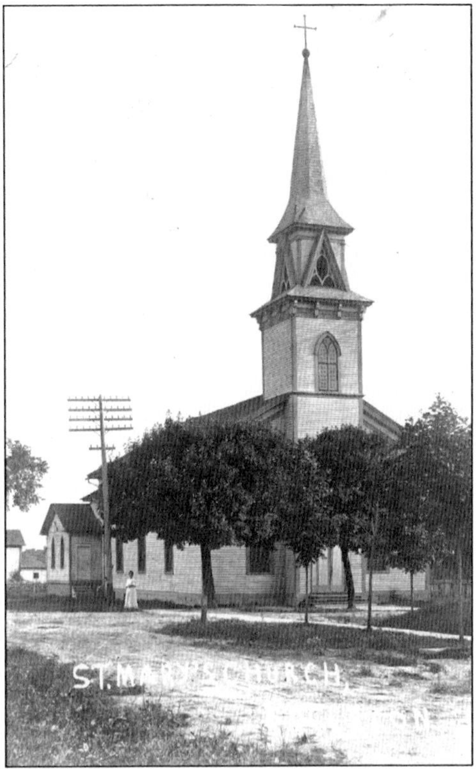

St. Mary's Catholic Church was organized as early as 1853. The congregation's first house of worship was erected southeast of Edgerton. In 1866, this ornate frame structure was erected on the southwest corner of Bement and Locust Streets in Edgerton. In 1940, the existing imposing church was constructed on the site, and this frame church was converted into a Knights of Columbus hall.

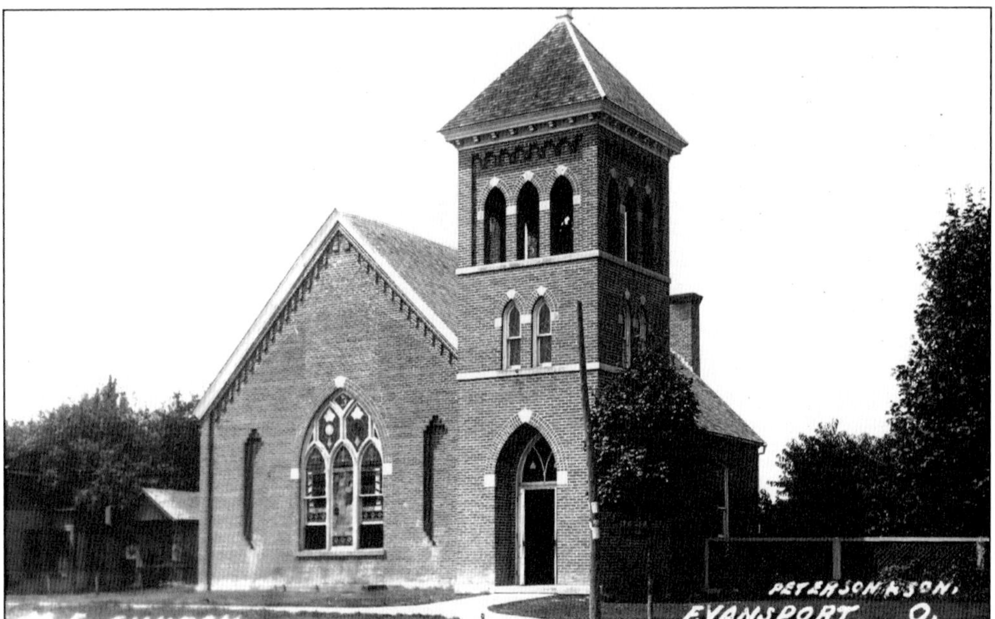

The Evansport United Methodist Church was organized as early as 1841 and constructed a house of worship along the Tiffin River two blocks east of the existing church. In 1874, the congregation erected this brick church on West Street. In 1991, a fellowship hall was added to the building's south side.

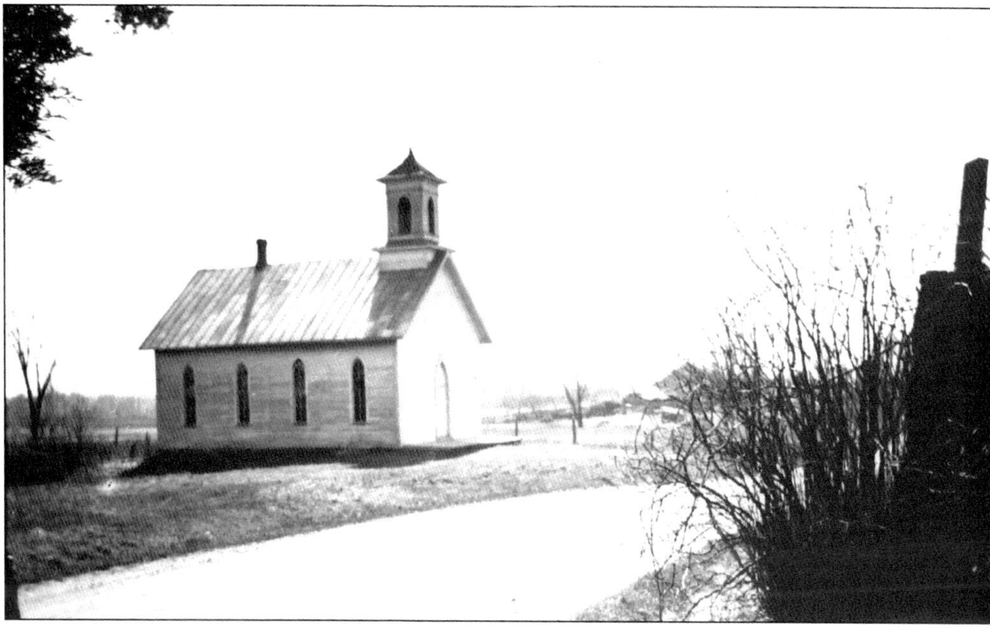

In 1861, the Nettle Lake Church of God was organized with 30 members. The congregation dedicated this frame church in 1875 near County Roads S and 5.5. Records indicate the congregation disbanded by 1920. The building was torn down, and in 1941, the site was sold. (WCPL Photographic Archives.)

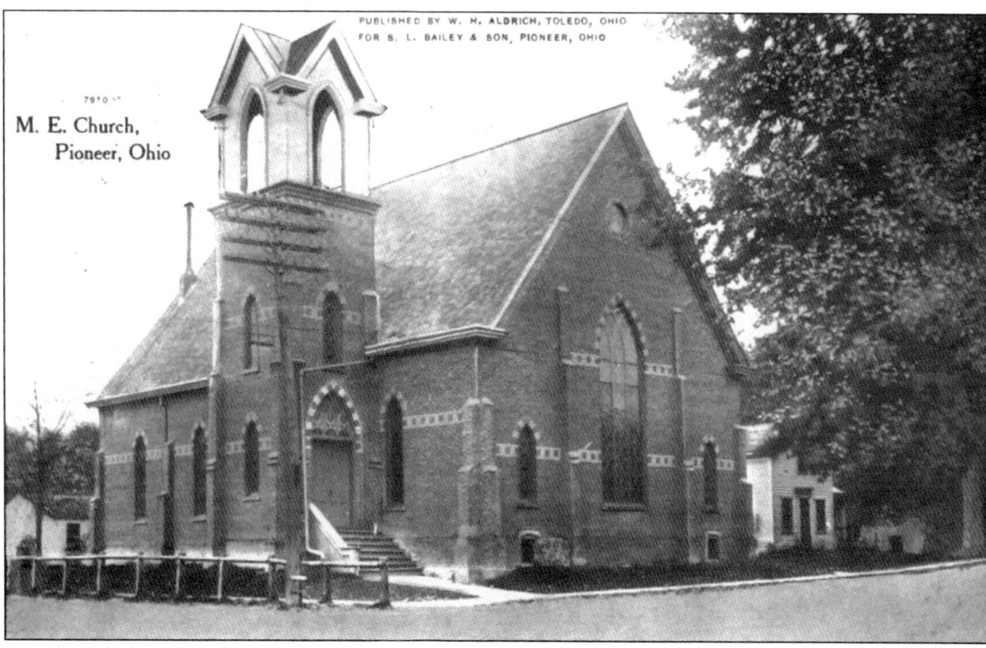

In 1879, the Pioneer Methodist Episcopal congregation constructed this brick church at South State and Church Streets, replacing a frame building erected 20 years earlier. It was probably Williams County's largest and most modern house of worship at the time and served the Pioneer United Methodist Church until the congregation completed a new facility on Baubice Street in 1975. The 1879 structure was razed in February 2000.

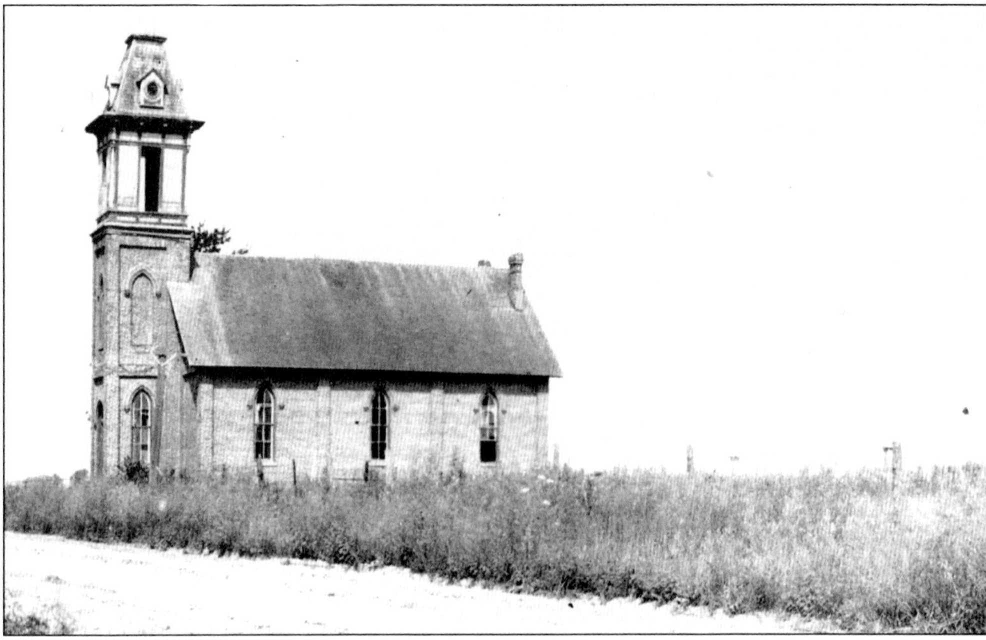

In 1881, the Beaver Creek German Reformed congregation built this brick structure to replace a log church on County Road M east of County Road 18. Its 70-foot tower held a 40-inch, 1,200-pound bell—the county's largest church bell. Declining membership closed the church in late 1926 or early 1927. In 1958, the Williams County Historical Society placed a marker at the site using the church cornerstone. (WCPL Photographic Archives.)

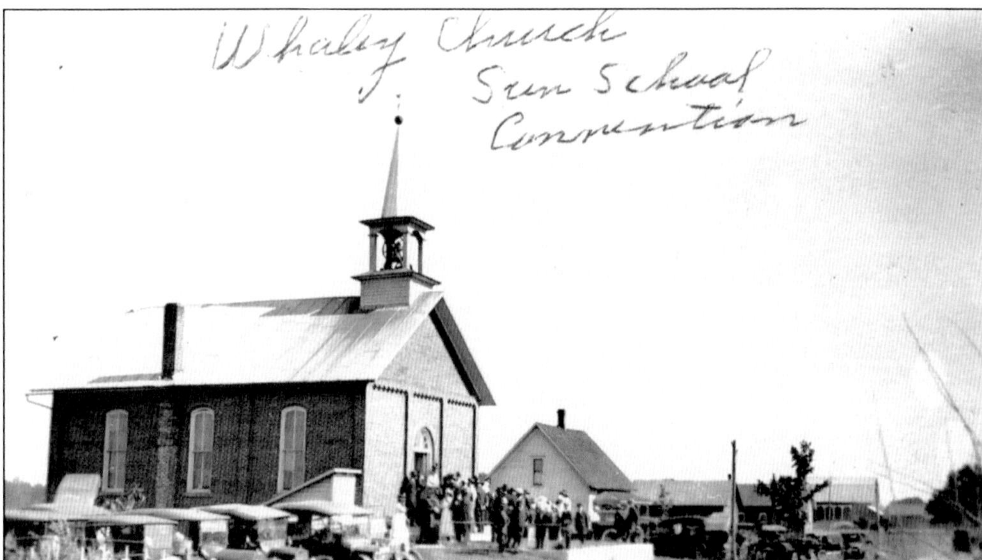

The Whaley United Brethren Church, two and a half miles north of Columbia, was dedicated in 1884. Worship services ceased in 1939, and in 1943, the church was sold to James Rogers, who dismantled the structure and sold its bricks to Lutterbein Lumber Company in Edgerton. The hip roof barn in the background was razed in 1991. (WCPL Photographic Archives.)

The Melbern Methodist Episcopal Church was organized as early as 1837, holding services at various places, including the Melbern Lutheran Church. In 1884, the congregation completed this church on the west side of Main Street. In 1911, extensive alterations were made to the church, including addition of a basement, Sunday school room, stained-glass windows, and relocation of its entrance.

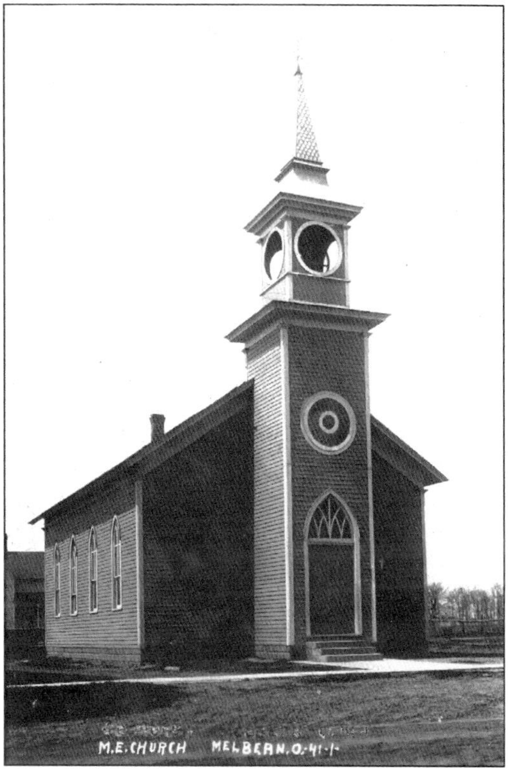

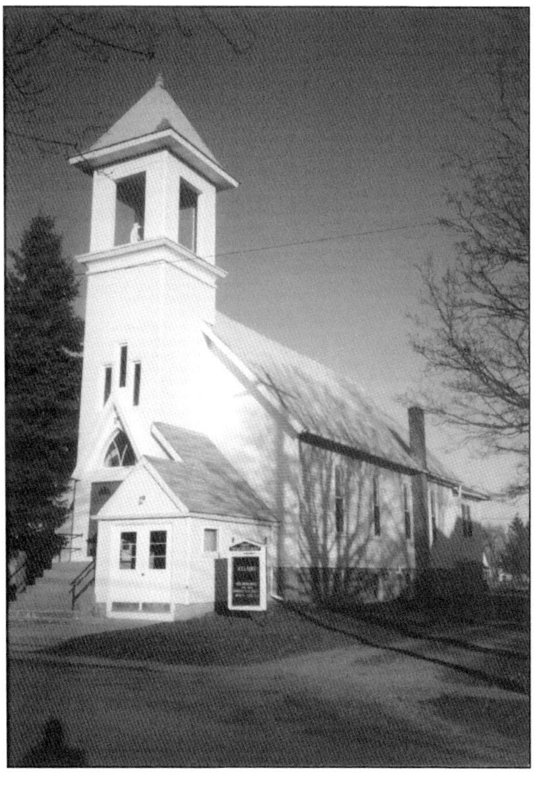

The First Presbyterian Church of Kunkle was organized in 1871 and erected a church on the west side of County Road 17. When the Wabash Railroad was extended through Kunkle, the church was so close to the tracks that it became a nuisance. This frame church was erected on Church Street and dedicated on June 5, 1887. The 128-year-old congregation disbanded in 1999.

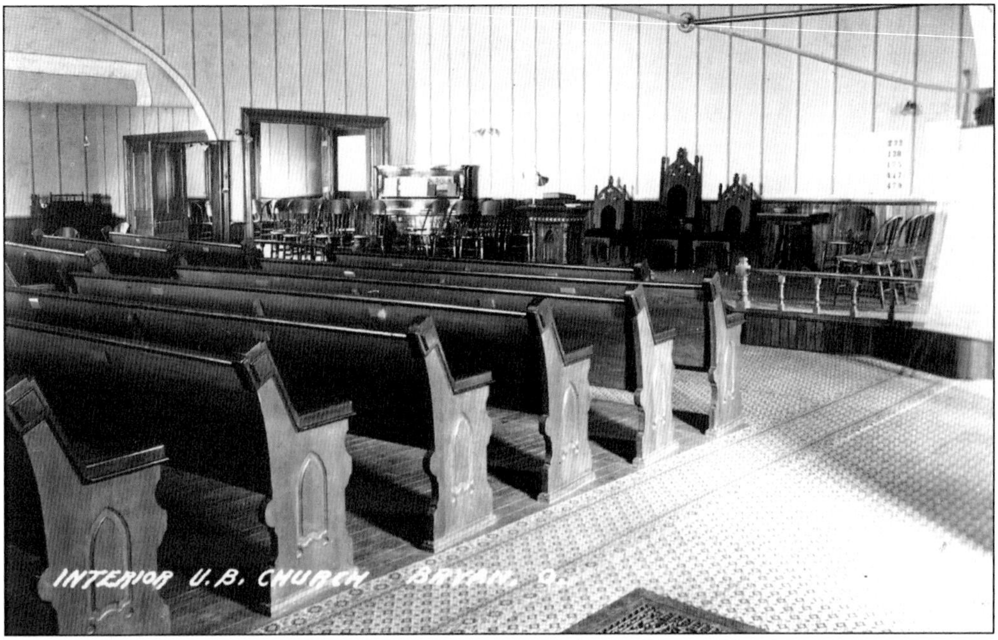

Bryan's Faith United Methodist Church was organized as a United Brethren congregation in the 1880s. This image shows the sanctuary of the frame church erected at Butler and Cherry Streets in 1891. When the Evangelical United Brethren and Methodist denominations merged in 1968, the congregation became Faith United Methodist Church. Groundbreaking for a new church was held on May 27, 1979, and the following week the old structure was demolished. (WCPL Photographic Archives.)

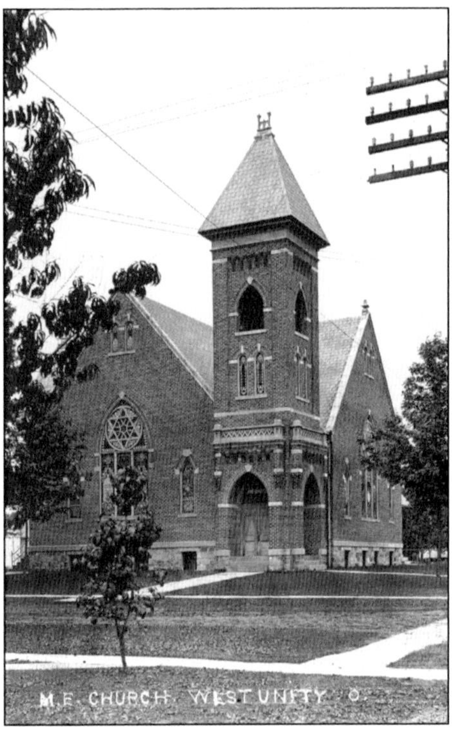

All three buildings that have served the West Unity United Methodist congregation occupied the northwest corner of Liberty and Church Streets. The first, a frame structure, was dedicated in January 1859 and was replaced by this brick house of worship in 1894. In 1969, this historic structure was replaced by the edifice that currently serves the congregation.

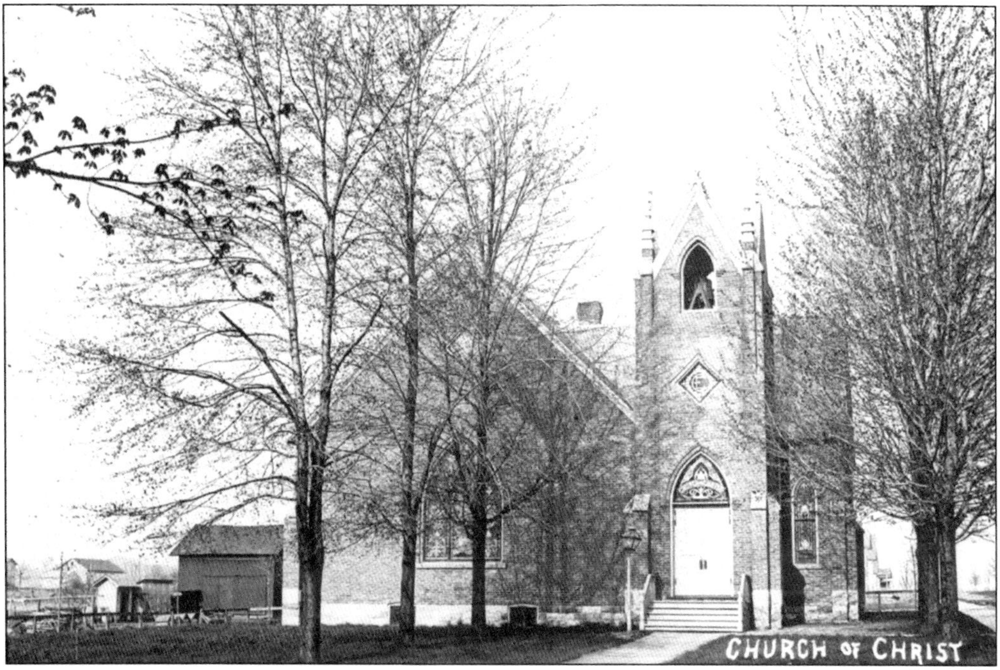

The Edon Church of Christ was organized on May 20, 1856. The congregation met at various locations before completing a frame church—believed to be Edon's first house of worship—at the southwest corner of Franklin and Michigan Streets around 1870. In 1895, the brick church above replaced the frame building. It was destroyed by fire on January 5, 1947. The present church was dedicated on July 15, 1951.

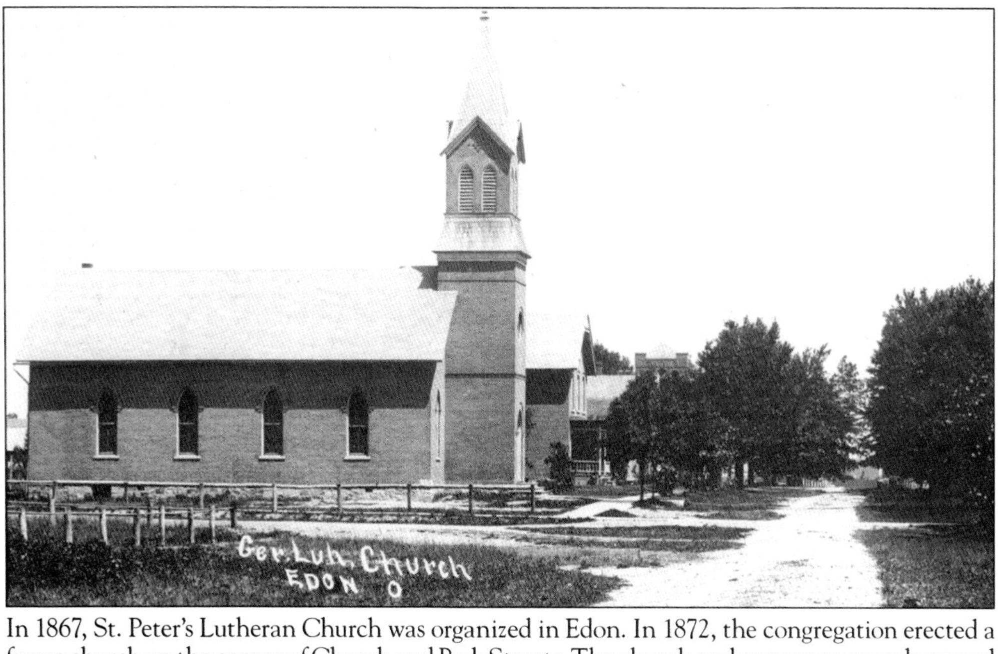

In 1867, St. Peter's Lutheran Church was organized in Edon. In 1872, the congregation erected a frame church on the corner of Church and Park Streets. The church and parsonage were destroyed in the great 1894 Edon fire. This brick church replaced the former structure on the site. The Edon United Methodist Church—destroyed by fire in 1916—can be seen in the background.

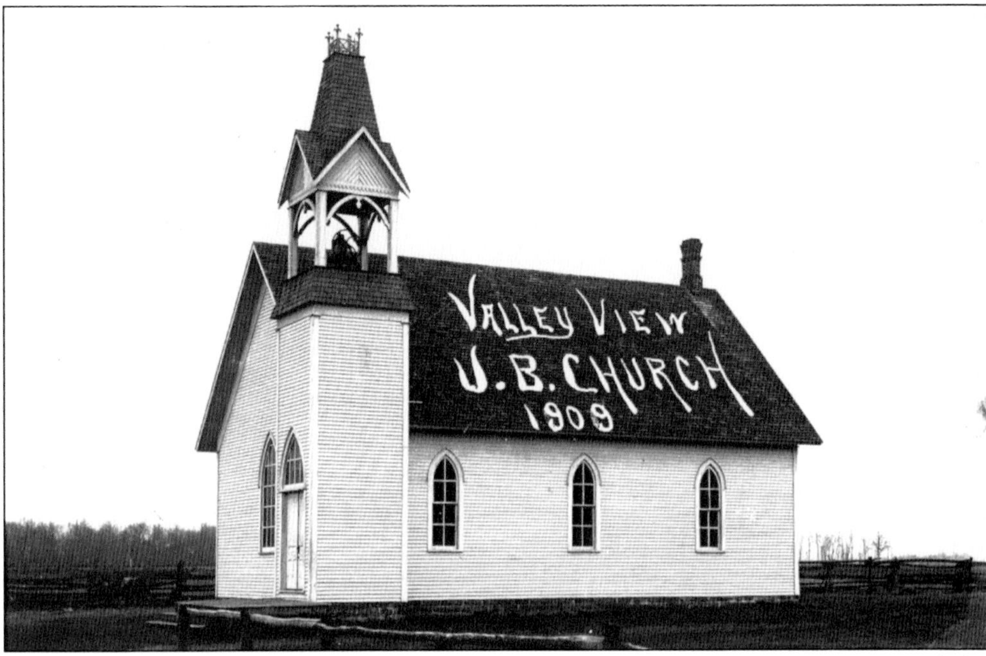

The Valley View United Brethren congregation, organized in March 1893, constructed this church in 1896–1897 at Ohio 107 and County Road 6. In 1944, the church closed due to declining interest and attendance. Two years later the Church of the Nazarene moved the building to South East Avenue in Montpelier. Since 1963 the structure has been home to the Williams County Playhouse.

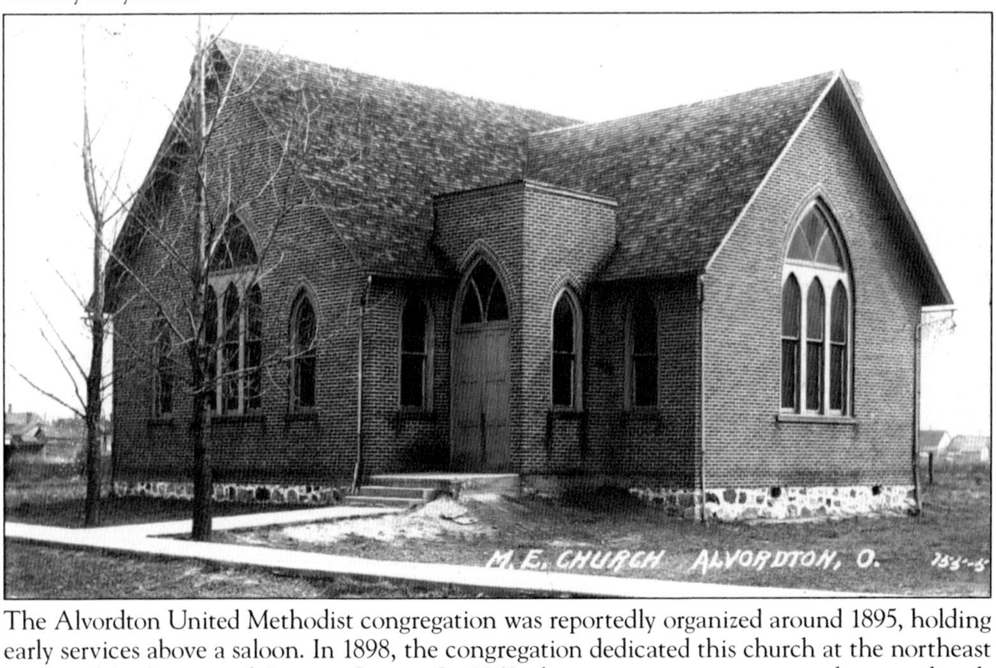

The Alvordton United Methodist congregation was reportedly organized around 1895, holding early services above a saloon. In 1898, the congregation dedicated this church at the northeast corner of Anderson and Summit Streets. In 1969, the congregation consecrated a new church north of the old building. On March 2, 2008, the final service was held at the Alvordton church, the congregation merging with the Pioneer United Methodist Church on March 9.

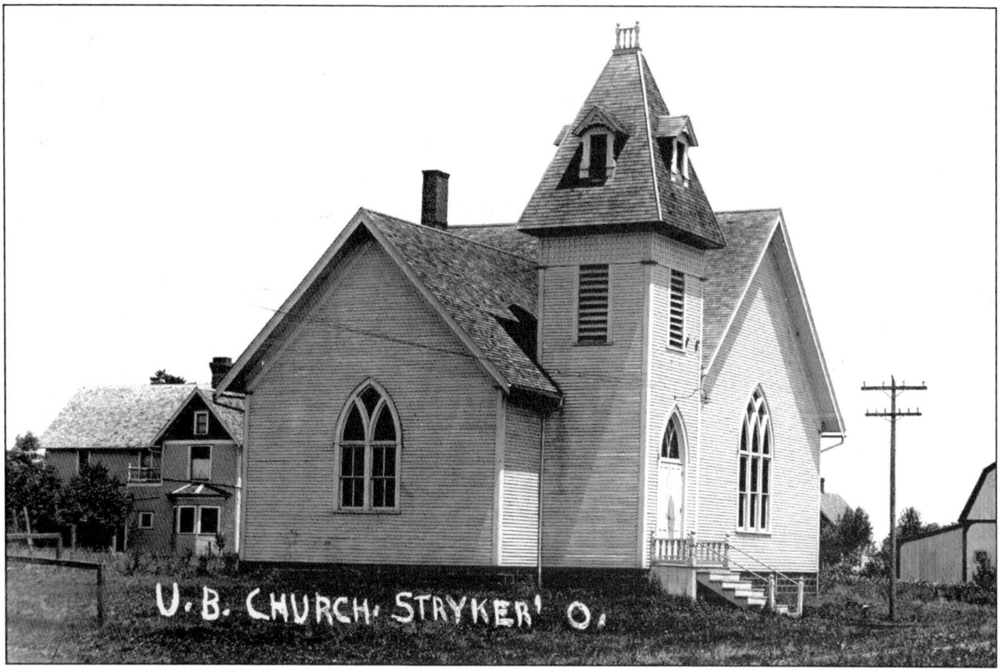

The Stryker United Brethren Church was organized by 1866. In 1873, the congregation moved the Thicket Chapel United Brethren Church southeast of Stryker to East Curtis Street. The question of secret society membership split the denomination nationally into Radical and Liberal factions, and Stryker's Radical United Brethren erected this frame building on East Church Street in 1898. In 1998, a brick church was built north of the old structure.

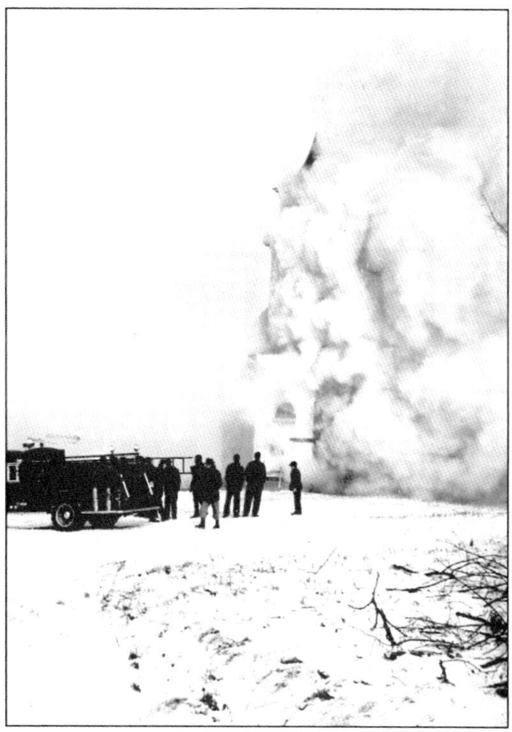

Calvary United Methodist Church was organized in 1842 as the Center United Brethren Church. In 1947, fire destroyed this church, erected in 1903, so the congregation moved the abandoned Emmanuel Lutheran Church to Williams Center. When the Evangelical United Brethren and Methodist denominations merged, Williams Center was left with two United Methodist churches. To distinguish them, the former United Brethren congregation adopted the name Calvary and the Methodists Asbury. (WCPL Photographic Archives.)

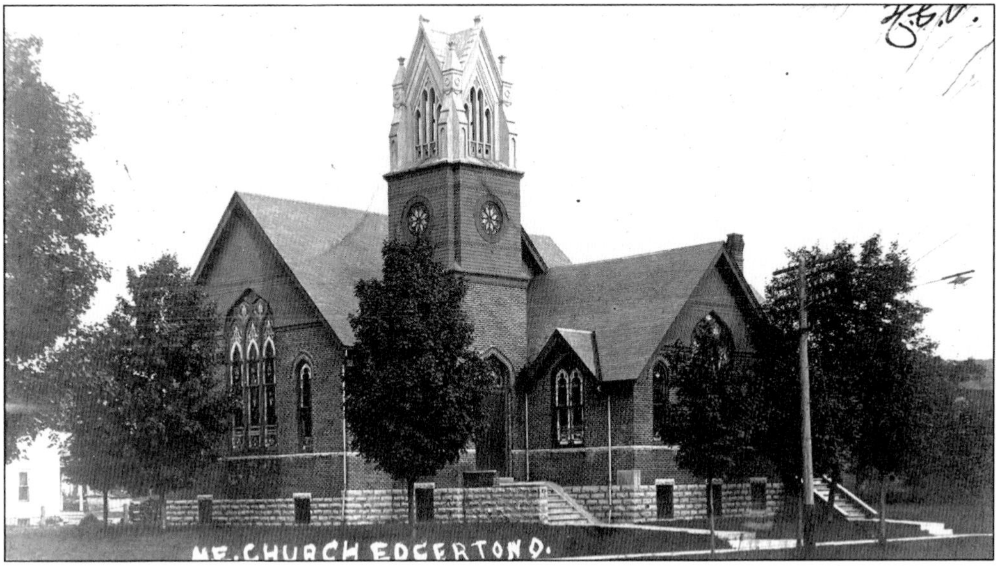

Edgerton's first house of worship was a one-room frame Methodist church with a tall steeple erected on the northwest corner of Michigan Avenue and Hull Street around 1861. On May 17, 1903, this beautiful $10,000 limestone and brick church was dedicated on the site that continues to serve the congregation. (WCPL Photographic Archives.)

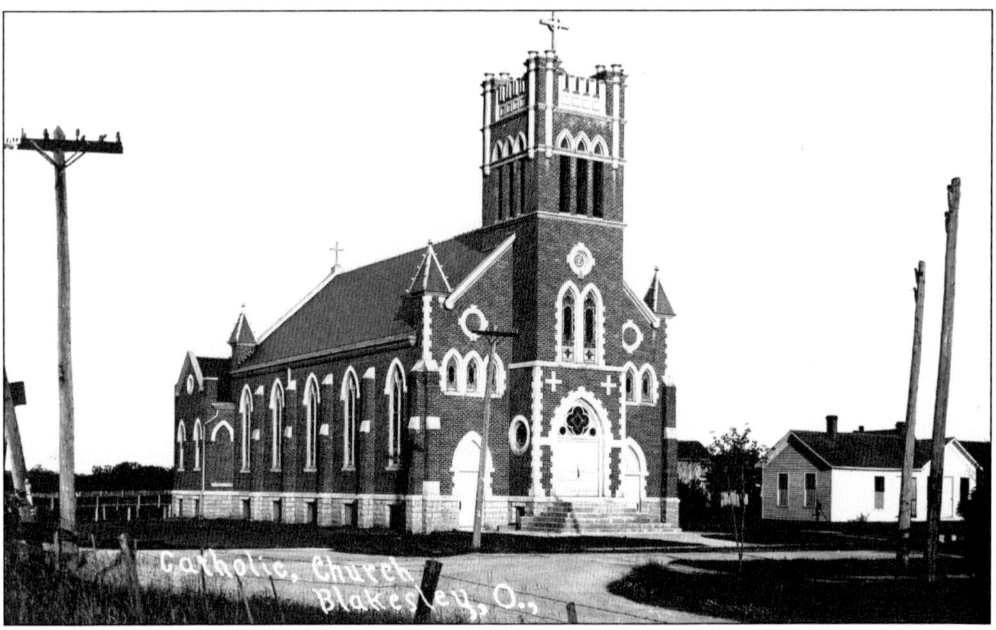

In 1865, the St. Joseph's Catholic congregation constructed a frame church one-half mile north of Blakeslee that was destroyed by arsonist Richmond Bennett in 1881. A brick church was built on the site in 1883. When the building became unsafe, it was dismantled and the bricks were used to construct this church in Blakeslee in 1906. (WCPL Photographic Archives.)

Seven

SOCIAL LIFE

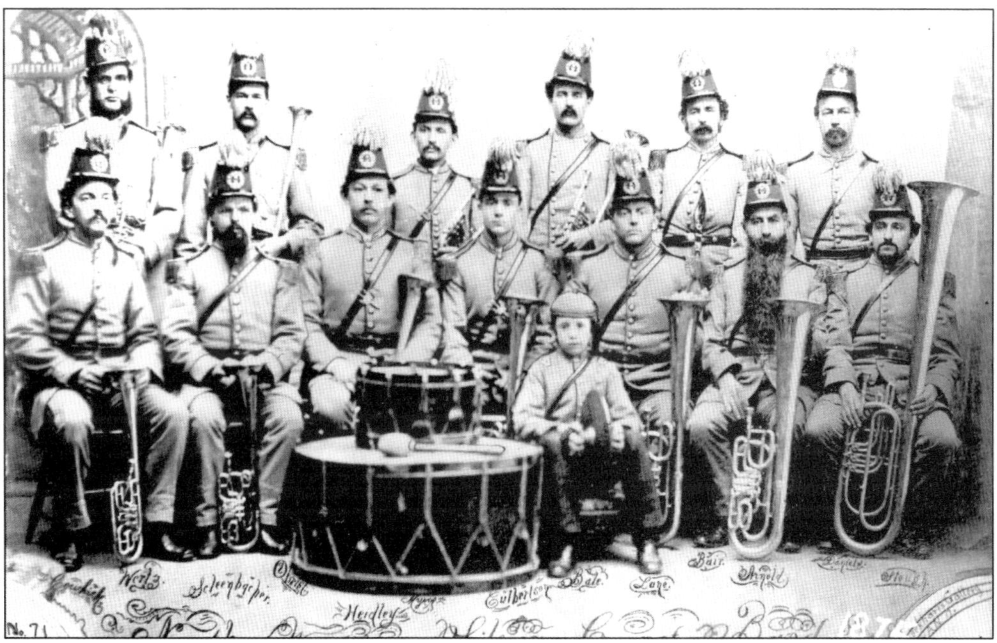

The Bryan City Band has long played an active role in the community. The band was founded in 1852, making it the second-oldest municipal band in the nation. This group, known as the North Western Silver Cornet Band, included Medary Patterson (the boy holding cymbals), son of Robert N. Patterson, who was editor of the *Bryan Democrat* newspaper. This image was taken in 1875 by William Lockhart, one of Bryan's early professional photographers, after the band was outfitted in new uniforms made by a Bryan tailor. (WCPL Photographic Archives.)

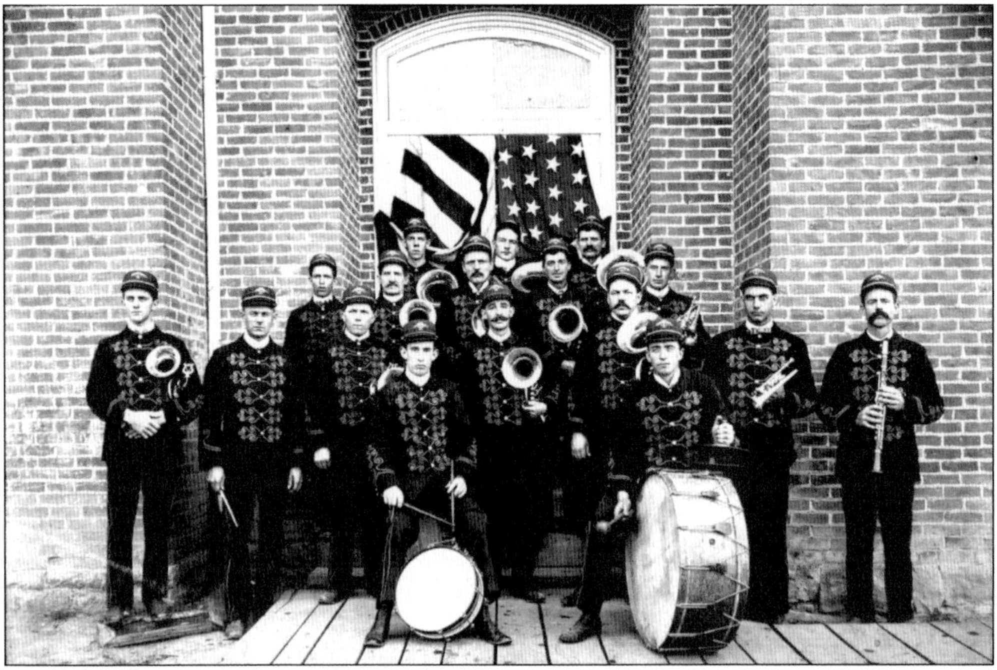

Evansport's town band was organized as early as 1875. Band members in this *c.* 1900 photograph are, from left to right, (first row) unidentified snare drummer and bass drummer John Christy; (second row) Charles Snyder, ? Wagner (leader), Ed Williams, Jim Christy, Jack Snyder, Claude Woodward, and Charles Schroeder; (third row) ? Mann, William Snyder, Sam Masters, Elmer Christy, and Ed King; (fourth row) Porter Cameron, Homer Hall, and Emery Snyder. (WCPL Photographic Archives.)

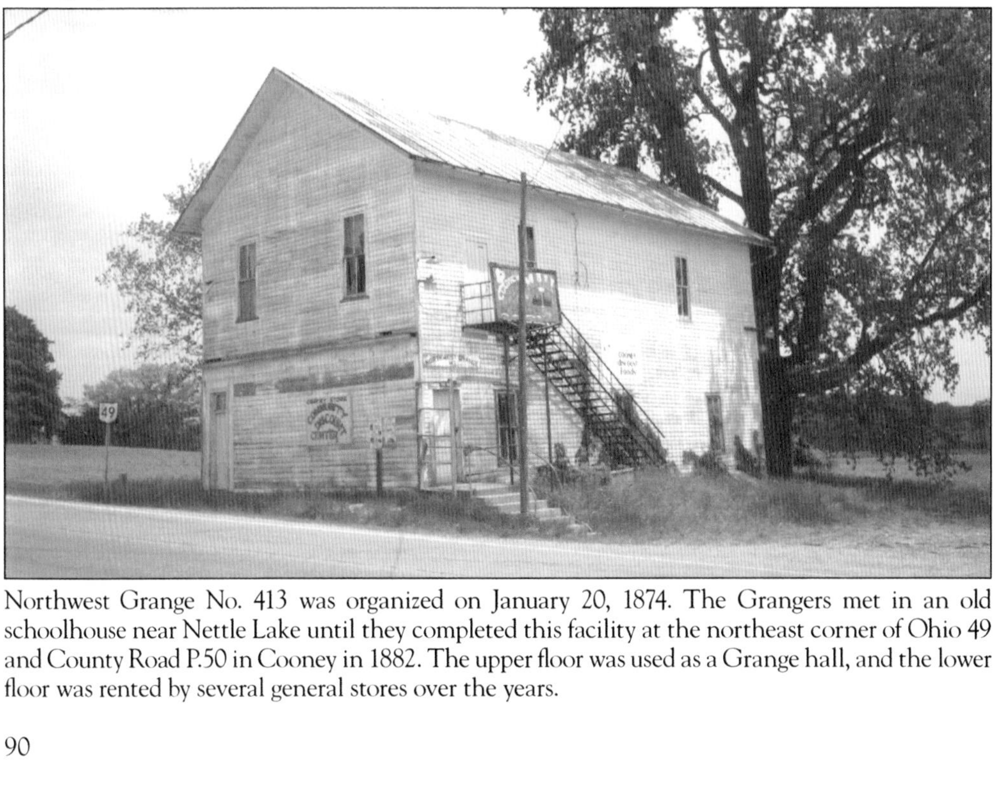

Northwest Grange No. 413 was organized on January 20, 1874. The Grangers met in an old schoolhouse near Nettle Lake until they completed this facility at the northeast corner of Ohio 49 and County Road P.50 in Cooney in 1882. The upper floor was used as a Grange hall, and the lower floor was rented by several general stores over the years.

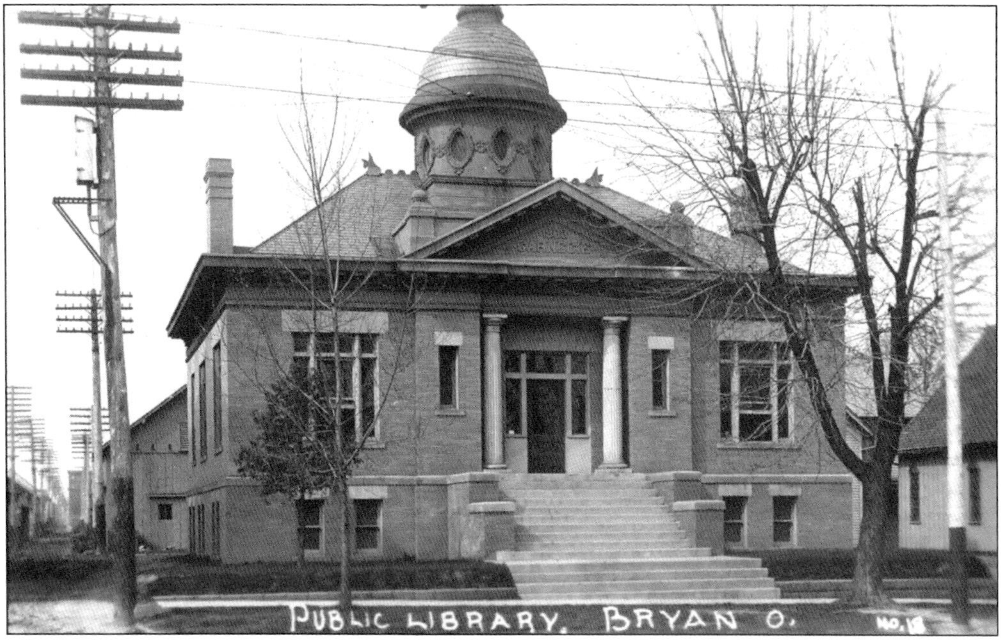

The Williams County Public Library began as a Bryan Taine Club project in 1882. The library was housed above a local bank and in the courthouse before this building—constructed using a $10,000 donation from Andrew Carnegie—opened in October 1904. By 1936, the library operated 15 branches across the county. Today the Williams County Public Library maintains branch libraries in Bryan, Edgerton, Edon, Pioneer, Stryker, and West Unity.

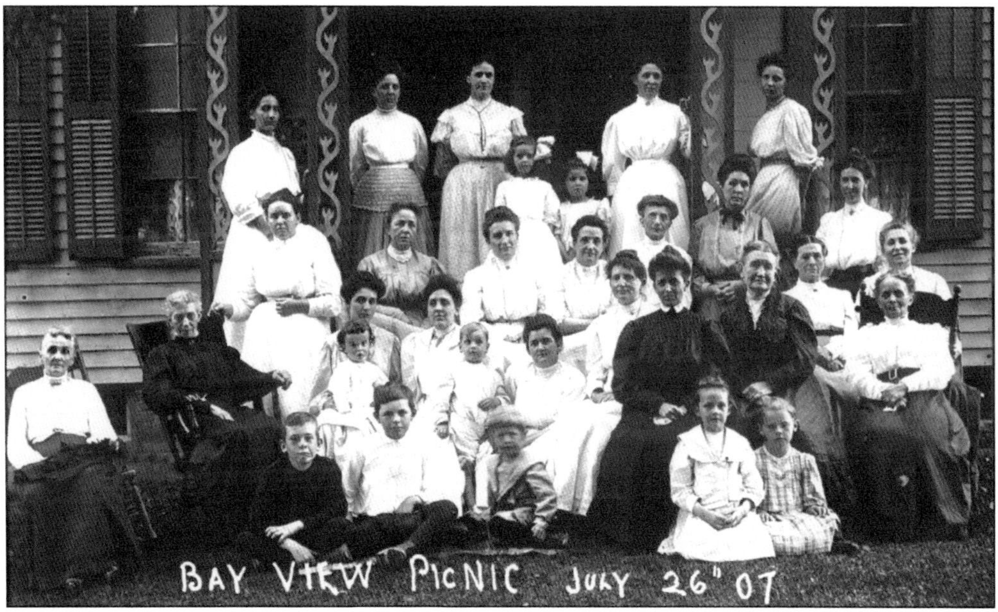

In 1880, the Reverend William Lance organized Bryan Circle of the Chautauqua Literary and Scientific Circle to provide a systematic reading course in history, literature, science, and art for those who were denied college opportunities or who wished to renew their studies. In 1901, the organization became Bay View Reading Circle, and in 1943–1944 Bay View Study Club. The group disbanded in the 1990s. (WCPL Photographic Archives.)

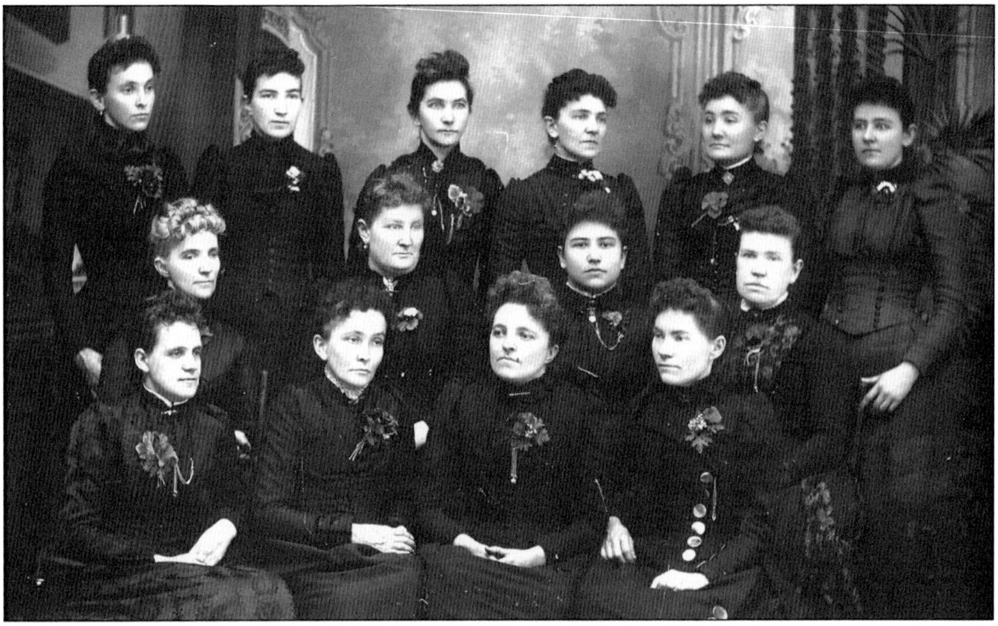

West Unity's first women's club, the Olive Literary Society, was organized on August 27, 1890, for study and research purposes. Members shown in this February 1892 photograph are, from left to right, (first row) Lydia Pettit, Alice Hoover, Josie Dodge, and unidentified; (second row) Mary Morrison, Nora Bowman, unidentified, and Mary Denman; (third row) Jessie Beatty, Nellie Carney, Ella Hollington, unidentified, Nettie Smith, and unidentified. (WCPL Photographic Archives.)

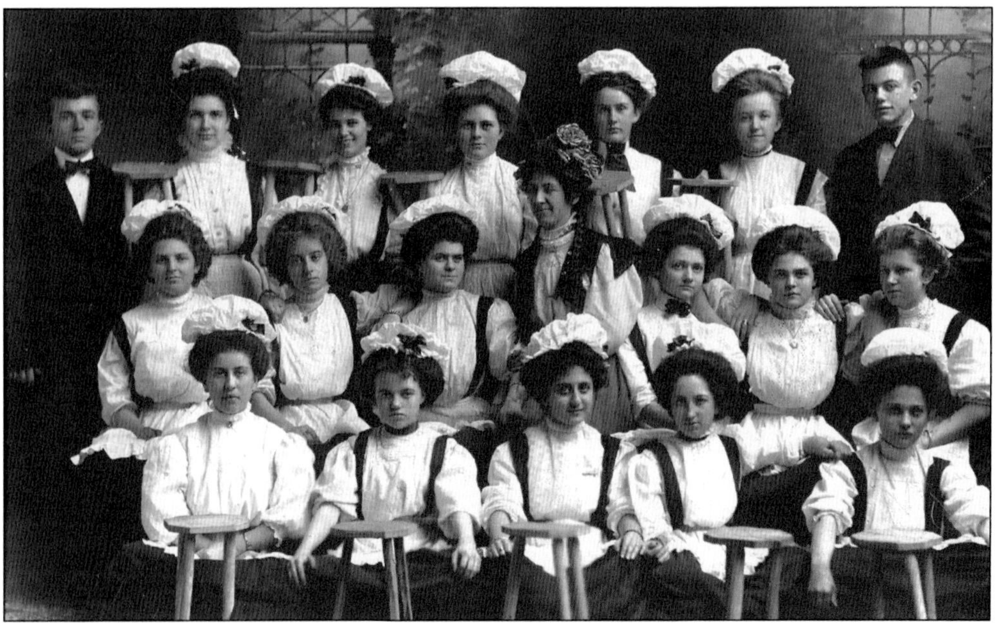

The cast of a Bryan High School play poses around 1906. Richard Cramer (third row, right) was born in Bryan in 1889 and became a Hollywood character actor, appearing in more than 200 films from the 1920s to the 1950s. Burly, menacing, and gravel-voiced, Cramer specialized in villainous roles in low-budget westerns but also appeared with Laurel and Hardy and W. C. Fields. He died in Los Angeles in 1960. (WCPL Photographic Archives.)

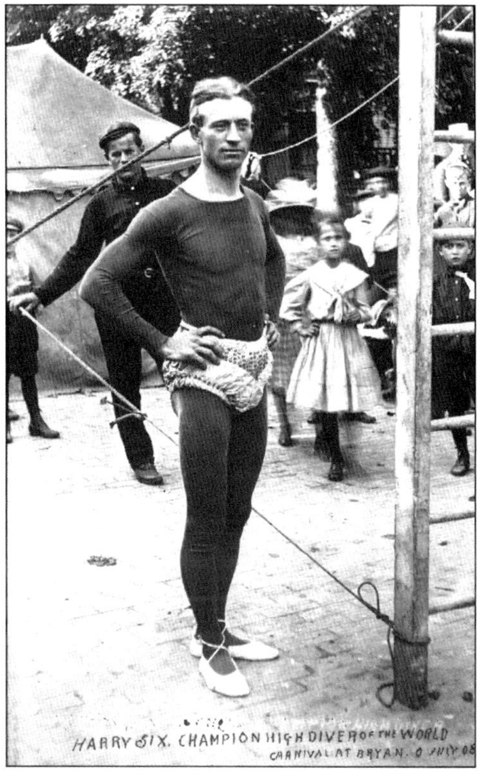

J. Harry Six, "the world's champion headforemost high diver," was born in Bryan in 1881 and by 1897 was touring with his act. By 1908, Six was diving blindfolded from a 110-foot ladder into a three-and-a-half-foot-deep water tank. Over time the battering Six's eyes took each time he hit the water began to cause problems. In 1913, a local newspaper reported Six was experiencing serious eye trouble, forcing him to abandon high diving. In 1917, after 20 years of showbiz fame, he returned to his hometown completely blind. Six ran a fish market and a restaurant in Bryan in the early 1920s. For many years Six and his wife owned and operated a traveling carnival company. He died at his East High Street home in Bryan in 1948 at the age of 67. (WCPL Photographic Archives.)

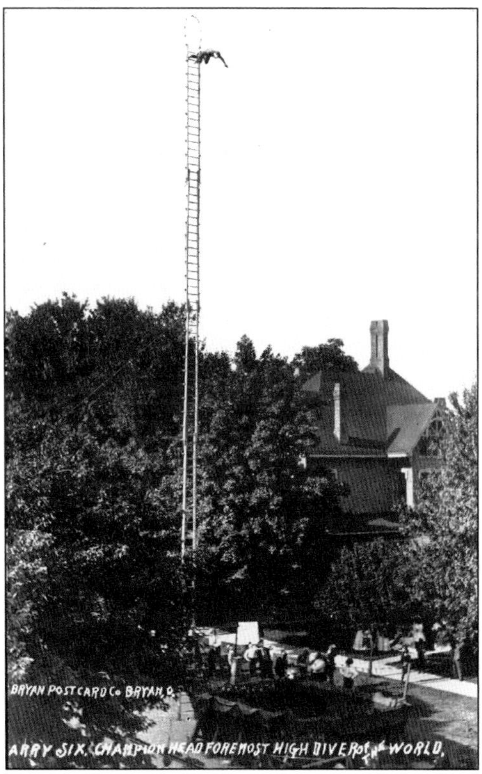

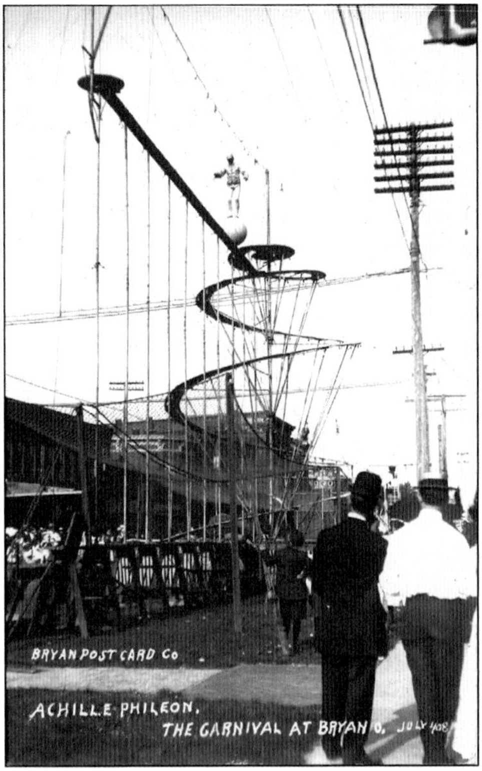

Summer carnivals have long been a Williams County pastime. A highlight of the Bryan Merchants' Carnival, held June 29 through July 4, 1908, was free shows provided twice daily by "equilibrist" Achille Phileon. Outfitted in flashy jacket, cap, and tights, Phileon balanced himself atop a large ball and, using his feet, maneuvered the ball to the top of a narrow, spiraling ramp erected on West High Street.

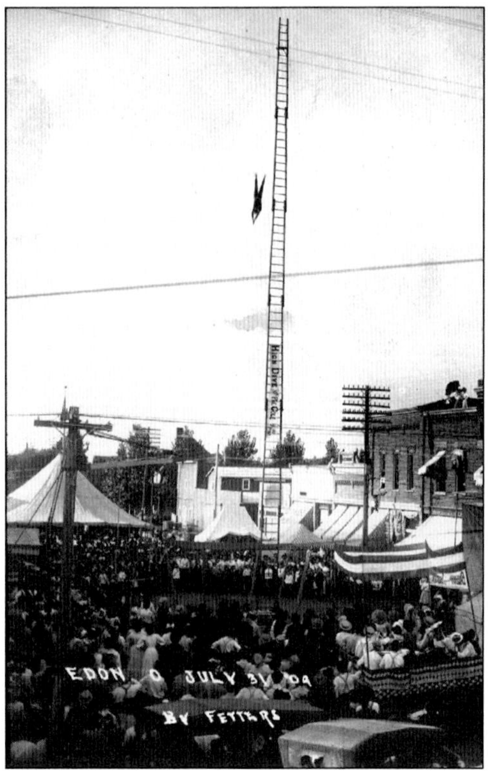

This photograph shows Professor Cole's high dive at the 1909 Edon Harvest Jubilee. The 1955 Edon centennial history states, "Perhaps the most thrilling event of the jubilee was the 'high dive.' Amid much breath-holding and a number of bloodcurdling screams from women spectators, the man made his dive into a net. Enormous crowds came from miles and miles to witness this daring feat."

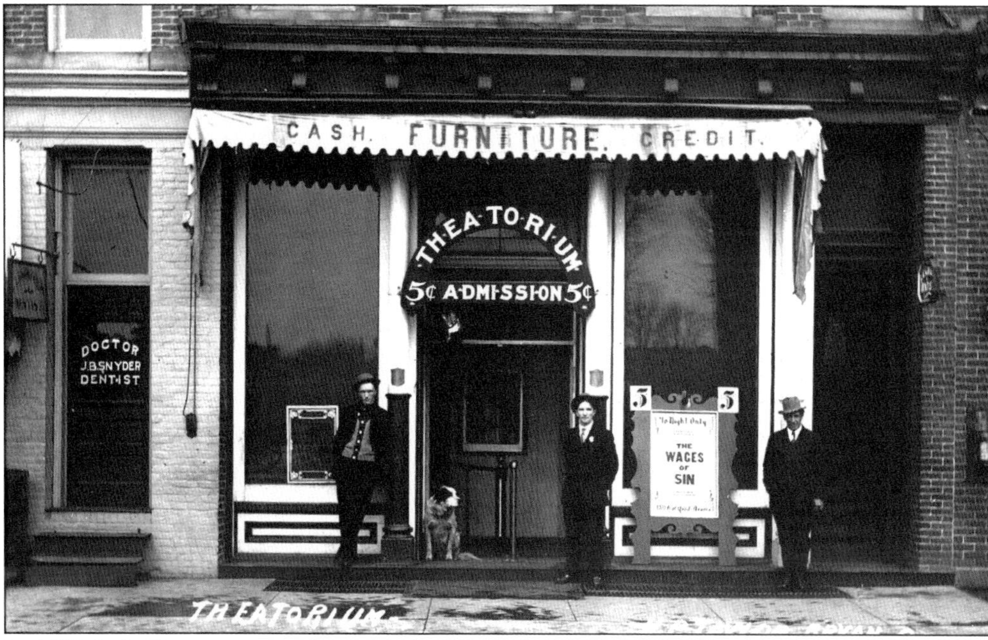

In 1907, J. C. Garnette, a professional photographer from Stryker, opened the Bryan Theatorium on the north side of the courthouse square. In 1908, the *Bryan Democrat* reported that "in addition to a thousand feet of film, a good vocalist sings illustrated songs and all for the small sum of five cents. Mothers with children can rest assured that nothing will be seen that could offend the most particular." (WCPL Photographic Archives.)

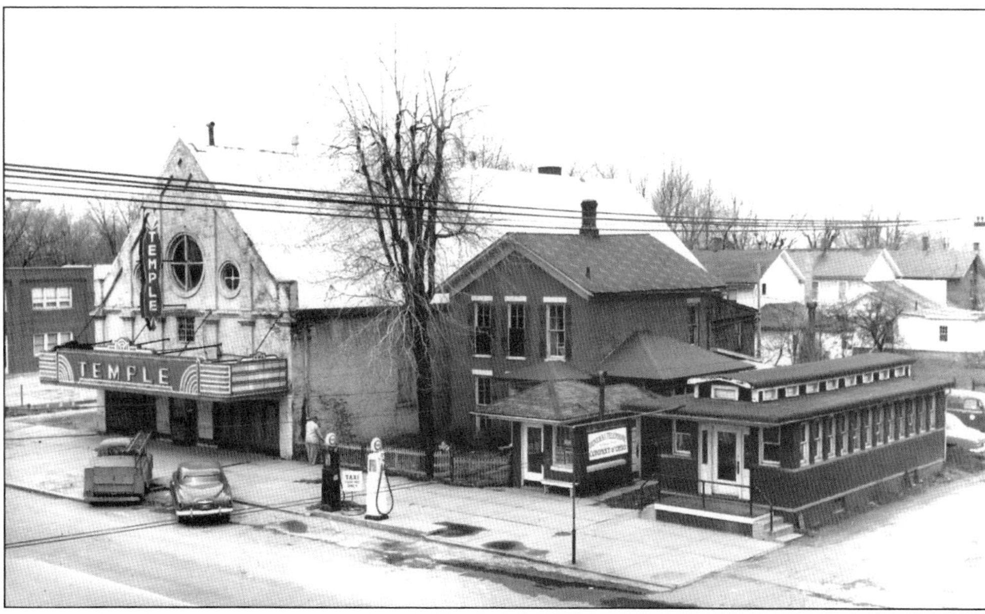

Bryan's Temple Theatre was originally a National Guard armory constructed in 1878. The armory was equipped with a stage and dressing rooms and hosted plays, dances, roller skating, high school commencements, and basketball games. In 1921, the Temple Theatre opened in the former armory, showing motion pictures for about 25 years. In April 1955, Carroll-Ames Hardware moved into the facility. (WCPL Photographic Archives.)

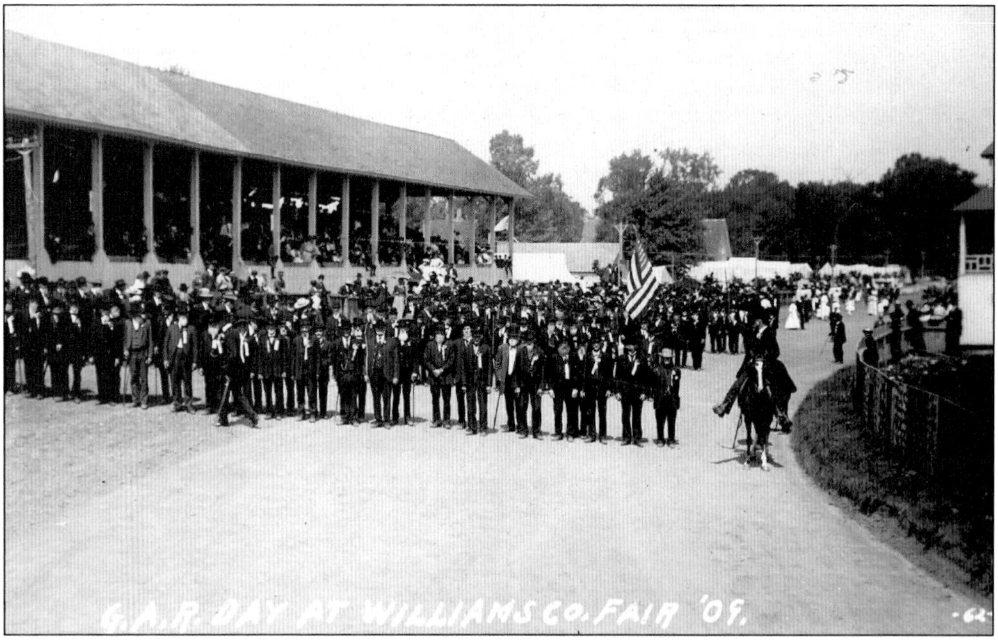

On September 11, 1909, the Williams County Fair hosted Soldiers Day, offering veterans free admission and a pork and beans dinner. The *Bryan Democrat* noted that each veteran was expected to bring a cane to be used in execution of the Manual of Arms. "Bear in mind the cane, as one man in ranks without a cane mars the harmony and greatly detracts from the appearance of the battalion."

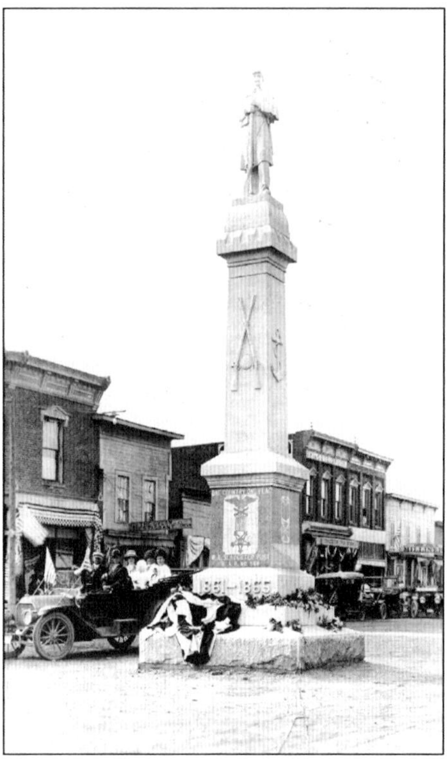

In 1911, Walter Slaughter Post Grand Army of the Republic sponsored efforts to erect Edgerton's veterans' monument, affectionately known as "Clem." On May 30, 1912, an American flag was unfurled, revealing the magnificent monument to a large crowd. As larger, faster motorized vehicles replaced horse-drawn conveyances, Clem's position in Edgerton's main intersection became less and less desirable. In 1972, the monument was relocated to the town hall's west lawn.

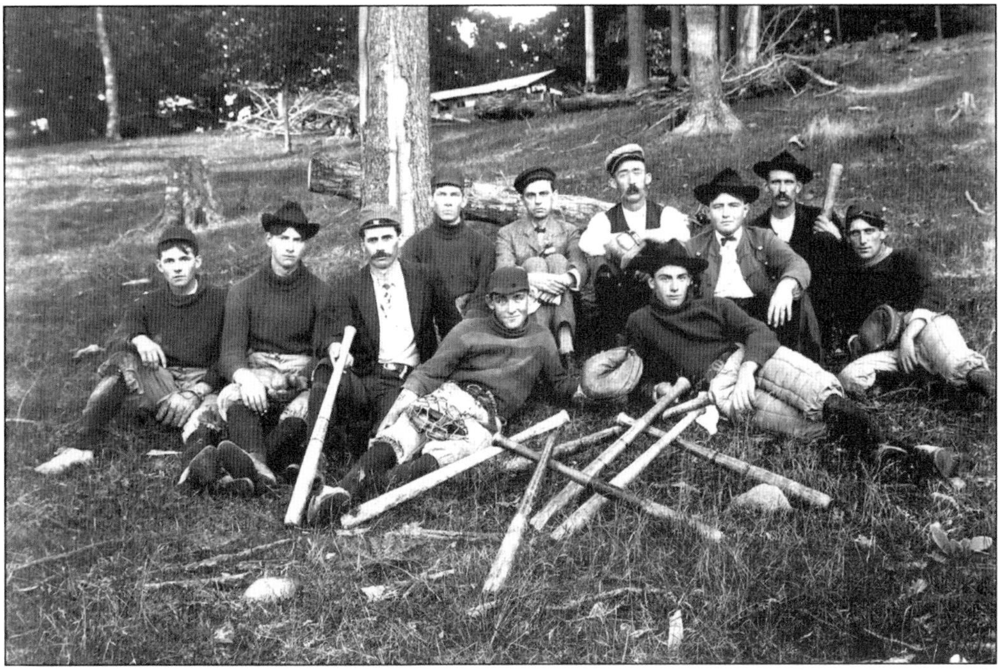

The 1904 Northwest Township baseball team poses at the Grange fairgrounds on Ohio 49 north of Cooney. From left to right are (first row) Bill Speaker and Ralph Ricketts; (second row) Thurman Walker, Henry Ricketts, Warren Ricketts, Ross Stickney, Joe Hershey, Bill Welch, Nate Townsend, Howard Carl, and Hurd Speaker. (WCPL Photographic Archives.)

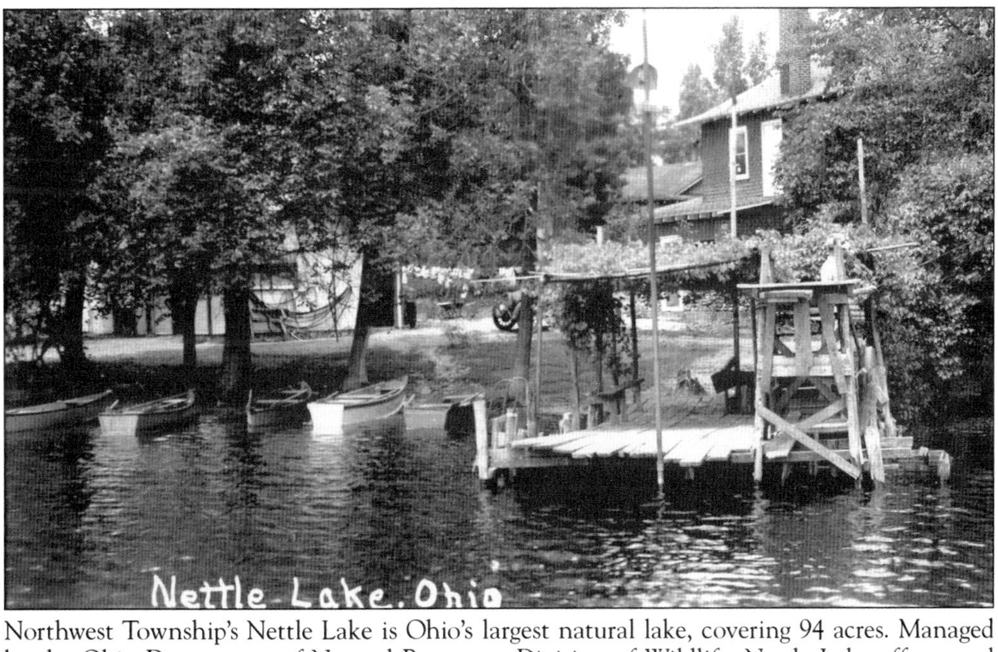

Northwest Township's Nettle Lake is Ohio's largest natural lake, covering 94 acres. Managed by the Ohio Department of Natural Resources Division of Wildlife, Nettle Lake offers good numbers of largemouth bass, crappie, channel catfish, and bluegill. Development around the lake began in earnest about 1916, and today numerous cottages, two campgrounds, and other facilities are available for public enjoyment.

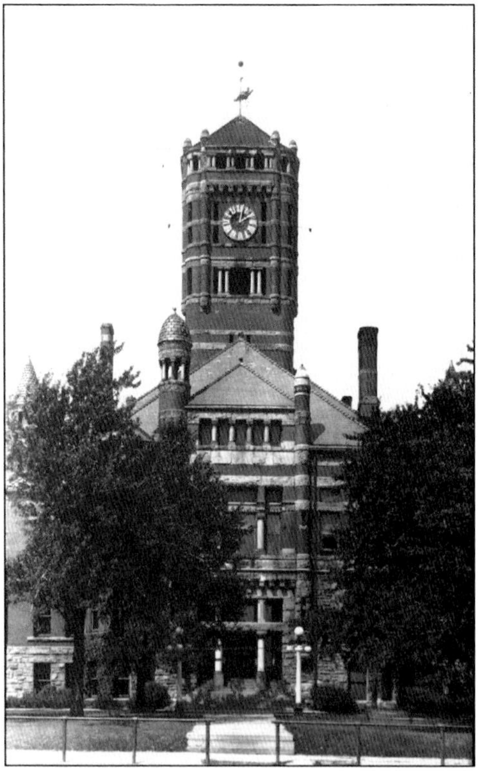

In 1927, Charles "Minor" Leichty set the world's flagpole sitting record atop the Williams County Courthouse. Leichty perched in an armchair for 21 days—from August 20 to September 10. Thousands of visitors flocked to Bryan to witness the stunt, which attracted national attention. In 1942, Leichty plunged three stories to his death while washing windows on the west side of the square. (WCPL Photographic Archives.)

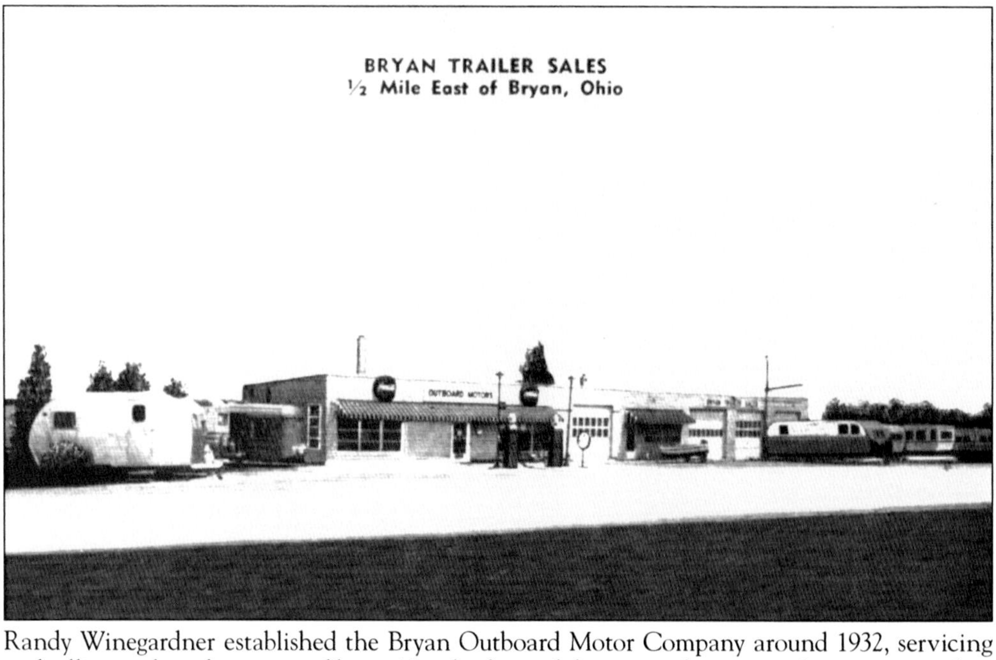

Randy Winegardner established the Bryan Outboard Motor Company around 1932, servicing and selling outboard motors and boats 18 miles from a lake or river large enough to accommodate motorboats. Winegardner constructed the brick and tile building above in 1939, adding mobile home sales and a Hi-Speed gasoline station. He later developed Woodland Estates Mobile Home Park on County Road 15.75, north of High Street.

Eight

TRANSPORTATION

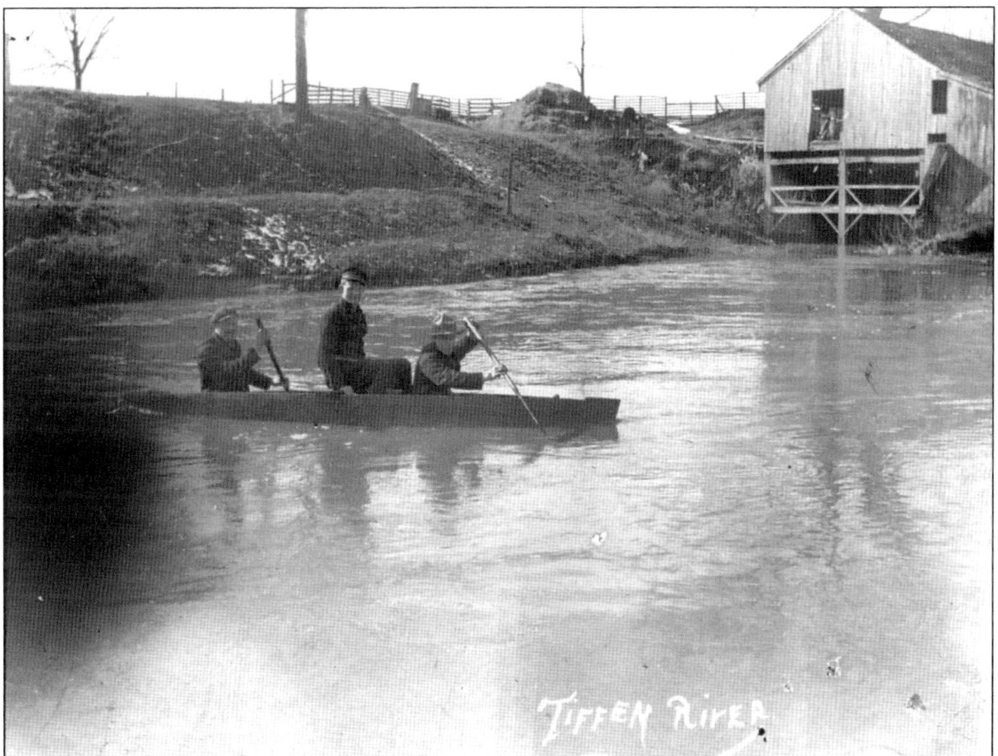

When Williams County's first settlers arrived in the 1830s, they found it nearly impossible to bring wagons through the thick, primitive forest and underbrush that had a stranglehold on the land. Journeying on waterways in a pirogue or "dug-out" canoe was comparatively easier than overland travel. Streams furnished power to operate the earliest sawmills and gristmills. In this undated photograph, a small party is shown traveling by boat on the Tiffin River.

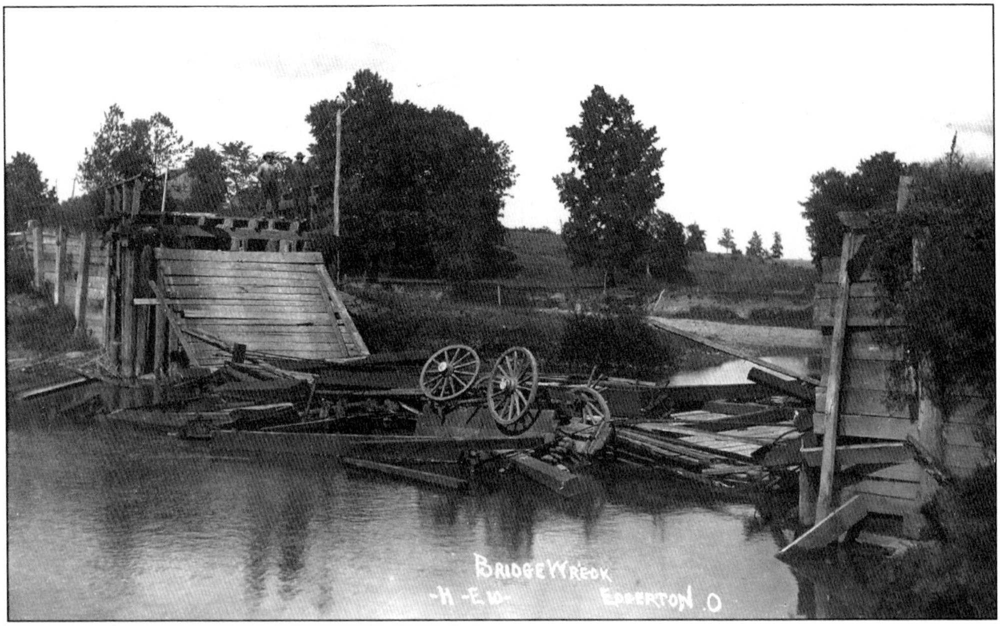

Pioneers forded local creeks and rivers while making their way through the unsettled wilderness. The area's first bridges were simple wooden spans that sometimes collapsed due to high water, ice, or structural issues. This c. 1910 image shows the aftermath of a bridge collapse near Edgerton.

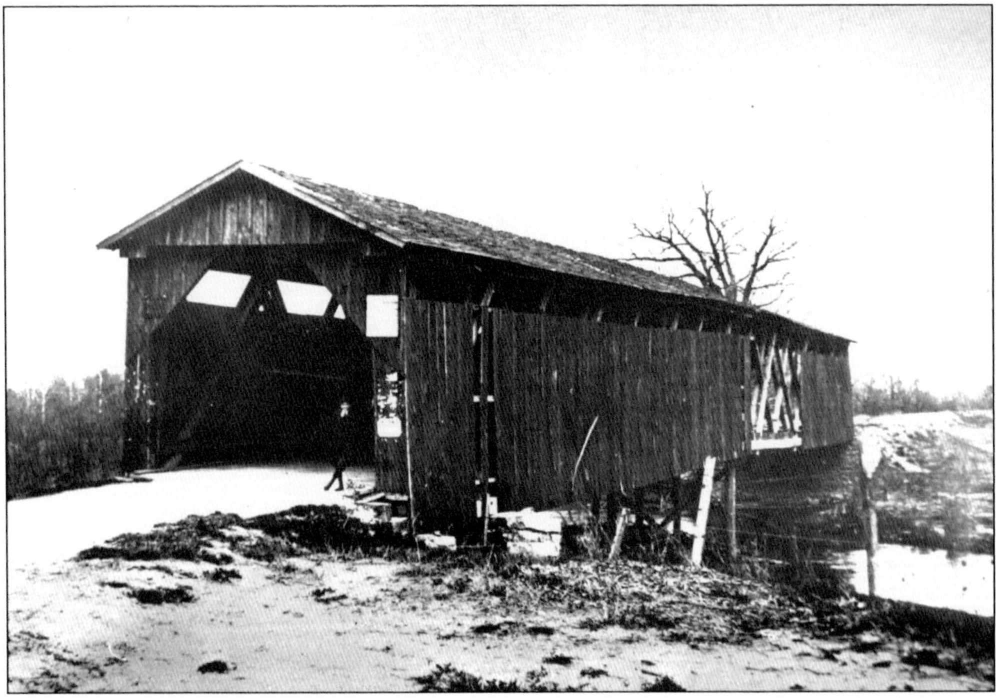

This remarkable series of photographs taken from the same vantage point illustrates the changes in construction methods of bridges spanning the Tiffin River at Lockport over the course of a century. The covered bridge above is believed to have been completed in 1871 and was a representative example of many local bridges of that time.

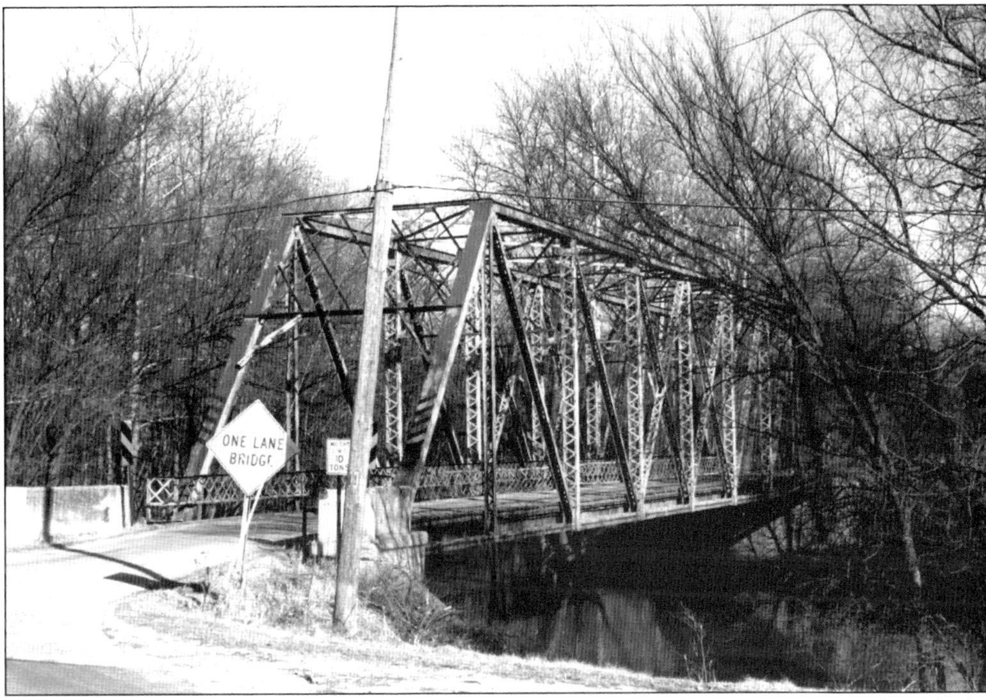

This covered bridge was replaced in 1919 by the steel truss bridge (also a once common local bridge design) shown above. The steel truss bridge was removed in 1998 to make way for construction of the modern covered bridge below.

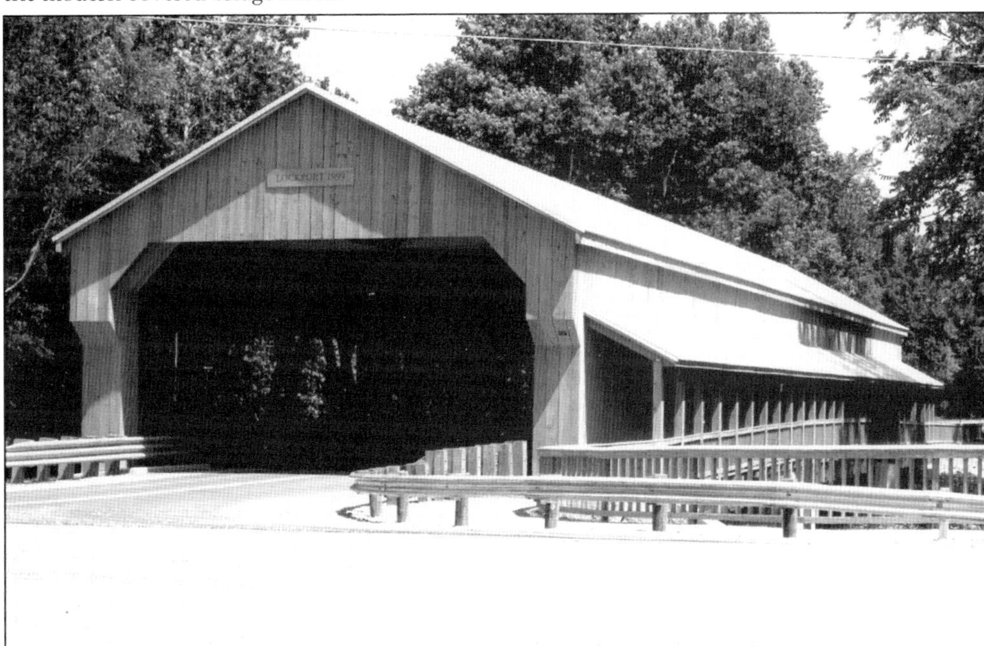

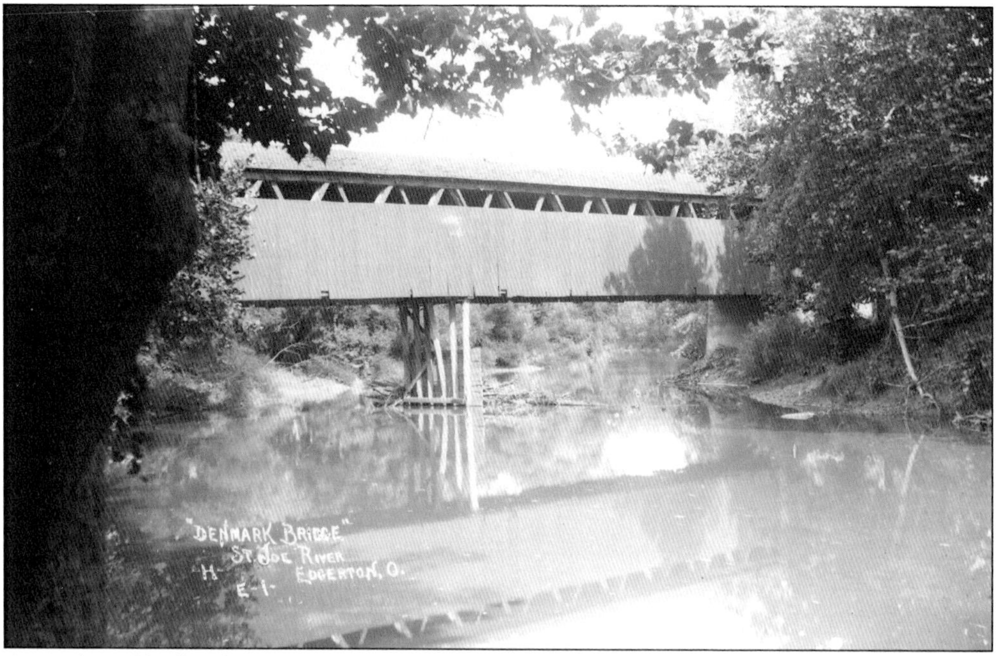

A number of bridges have spanned the St. Joseph River near the ghost town Denmark. Bridges were constructed in 1841 and 1865 before this wooden covered bridge was completed in 1869. The Denmark Bridge—replaced by a steel span in 1939—was Williams County's last covered bridge until Lockport's modern covered bridge was completed in 1999. (Richard L. Cooley.)

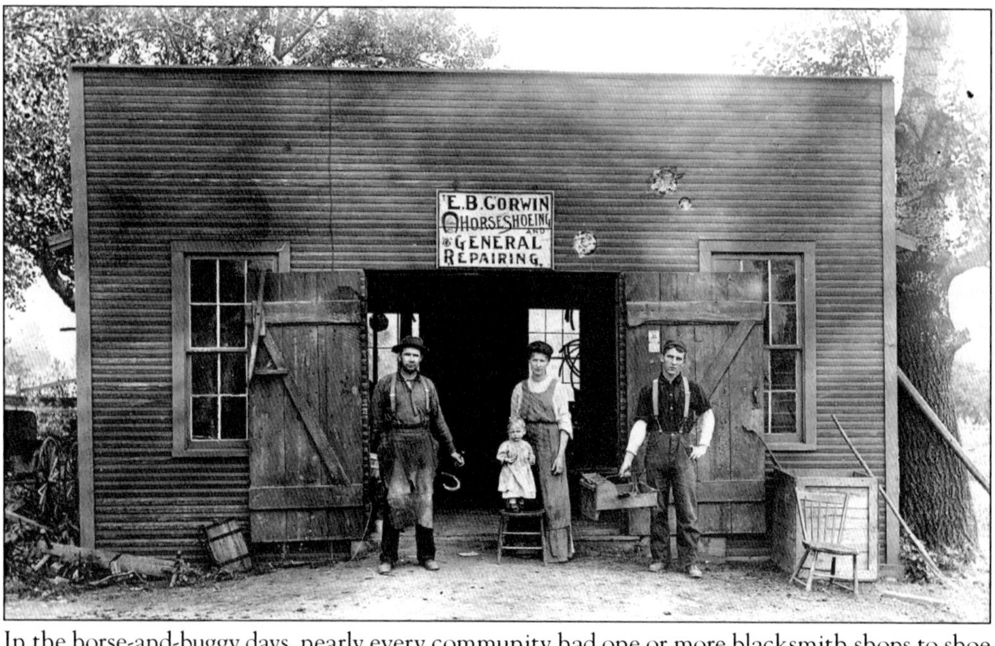

In the horse-and-buggy days, nearly every community had one or more blacksmith shops to shoe horses and to fabricate or repair metal items. Several generations of the Corwin family were blacksmiths. Shown at the Williams Center Blacksmith Shop around 1908 are Edgar Corwin, Stephen Corwin with his mother, Adelpha Corwin, and Stephen's father, Hugh Corwin. (WCPL Photographic Archives.)

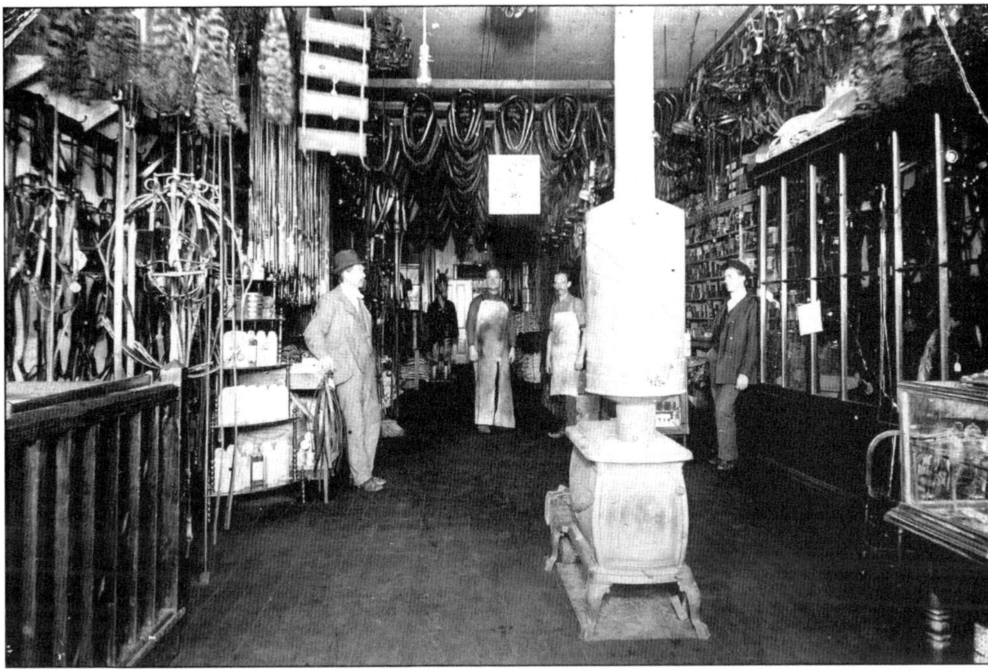

When horses were a primary means of transportation, harness shops sold and mended saddles, bridles, harness, and other leather goods. William H. Riley and his son, Harold "Hal" Riley, operated this harness shop on the east side of Bryan's square from 1894 to 1917. The pair manufactured leather goods—employing more than 20 craftsmen—and maintained a Des Moines, Iowa, warehouse until competition from automobiles forced them out of business. (WCPL Photographic Archives.)

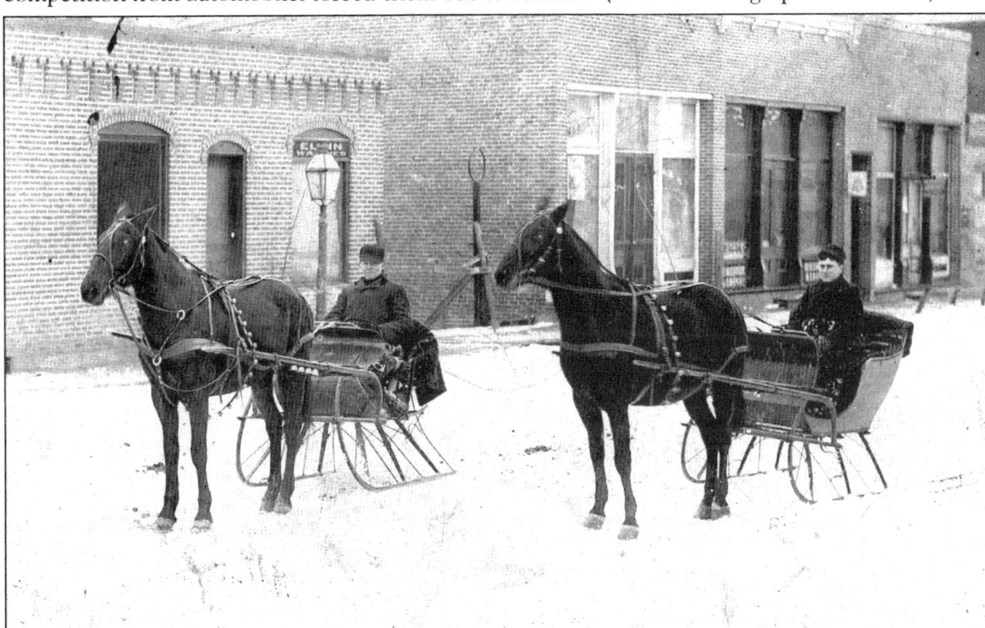

Before motorized vehicles, improved roads, and snowplows, horse-drawn sleighs or bobsleds often provided winter transportation of people and goods. In this undated photograph, two young men are shown using sleighs on Baubice Street in Pioneer. (WCPL Photographic Archives.)

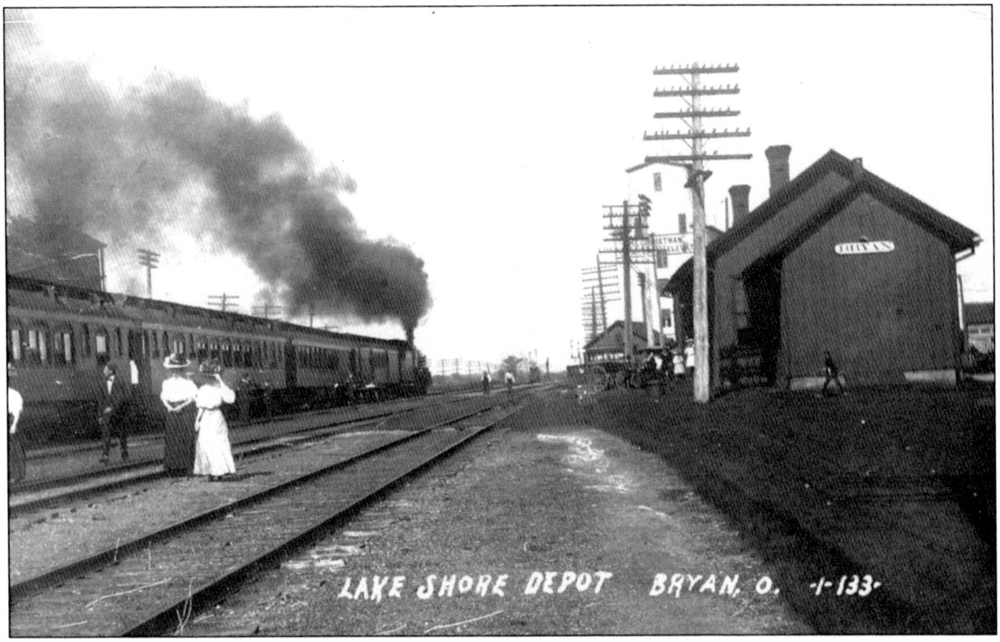

In 1871, the Lake Shore and Michigan Southern Railroad constructed this Bryan passenger depot on the north side of the tracks one and a half blocks west of its present location. This site proved inconvenient and dangerous, requiring passengers to run a gauntlet of trains. In 1888, the depot was moved to its present site.

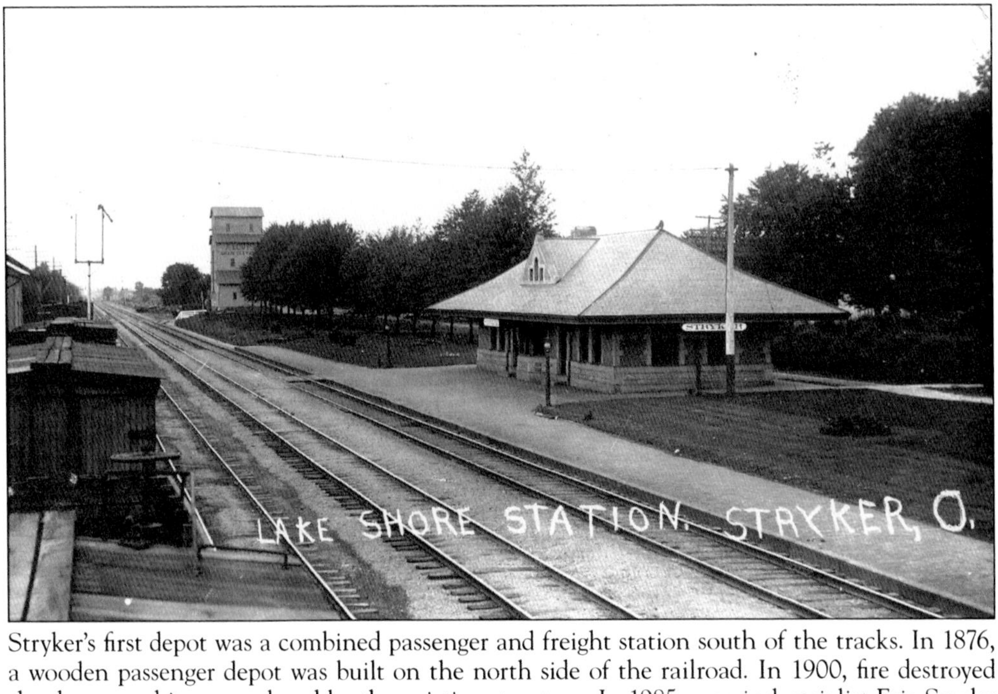

Stryker's first depot was a combined passenger and freight station south of the tracks. In 1876, a wooden passenger depot was built on the north side of the railroad. In 1900, fire destroyed the depot, and it was replaced by the existing structure. In 1985, area industrialist Erie Sauder donated the depot to the Village of Stryker. It was placed on the National Register of Historic Places in 1989.

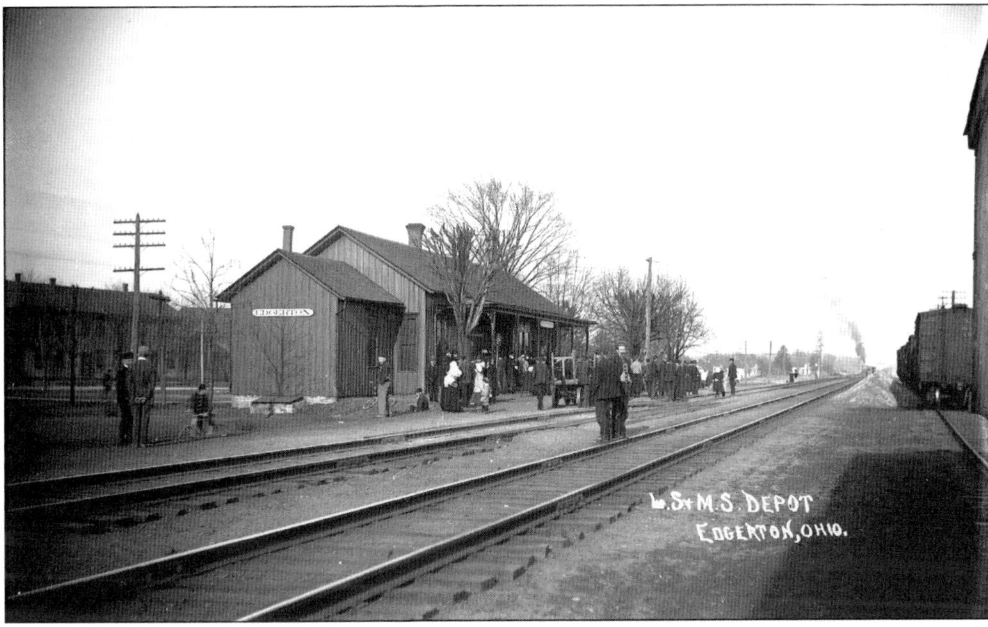

In 1869, the Michigan Southern and Northern Indiana Railroad became the Lake Shore and Michigan Southern. Later name changes included the New York Central (1913), Penn Central (1968), Conrail (1976), and Norfolk Southern (1999). In 1870, the Lake Shore and Michigan Southern constructed this frame depot north of the tracks near the foot of Oak Street in Edgerton. The Hotel Mortland is visible on the left. (WCPL Photographic Archives.)

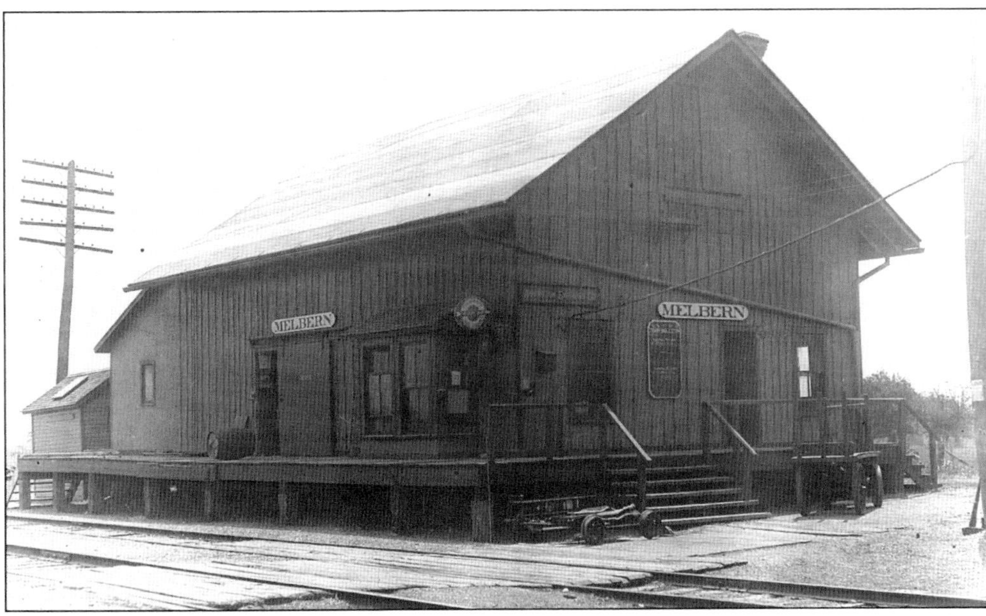

Melbern was originally platted as Kansas in 1856 but experienced little growth until the railroad established a station in 1867. In 1869, the village was resurveyed as Melbern, taking its name from the local post office created in 1866. In 1868, this combined passenger and freight depot was erected on the south side of the tracks. The depot sat unused 10 years before it was razed in 1942. (Allen County, Ohio, Historical Society.)

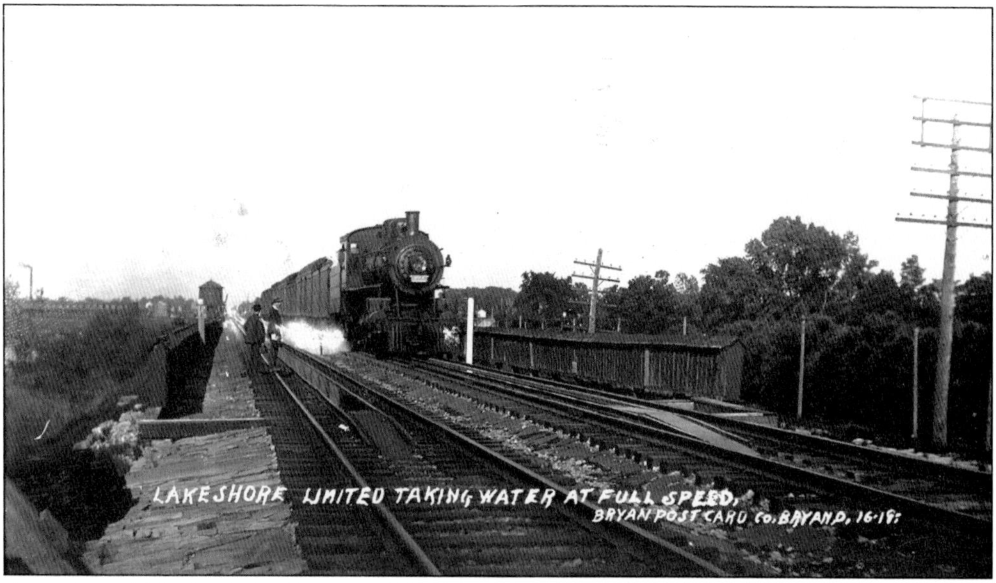

As early as 1890 the Lake Shore and Michigan Southern Railroad installed track pans at the Tiffin River west of Stryker to allow steam locomotives to scoop up needed water without stopping, shaving precious time from railroad timetables. In 1910, the pans were moved about a mile east of town. As steam locomotives gave way to diesels, track pans became obsolete; Stryker's facility ceased operation about March 1, 1954.

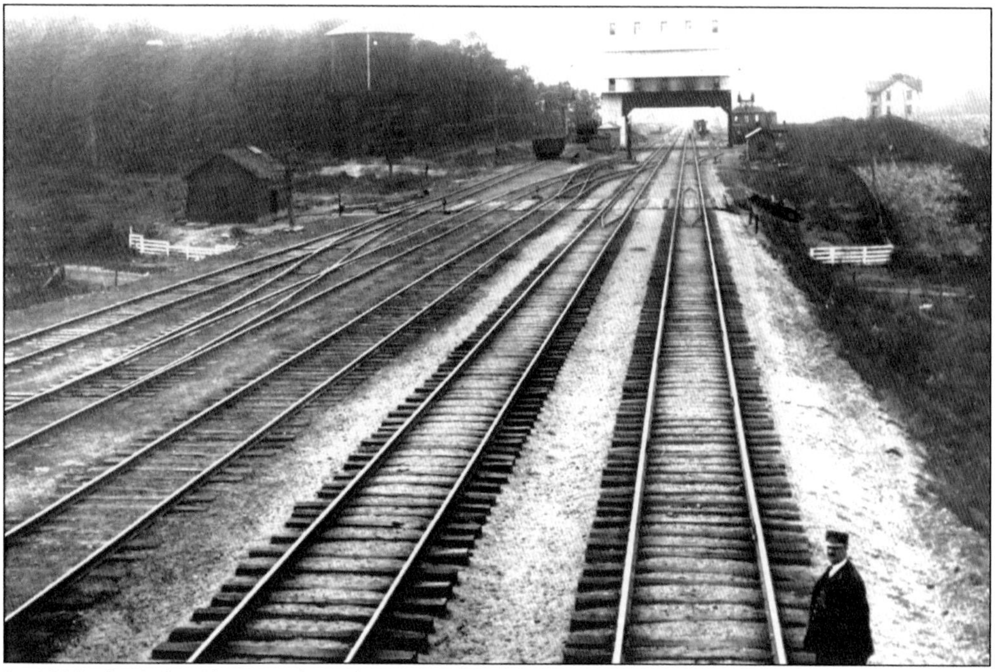

In 1905, the Lake Shore and Michigan Southern Railroad constructed the Mina coaling and watering station near County Road 6 east of Edgerton at a cost of about $100,000. The coaling station burned in 1907 and was rebuilt. Coal filled a locomotive's tender from the overhead structure in about three minutes. The change from steam to diesel locomotives made Mina obsolete, and the station closed in 1954.

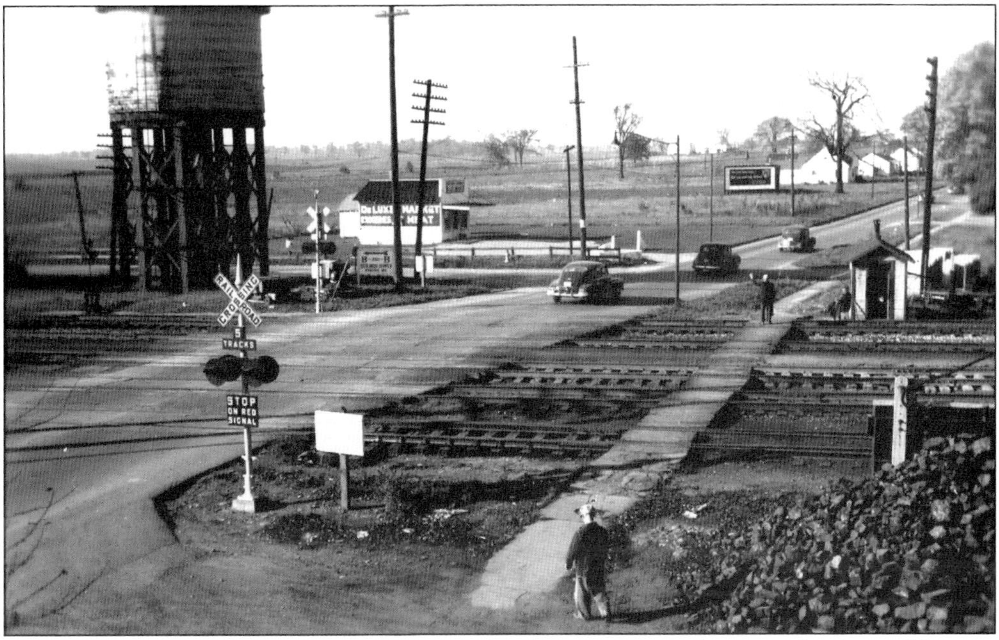

Completion of the New York Central Railroad underpass in 1962 dramatically changed Bryan's North Main Street. The railroad's water tower, removed in 1956, and Goldie Newman's Deluxe Market are shown on the left in this 1950 photograph. The crossing watchman's shack stands on the right. Watchmen were eliminated when automatic crossing gates were installed in 1951. (WCPL Photographic Archives.)

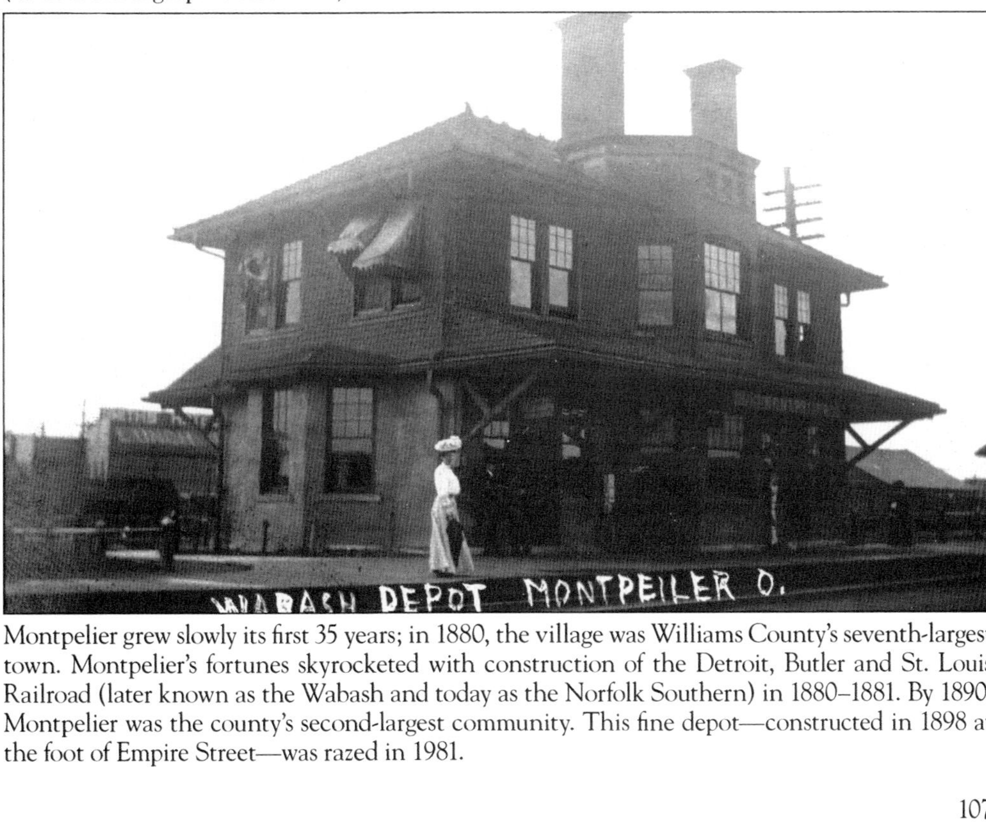

Montpelier grew slowly its first 35 years; in 1880, the village was Williams County's seventh-largest town. Montpelier's fortunes skyrocketed with construction of the Detroit, Butler and St. Louis Railroad (later known as the Wabash and today as the Norfolk Southern) in 1880–1881. By 1890, Montpelier was the county's second-largest community. This fine depot—constructed in 1898 at the foot of Empire Street—was razed in 1981.

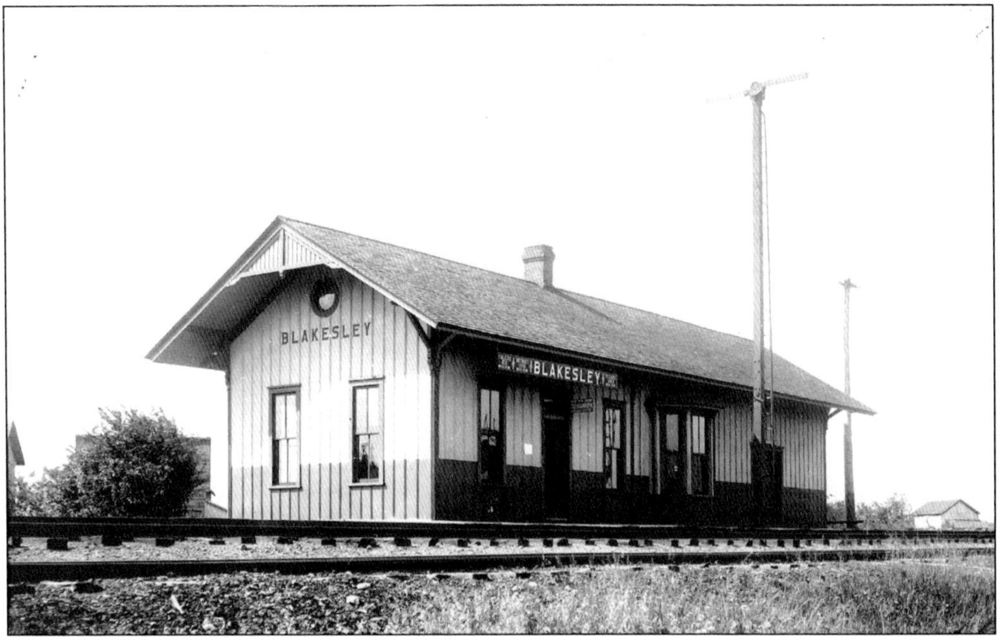

Blakeslee owes its existence to the Wabash Railroad's arrival in 1880–1881. This frame depot was completed in June 1881 south of the tracks west of Washington Street. At the time, railroad communication relied on telegraphic dots and dashes to relay information. The Wabash spelled Blakeslee as "Blakesley" on its depot, changing the double *e* ending to one *e* and a similar sound, *y*, to avoid miscommunication. (WCPL Photographic Archives.)

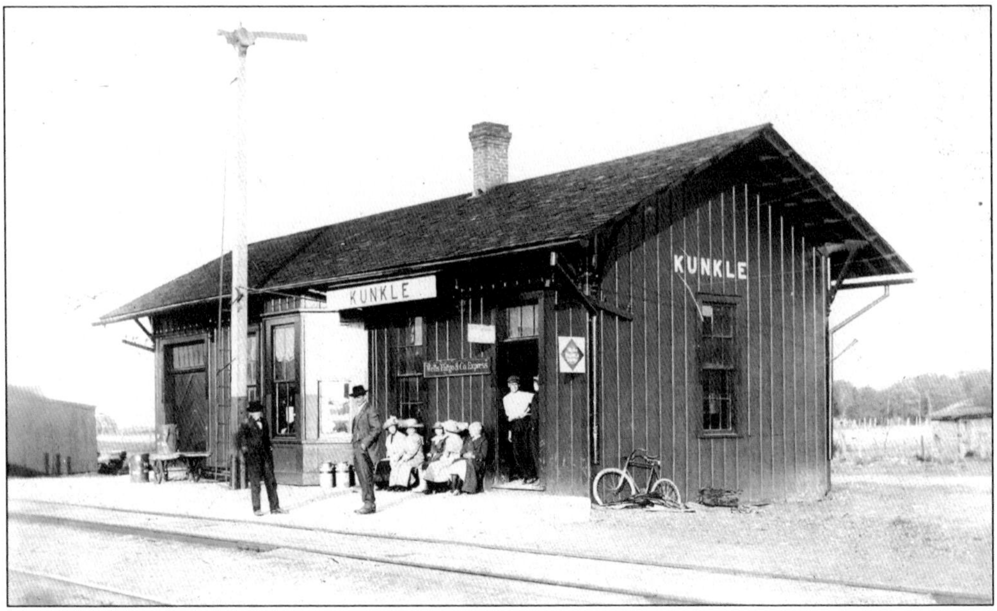

Kunkle remained a minor business point until the Wabash Railroad was built through the village. In 1884, Kunkle's population was estimated at 140 people with 23 buildings erected in the previous year, including this frame depot south of the tracks east of Pleasant Street.

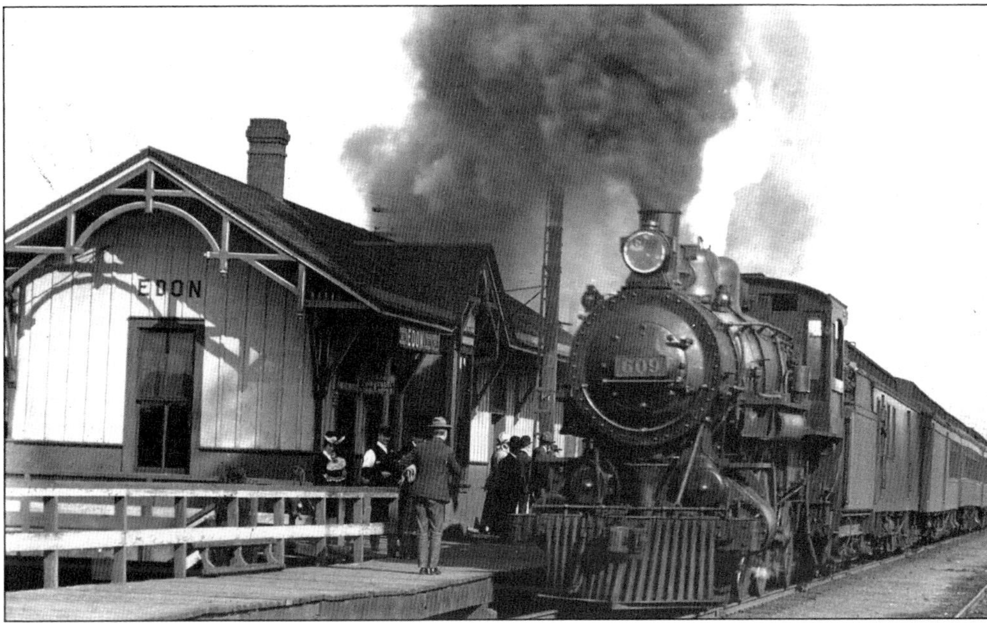

In 1892, the Wabash Railroad extension from Chicago to Montpelier was built through Edon, spurring local growth. Edon's historic Wabash depot—now located in Walz Park—was built that summer north of the railroad east of Michigan Street where it was a hub of local activity for many years.

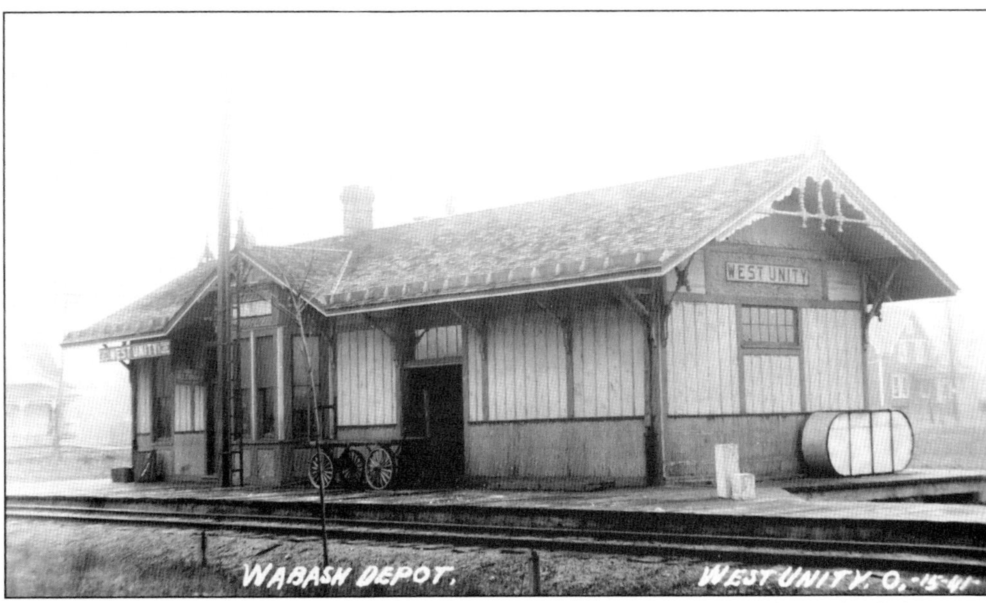

In 1901, the Wabash Railroad constructed a direct rail link between Montpelier and Toledo, giving West Unity a second railroad. This frame Wabash depot stood north of the tracks east of Main Street. The Montpelier-to-Toledo rail line was abandoned around 1990 and was acquired by the Northwest Ohio Rails to Trails Association. The Wabash Railroad became the Norfolk and Western in 1964 and Norfolk Southern in 1982. (WCPL Photographic Archives.)

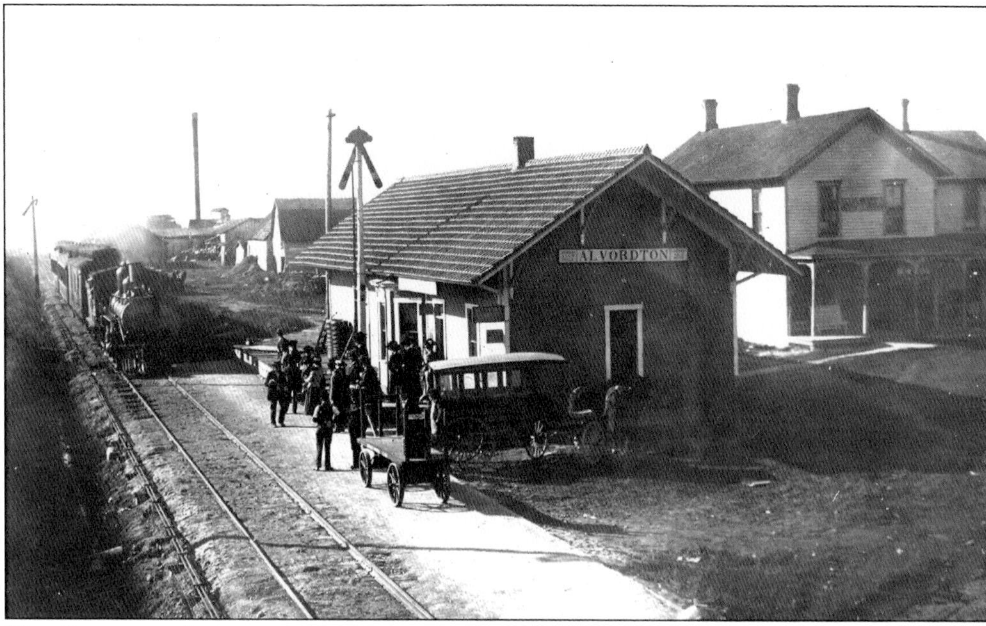

The Cincinnati, Jackson and Mackinaw Railroad was extended through Williams County in 1887. The Mackinaw's arrival gave Alvordton a second rail line, further boosting the town's early economy. This frame depot was constructed west of the tracks between Ames and Main Streets in 1888. The Cincinnati, Jackson and Mackinaw became the Cincinnati Northern Railroad around 1897. Passenger service ceased in 1936, and the railroad was abandoned in the late 1970s.

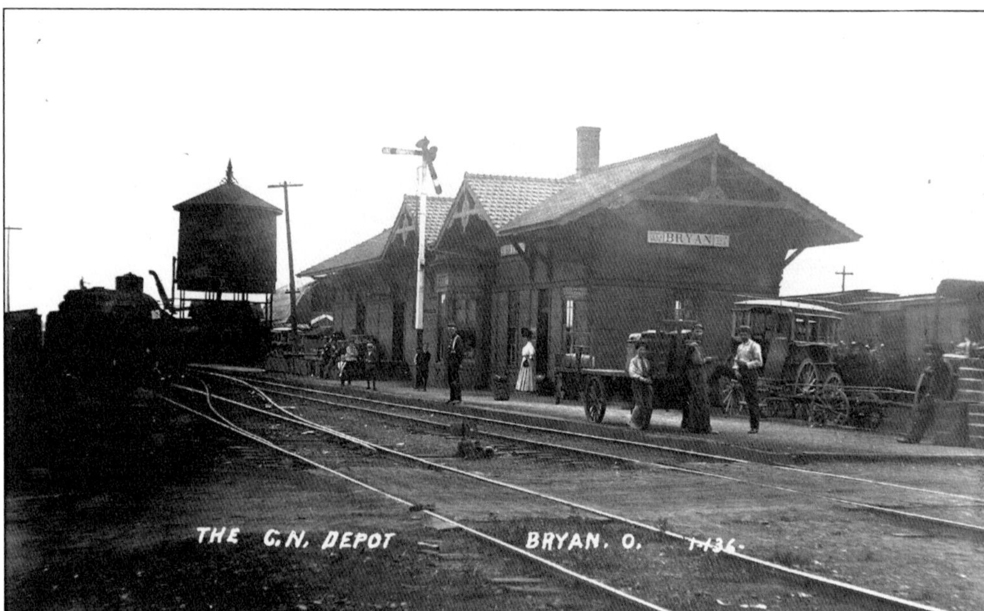

Cincinnati, Jackson and Mackinaw Railroad tracklayers reached Bryan on September 24, 1887, giving the Fountain City access to a second rail line. This ornate frame depot was completed in late 1887 west of the tracks south of Wilson Street. In 1943, the railroad removed the north half of the station. The elevated water tank behind the depot replenished steam locomotive boilers.

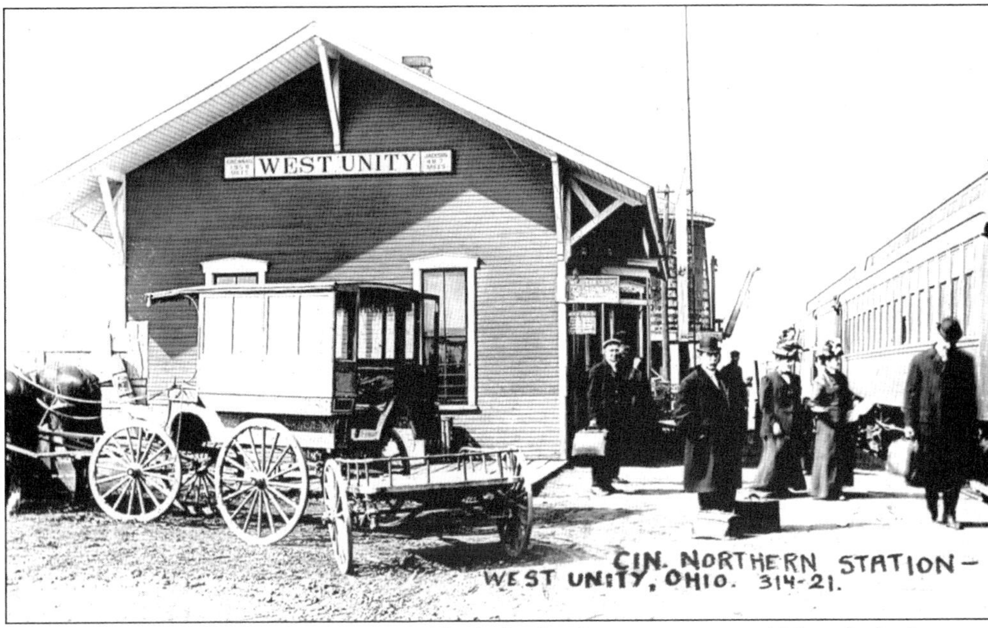

West Unity's early growth was hampered by lack of rail transportation. Although the Junction Railroad extension from Toledo was proposed through West Unity in 1852, it was not until 1887 that the Cincinnati, Jackson and Mackinaw Railroad arrived. The railroad's coming was cause for a great celebration in the village. This frame depot was constructed where the railroad crossed U.S. 127 at the northeast edge of West Unity.

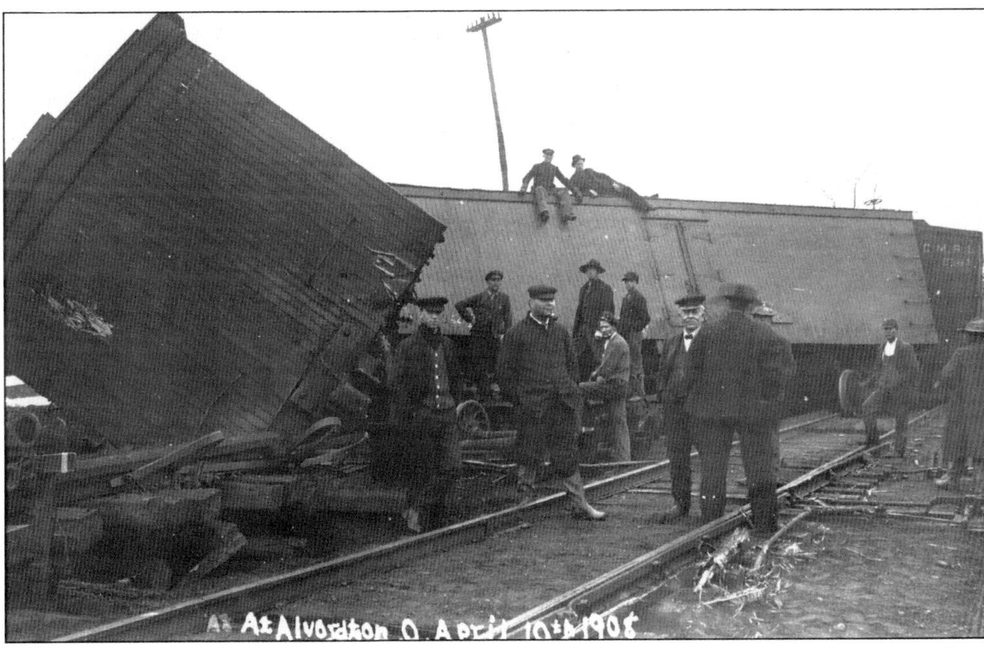

On April 10, 1908, seven cars of an eastbound Wabash freight train traveling 60 miles per hour derailed near the Alvordton depot. An arch bar under one of the cars broke, throwing out its rear trucks and dropping the car on the track. The Montpelier Wabash wrecking crew and local section crews worked two days to clear the wreck and rebuild damaged track.

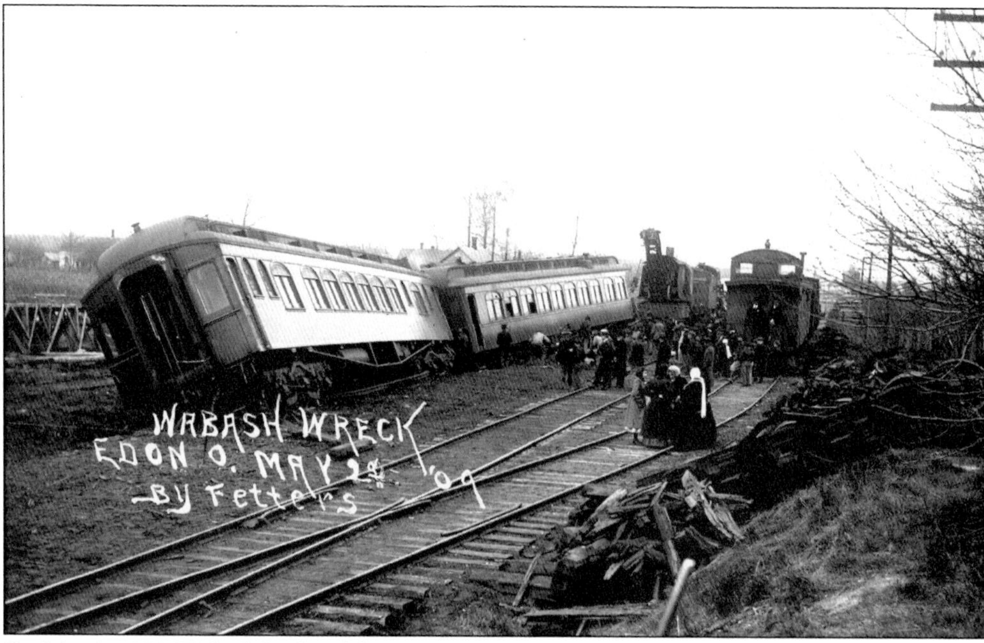

On May 2, 1909, Wabash Railroad fast train No. 6 derailed east of Edon's depot. All eight coaches were thrown from the track, with the baggage car coming to rest in a ditch. A relief train carrying doctors and nurses was dispatched from Montpelier, but no serious injuries were reported. Passengers and baggage were taken to Montpelier on the relief train while crews cleared the wreckage and laid temporary rails.

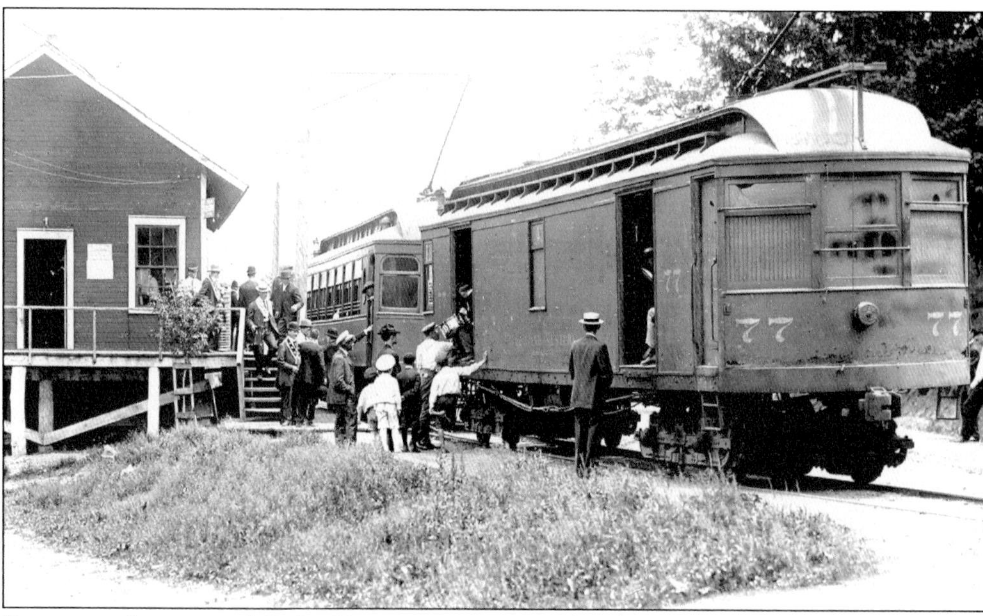

Pioneer tried unsuccessfully for 50 years to attract a railroad. On December 3, 1903, the Toledo and Western Railway—Williams County's first electric interurban railway—reached the community. Its arrival was welcomed with a grand celebration in Pioneer. This frame depot was erected on the east side of South State Street. The depot was later moved north and became part of a local grocery store.

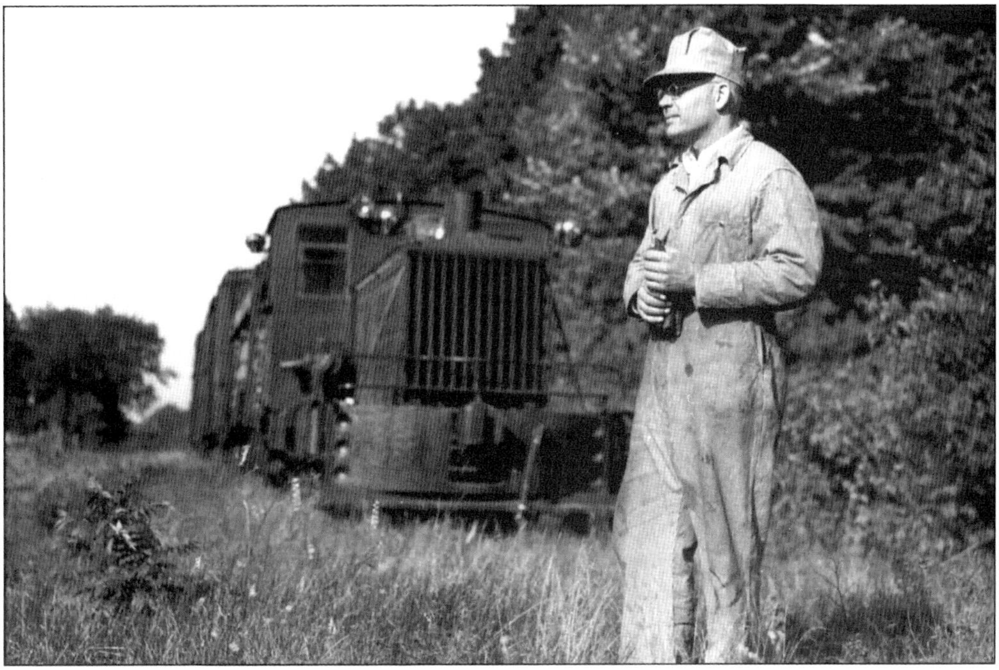

When the Toledo and Western interurban railway ceased operations, Pioneer and Fayette citizens led by Earl S. Snyder (above) purchased the tracks between their towns and created the Pioneer and Fayette Railroad. The Pioneer and Fayette began operations on September 2, 1933, and was believed to be the shortest rail line in the country. The company ceased running trains in the early 1940s but continued its trucking business until 1992. (WCPL Photographic Archives.)

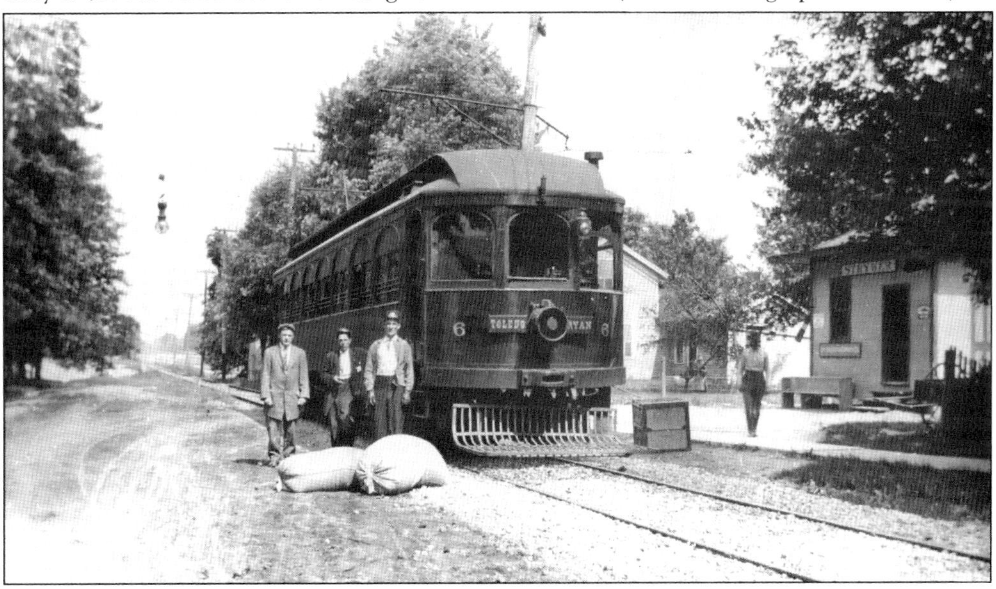

The Toledo and Indiana Railway operated between Toledo and Bryan from 1905 to 1939. Its interurban cars' electric motors were powered through a "kite" extending to an overhead power line. The Toledo and Indiana provided more convenient schedules, and more stops, and was less expensive than "steam" railroad passenger service. A Toledo and Indiana car pauses at the Stryker depot on East Lynn Street in this undated photograph. (WCPL Photographic Archives.)

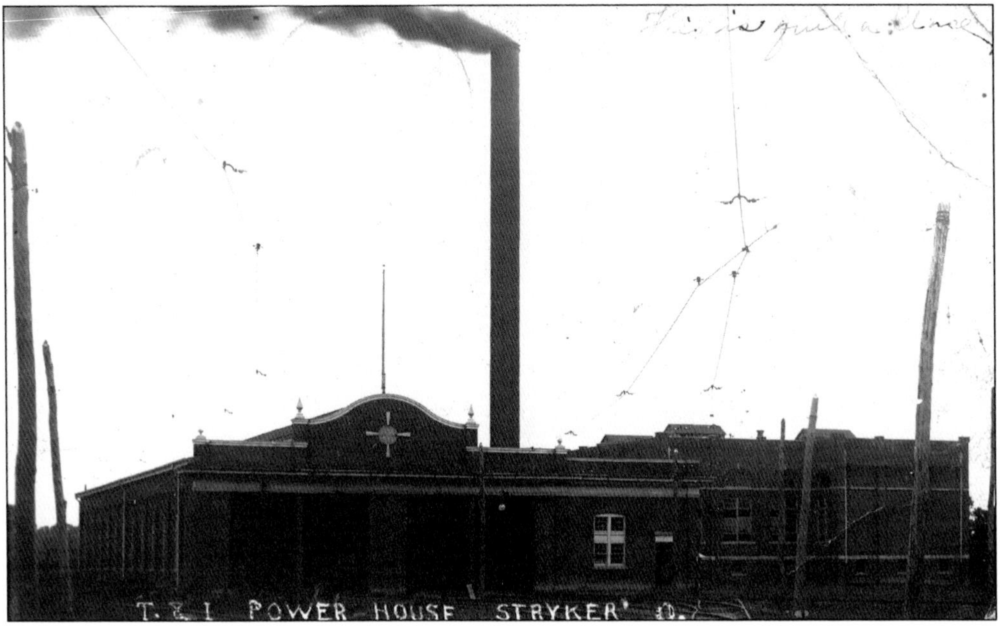

In the spring of 1905, the Toledo and Indiana Railway constructed this generating station (right) at Stryker to power its interurban cars. The generating station also provided electricity to many northwest Ohio communities, helping bring the area into the "modern age." Later that year, the Toledo and Indiana completed its car maintenance and storage facility (left) east of the generating station.

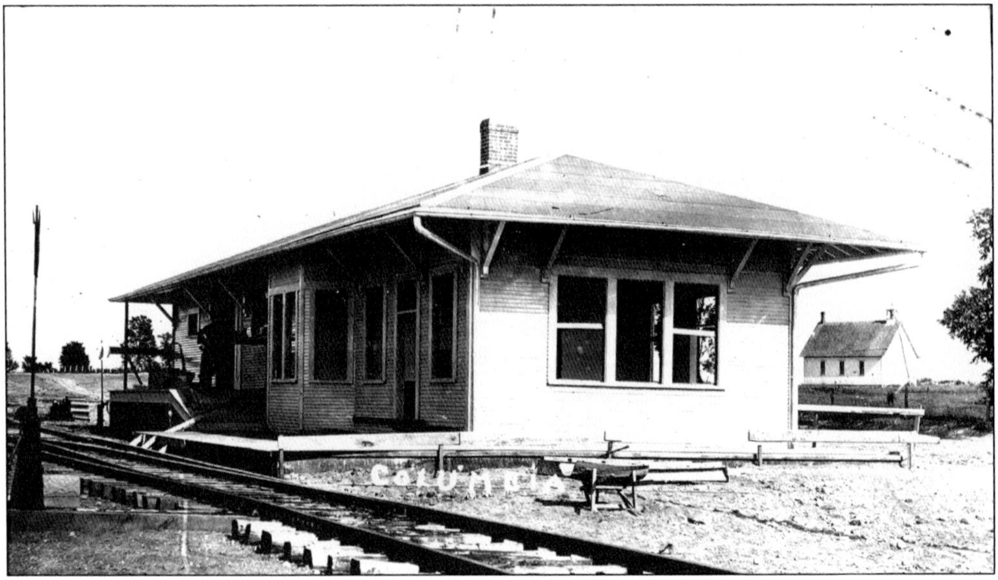

The St. Joseph Valley Railway was organized to provide an interurban rail link between Chicago, Toledo, and Cleveland. In 1915, Columbia became a boomtown with the railroad's arrival. Fairview Addition—consisting of 117 lots—was surveyed, and a bank, stockyard, elevator, pickle factory, and lumber shed were established. This depot was constructed on the east side of North Main Street northwest of the Columbia schoolhouse. Trains ceased running in 1918. (WCPL Photographic Archives.)

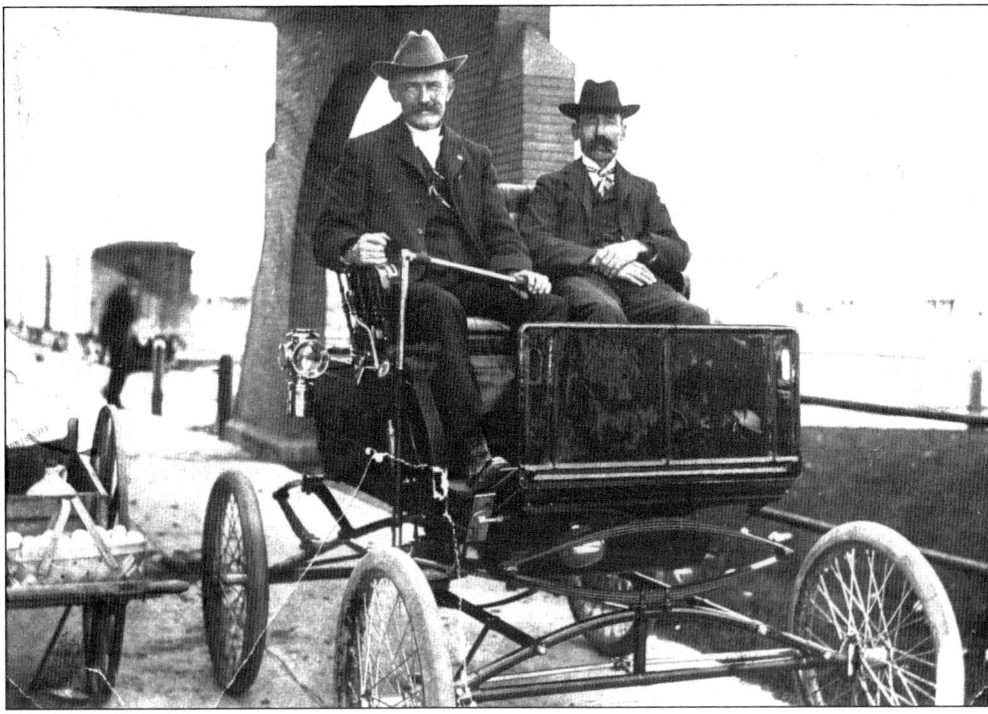

Montpelier undertaker and furniture dealer Nathan Lash owned the town's first automobile, a steam-powered vehicle. Lash gives Everitt Holloway a lift at the Wabash depot in this undated photograph. (Williams County Historical Society.)

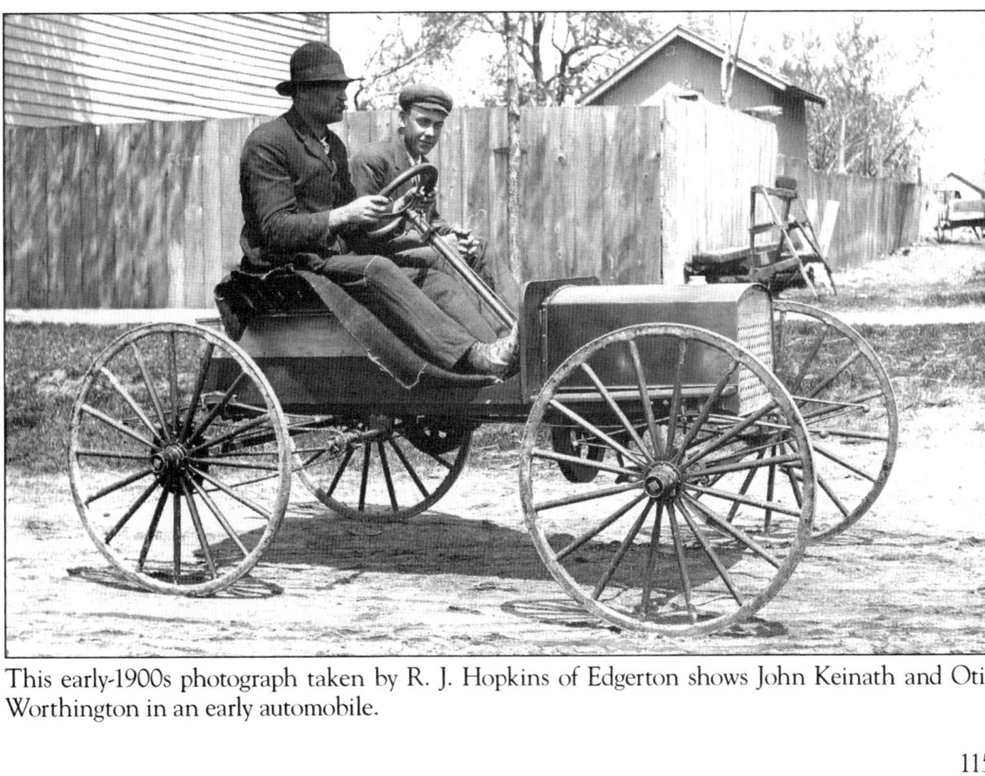

This early-1900s photograph taken by R. J. Hopkins of Edgerton shows John Keinath and Otis Worthington in an early automobile.

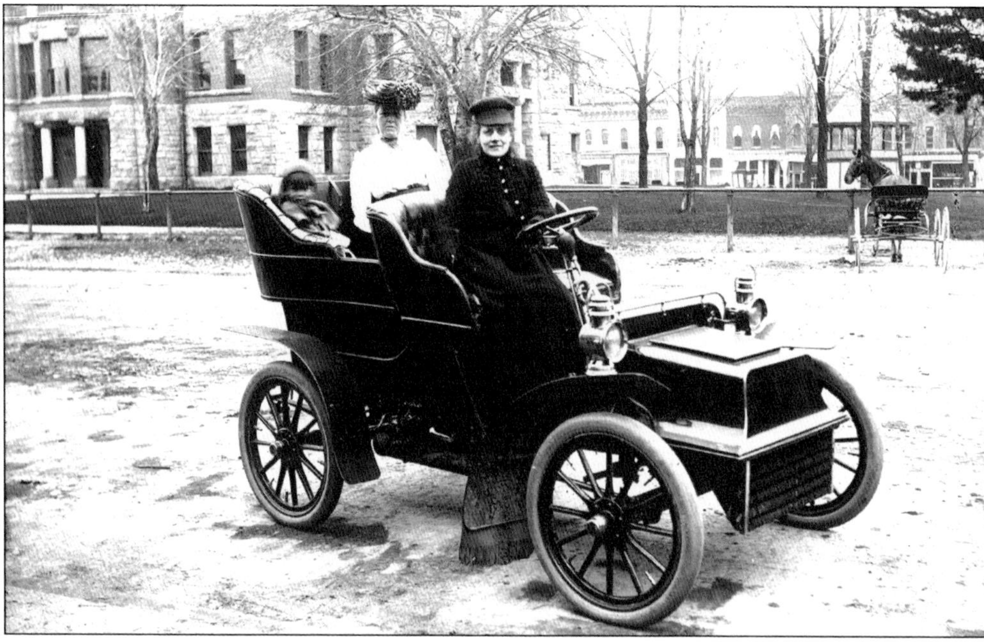

Arthur Snyder, Rose Beach, and Lillion Snyder pose in an early automobile on the west side of Bryan's square. Note the iron hitching rail surrounding the Williams County Courthouse, brick paving on South Lynn Street, and the bandstand in the southeast corner of the courtyard. John E. Beach, a professional photographer who also owned the Bryan Postcard Company, took this photograph near his South Lynn Street studio. (WCPL Photographic Archives.)

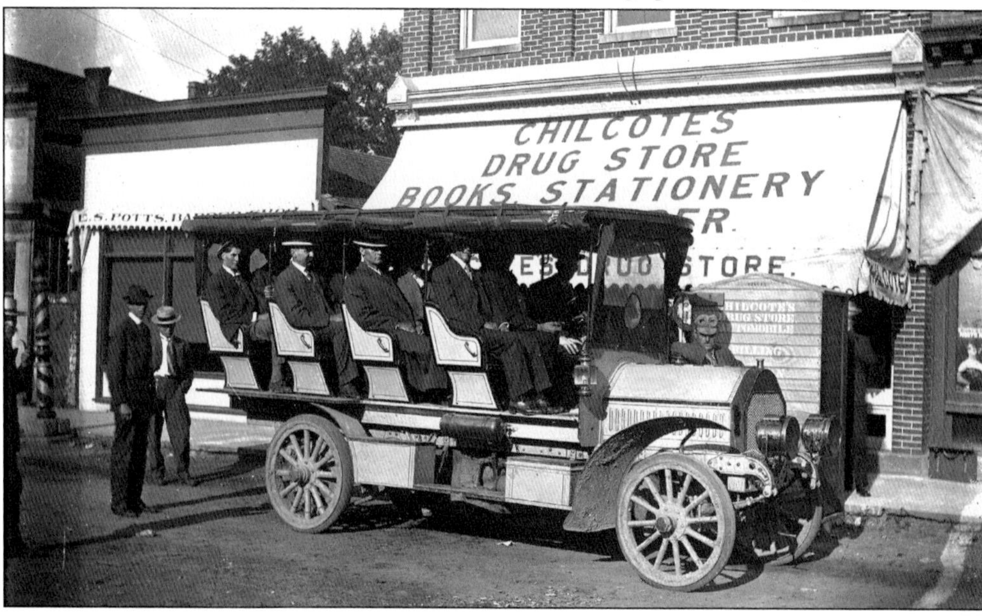

This early-1900s bus is parked at the filling station in front of William H. Chilcote's drugstore on the east side of Edgerton's North Michigan Avenue. Chilcote was an Edgerton businessman for nearly 60 years, selling his drugstore in 1939. He also served as Edgerton postmaster from 1885 to 1889 and 1914 to 1919. E. S. Potts's barbershop can be seen on the left behind the bus. (WCPL Photographic Archives.)

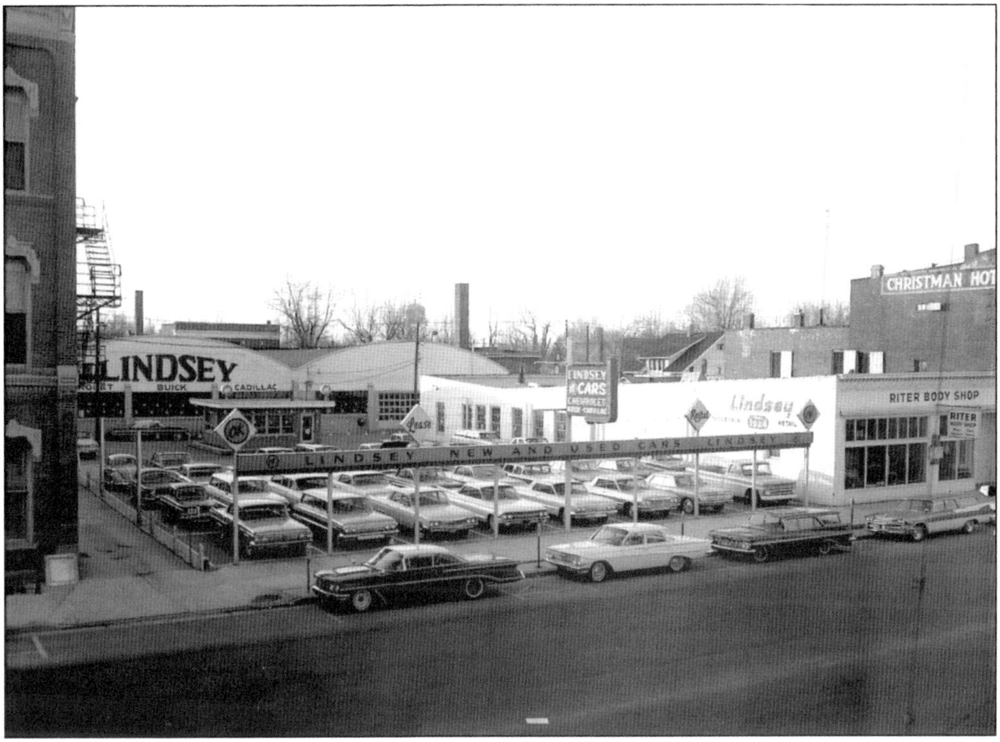

The evolution from horses to automobiles in the early 1900s gave birth to a new business—automobile sales. Early automobile dealers often sold vehicles as a sideline; as demand grew automobile sales and service became a significant business itself. This photograph shows H. A. Lindsey's car lot on Bryan's North Main Street after the Dining Car was removed in 1960. In 1970, Stan Pepple Motors purchased Lindsey's business. (WCPL Photographic Archives.)

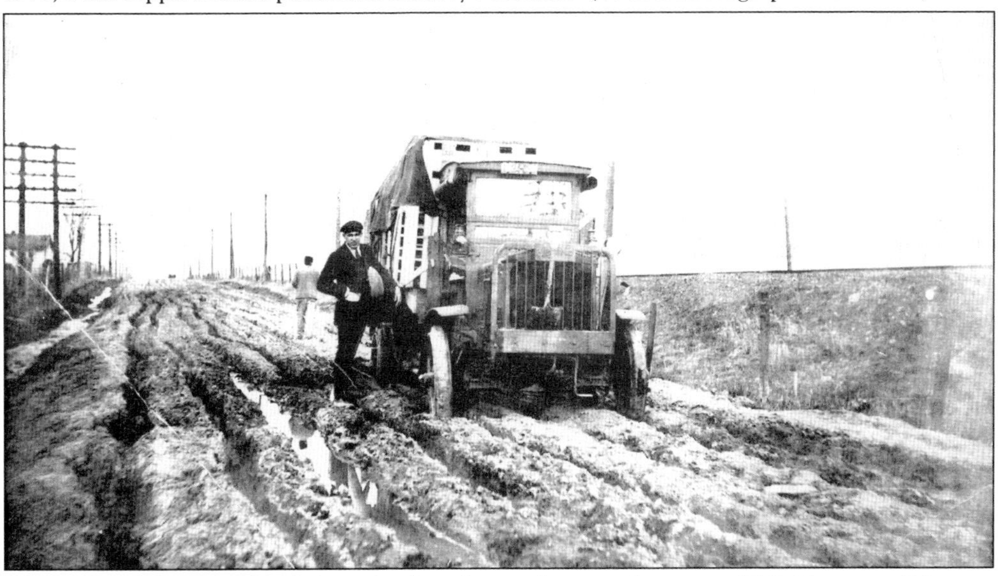
This undated photograph is believed to have been taken on what is now U.S. 6 between Edgerton and Butler, Indiana. Prior to roadway paving and ditching, mud was a regular and significant hindrance for local travelers. (WCPL Photographic Archives.)

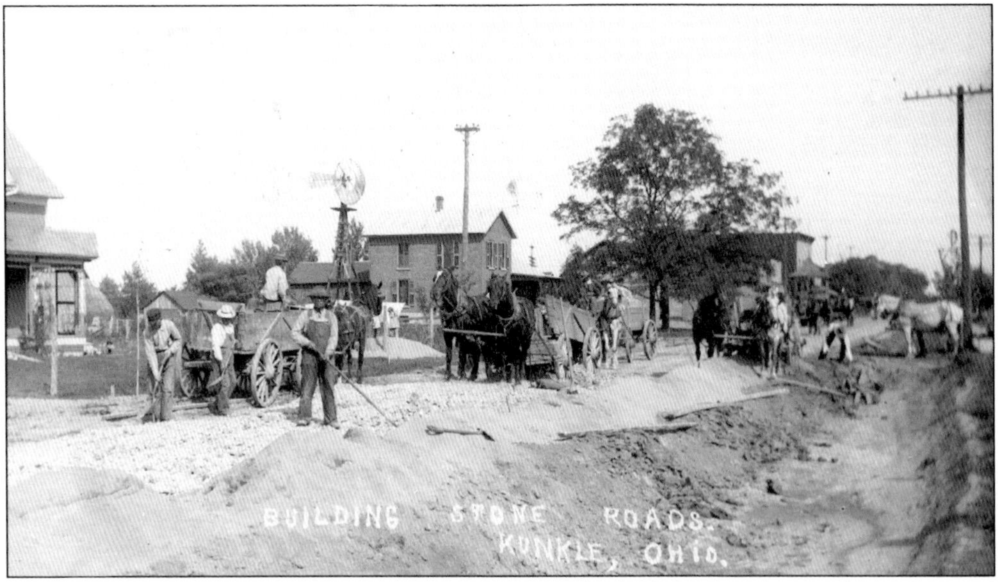

Williams County's first roads were little more than trails hacked through the woods. By the Civil War, dirt roads were constructed nearly every square mile. Around 1900, as automobiles gained popularity, demand for better roads increased. Macadamized stone roads and roadside ditches were constructed throughout the area, and many villages installed brick pavement on primary thoroughfares. This undated photograph shows a crew building a stone road with ditches at Kunkle. (WCPL Photographic Archives.)

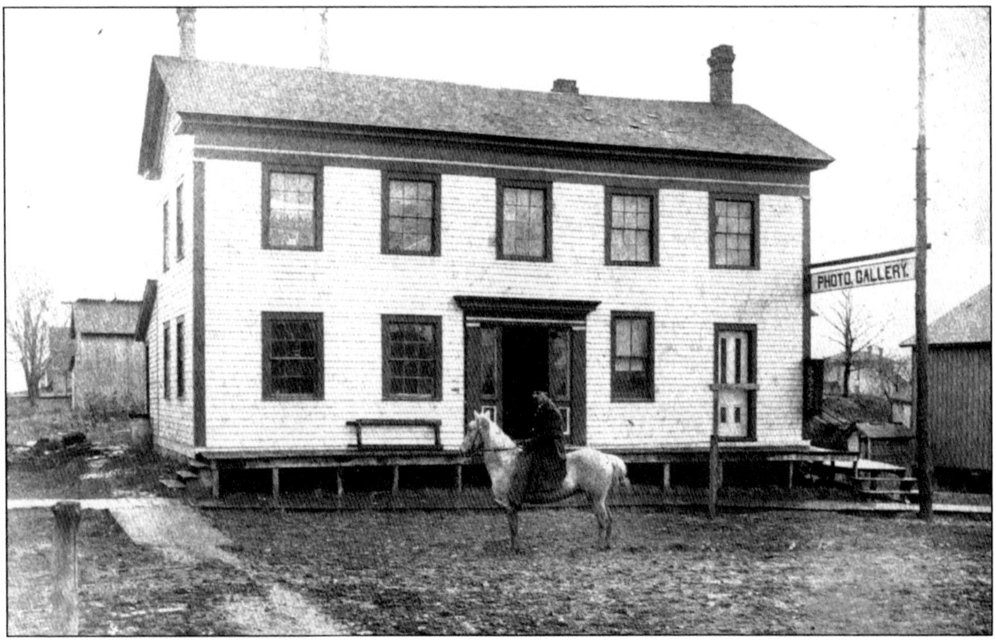

In 1854, Andy Irwin built the Pioneer Hotel at the southeast corner of State and Mulberry Streets. Pioneer's second hotel was constructed by George R. Joy on First Street later that year. The 1882 Goodspeed Williams County history states, "The Pioneer House tried to kill out Joy's Hotel, but after 21 different proprietors had vainly struggled through a period of 20 years to accomplish that result, the attempt was abandoned." (WCPL Photographic Archives.)

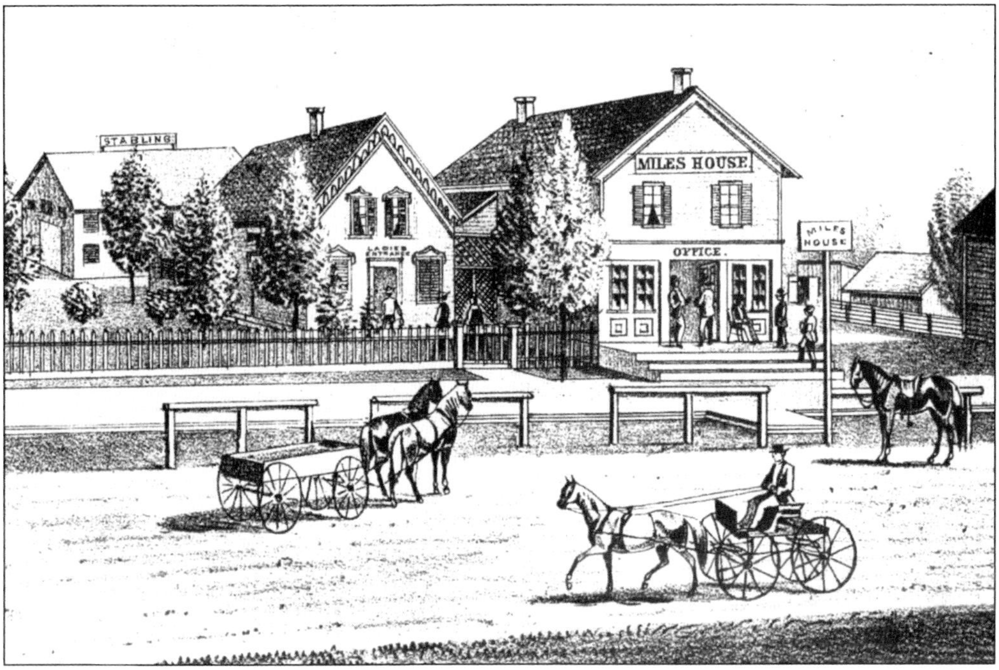

In 1869, James A. Miles opened the Miles House Hotel at the northeast corner of Stryker's Defiance and South Depot Streets, operating it for about 40 years. The building was later used as a feed mill, for public auctions, automobile storage, a hatchery, and a machine shop. The old hotel was razed in 1960 to make room for Rolland and Delilah Wyse's Stryker Dairy Isle/Polly's Drive-In. (Williams County atlas of 1874.)

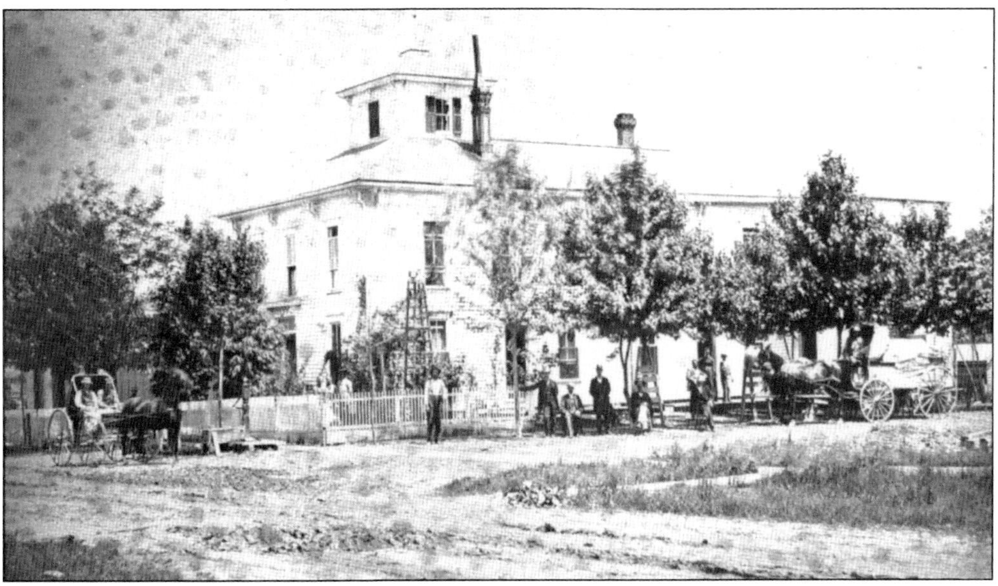

Montpelier's first hotel, the Empire House, was erected around 1850 near Monroe and Main Streets. By 1878, the Lattanner House above—also known as the Globe Hotel—served travelers at the northwest corner of Empire and Jefferson Streets. Fire destroyed the hotel in 1891, and it was replaced the following year. The hostelry was later known as the Louden Hotel and the Allen Hotel before it was razed in 1961. (WCPL Photographic Archives.)

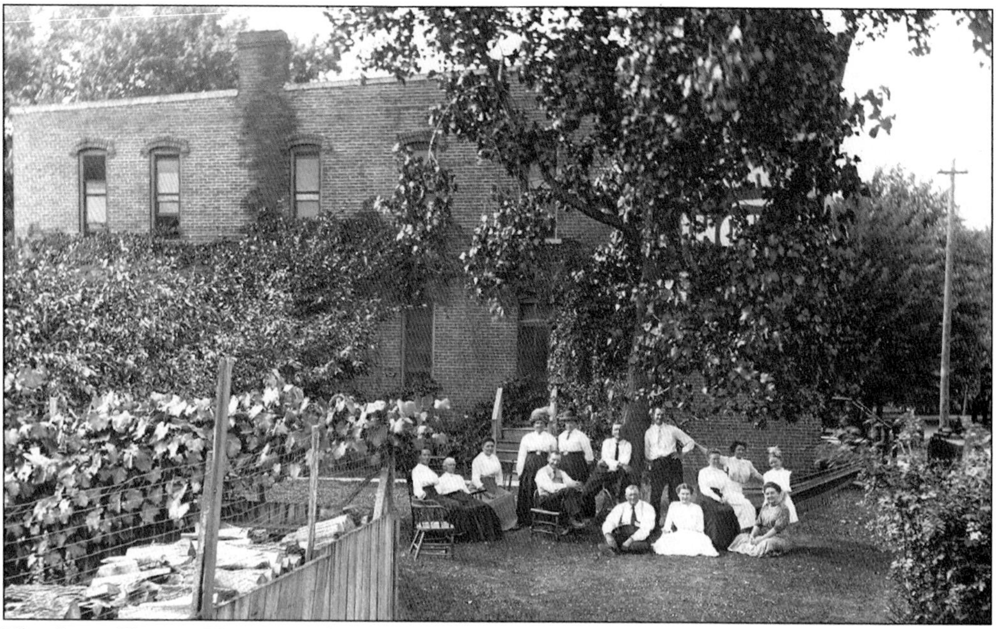

The frame Kenyon House Hotel was constructed at the southwest corner of West Unity's Main and North Streets around 1874. In 1888, Sidney Dodge, a Williams Center blacksmith and sawmill operator, purchased the hotel. When the hostelry was destroyed in the great August 1888 West Unity fire, Dodge erected this two-story brick hotel that still occupies the site.

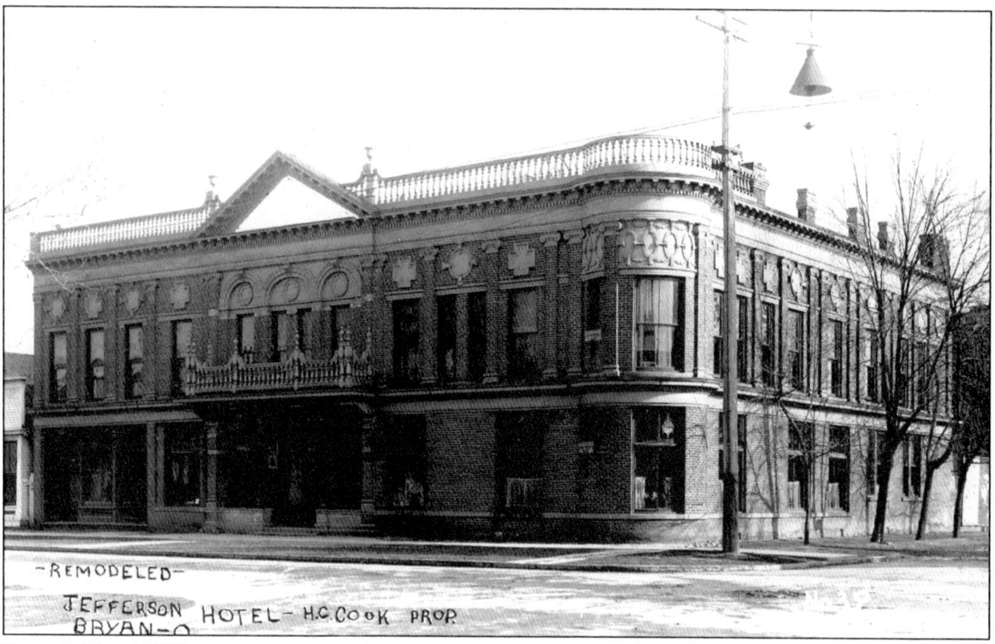

Bryan's Hotel Williams opened on the southeast corner of High and Beech Streets in April 1892, the *Bryan Press* declaring it the finest hotel between Toledo and Chicago. Edward Oscar Fallis, who designed the Williams County Courthouse, prepared the building's plans and specifications. The hotel went through several name changes—including the Closs and the Jefferson—becoming the Hotel Elder in 1934. It was razed in 1972.

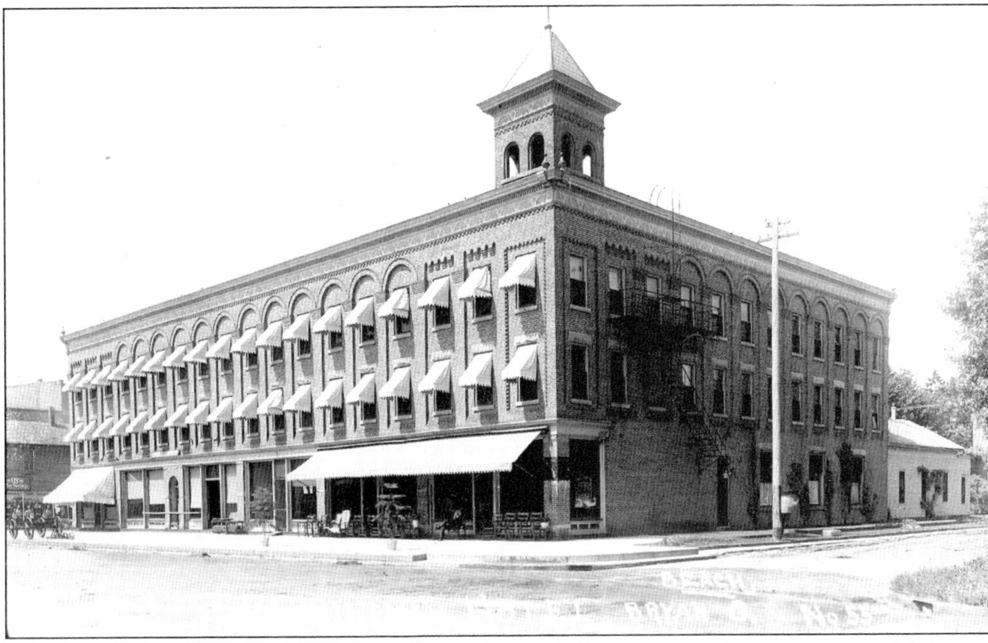

Bryan's stately Christman Hotel opened on July 10, 1895, at the southwest corner of Main and Bryan Streets. The 80-by-132-foot structure cost $25,000, including furnishings. Most of the hotel's 50 rooms were located on the second and third floors, with four business rooms on ground level. The Christman hosted distinguished guests, including Gov. William McKinley and Sen. Warren G. Harding. The hotel was razed in March 1979.

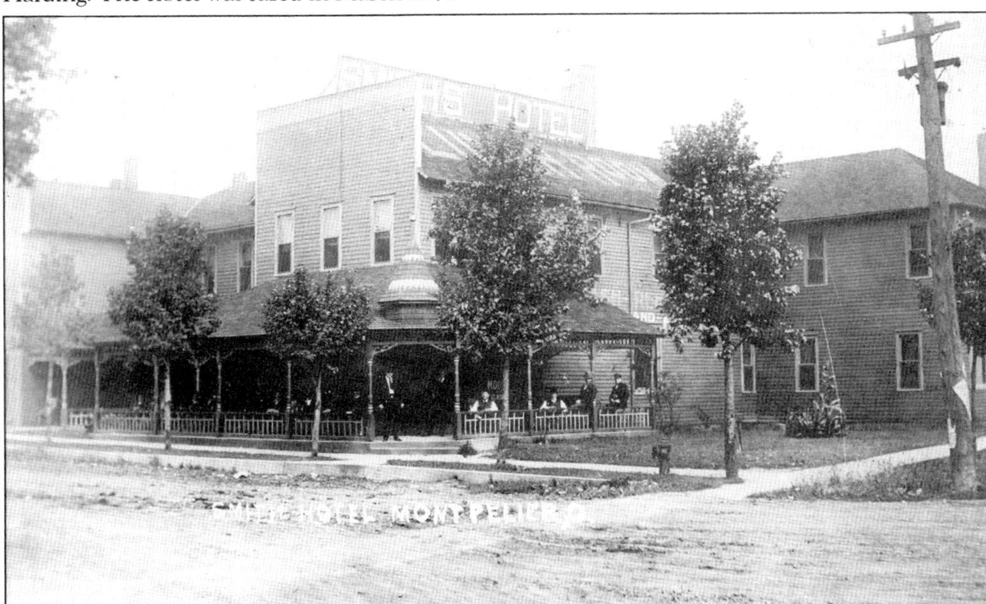

In 1900, William Gause built this two-story, 40-room hotel next to his restaurant on the northeast corner of Montpelier's Empire and Depot Streets. Its location near the Wabash depot was convenient for travelers, salespeople, and railroad employees. In 1905, the hotel was purchased by Smith Brothers from Indiana and renamed Smith's Hotel. The hotel was destroyed by fire in February 1972.

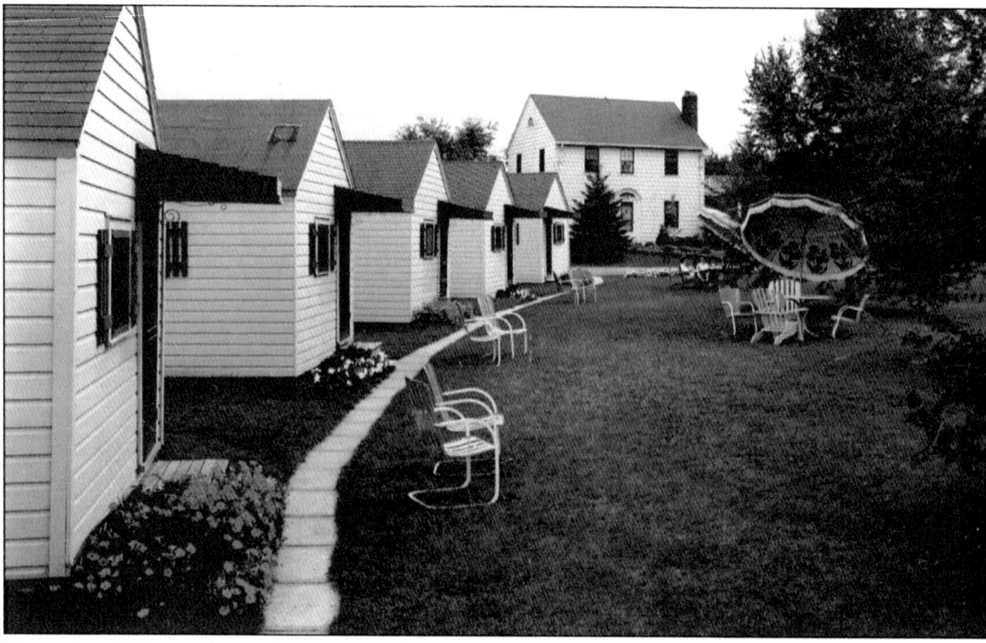

From the 1930s to the 1950s, improved roads and automobiles spurred growth of tourist camps along highways. Small cabins with few amenities provided travelers with affordable overnight accommodations. By 1948, the Green Acres tourist camp at Bryan's Mulberry and Union Streets offered travelers a deluxe double cabin, nine single cabins, and four rooms in the home on the right. Development of the motel industry led to tourist camps' demise.

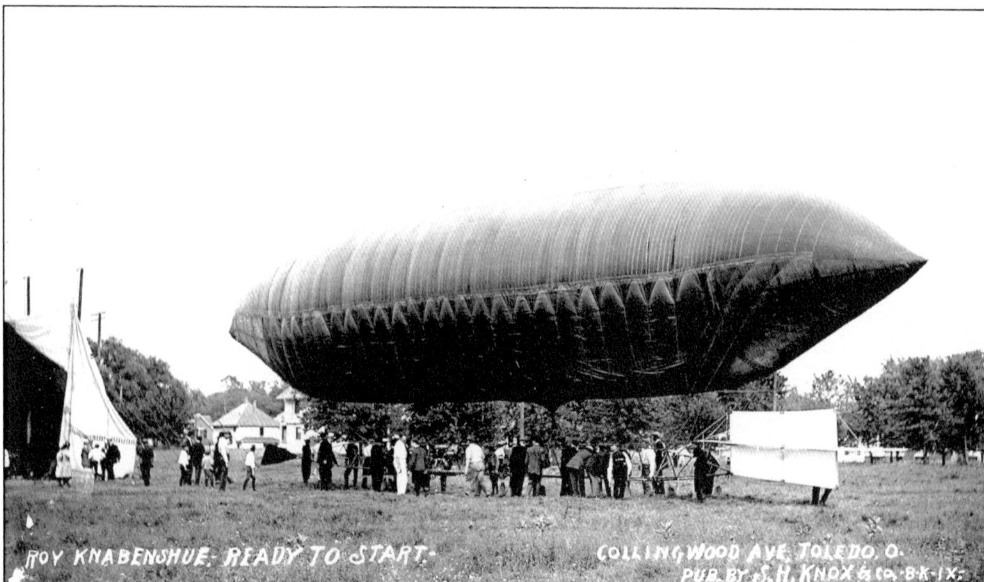

Aviation pioneer A. Roy Knabenshue worked for Bryan's Bell Telephone Company, probably in the 1890s. He launched small balloons from "Beer Cellar Hill" west of Bryan and from the opera house stage. In 1905, Knabenshue amazed Toledoans by piloting his airship from the fairgrounds to the roof of the 10-story Spitzer Building.

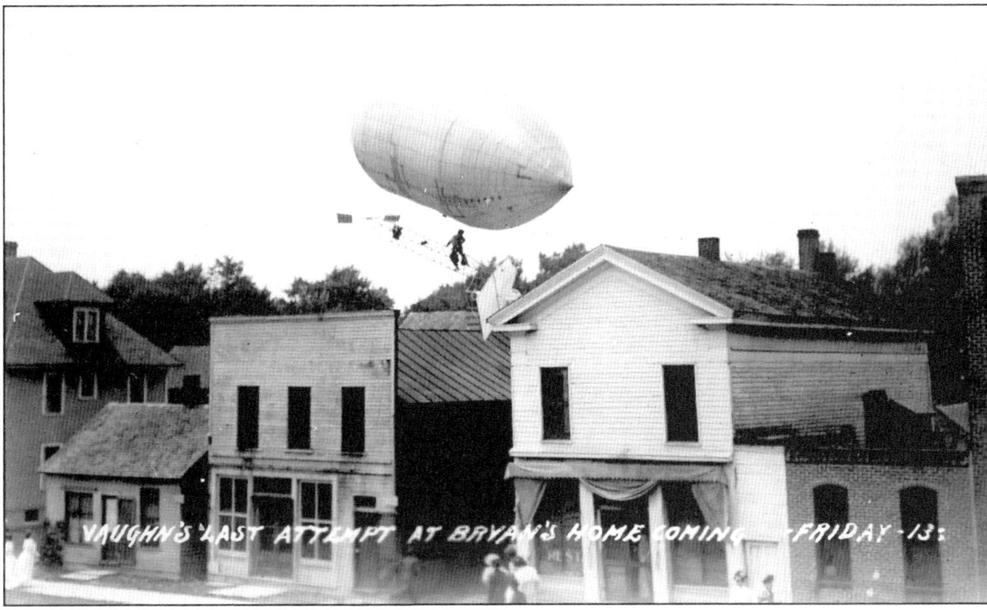

Many Williams County residents got their first glimpse of a flying machine at the 1909 Bryan homecoming. Charles J. Strobel of Toledo manufactured airships with a gas-filled bag that provided lift. The pilot straddled a sparse metal frame equipped with an engine, propeller, and rudder that was suspended from the gas bag. Stanley Vaughn piloted the *Airship Strobel* in two demonstrations on August 12, circling the Williams County Courthouse's tower numerous times and maneuvering the aircraft at will. Thousands gathered to witness a third exhibition on Friday the 13th. As the machine slowly rose from the pavement, a gust of wind forced it to collide with buildings on Main Street, breaking the rudder and puncturing the gas bag. Unable to steer, Vaughn stopped the engine, and the airship floated down behind a South Lynn Street residence. Vaughn escaped unharmed.

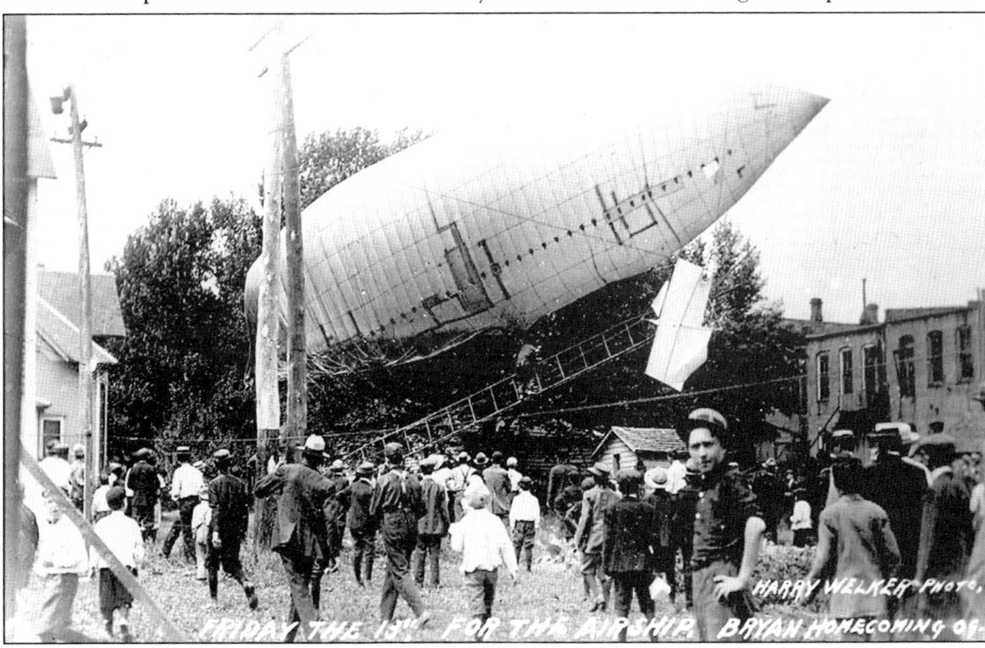

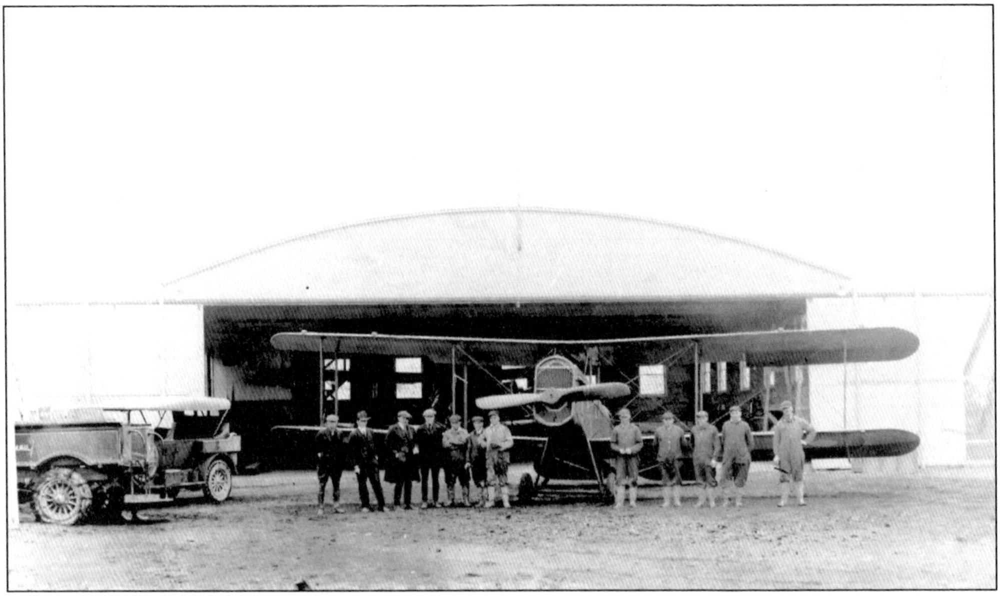

In 1918, U.S. Airmail service was established between New York and Chicago, significantly reducing mail transportation time. One of only three stops on the airmail route, Bryan's U.S. Airmail field began operations on September 6, 1918. By May 1926, more efficient airmail planes bypassed Bryan, and the local airmail field was relegated to emergency landing site status. (WCPL Photographic Archives.)

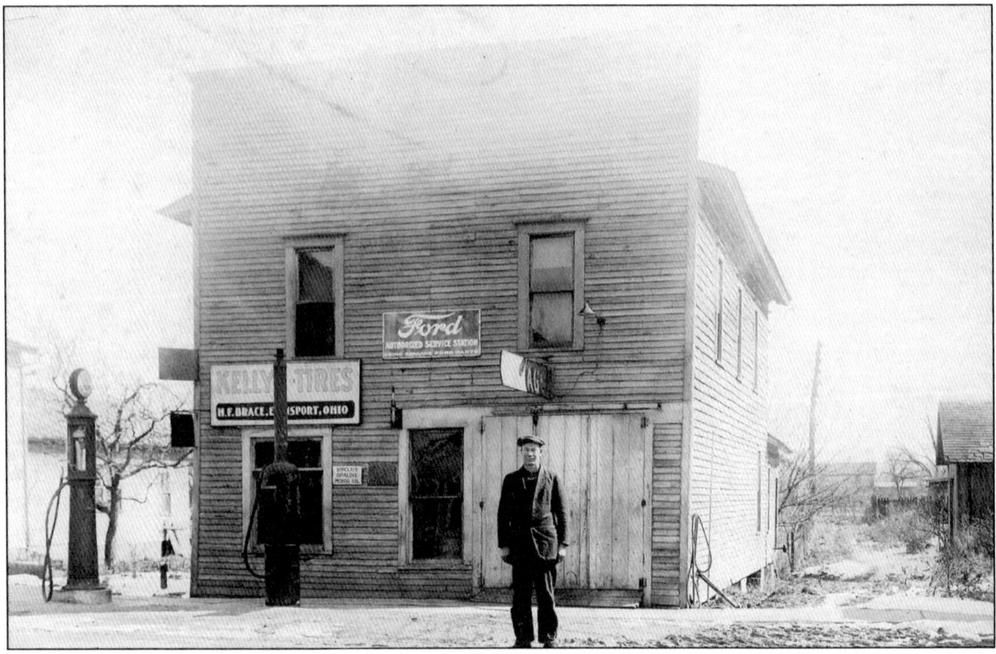

In March 1925, Harry Brace posed in front of the Evansport garage he operated for 50 years. Brace's garage was an authorized Ford service station and sold gasoline, Kelly Tires, and Sinclair Opaline Motor Oil. The building still stands; its second story was removed after being badly damaged in two 1925 fires that destroyed the remaining buildings on the east side of Evansport's business district.

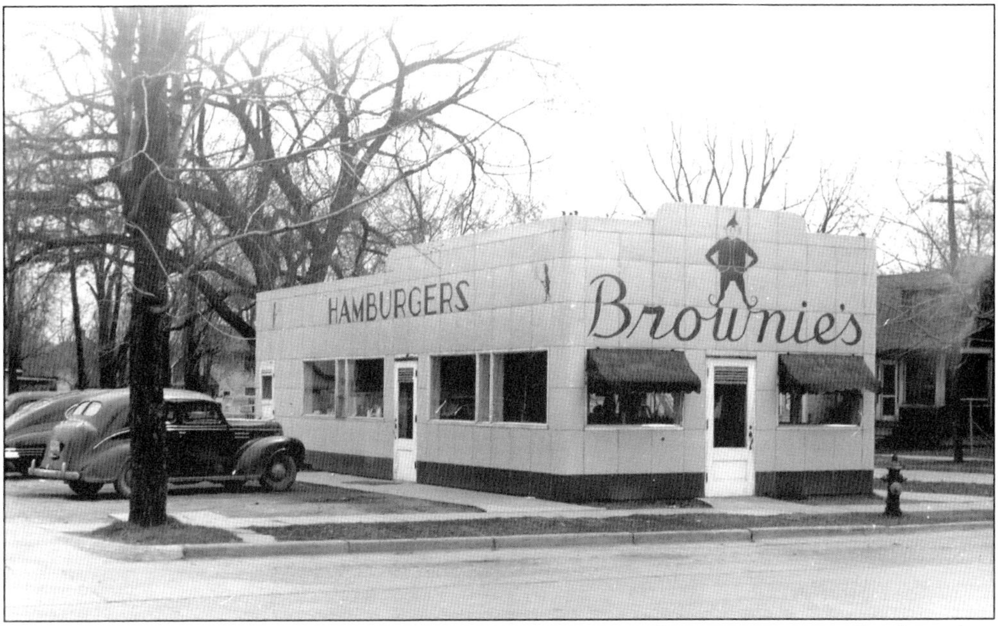

When Grant Brown opened Brownie's Drive-In in Bryan in June 1946, it was the first of its kind in the area—a fast-service restaurant where patrons could dine inside or be served in their automobiles. On summer nights, young people enjoyed dancing to a jukebox under a large elm tree behind Brownie's. By the time Grant Brown retired in 1975, Brownie's had become a Bryan institution. (WCPL Photographic Archives.)

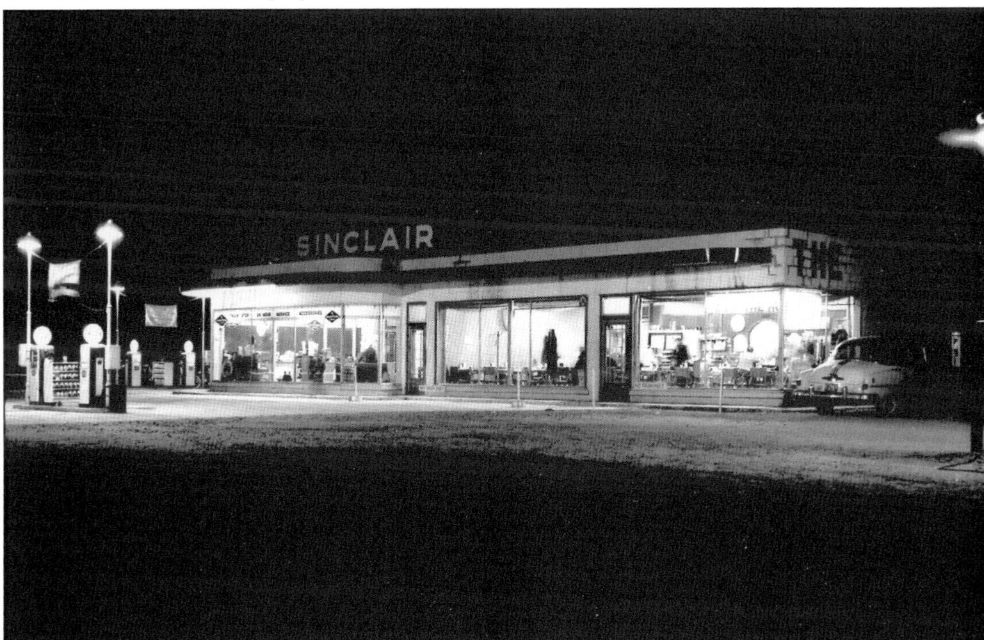

The Hub super-service station, restaurant, and truck stop opened in January 1950 at the northeast corner of High and Union Streets in Bryan. Featuring Sinclair products, customers were offered the best in automotive attention. The service station included a restaurant that offered the best in home-cooked meals at popular prices. (WCPL Photographic Archives.)

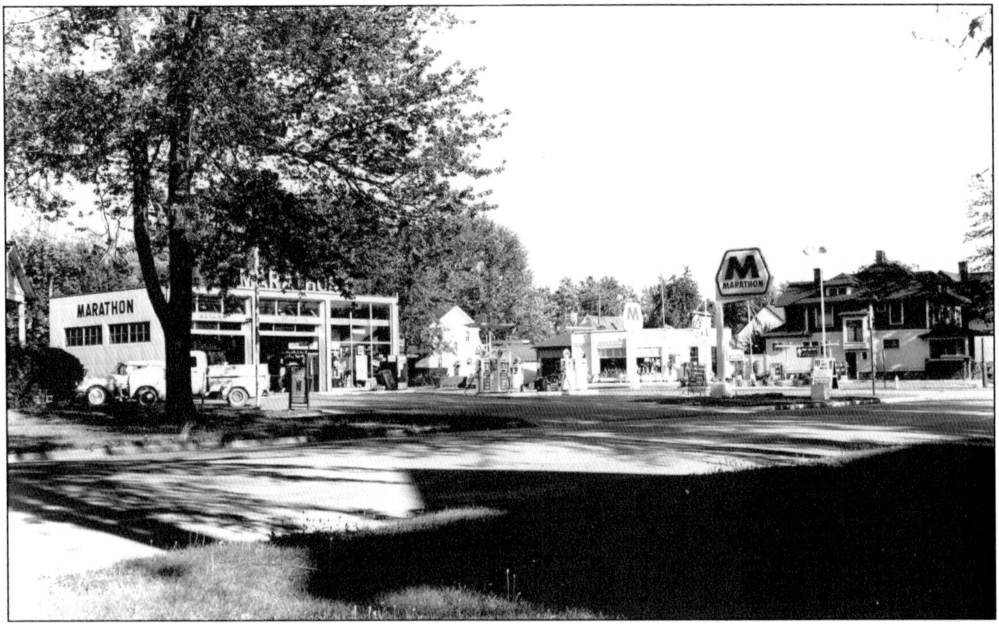

Willis Meyer opened this Marathon service station on the northeast corner of Main and Mulberry Streets in Bryan in August 1957. Meyer and his skilled mechanics offered a full range of automotive services, including tune-ups, generator rebuilding, glass replacement, radiator repair, brake work, clutch replacement, rust proofing, and valve grinding. In 1985, Robert Mattingly leased the station and operated it until his retirement in 1994. (WCPL Photographic Archives.)

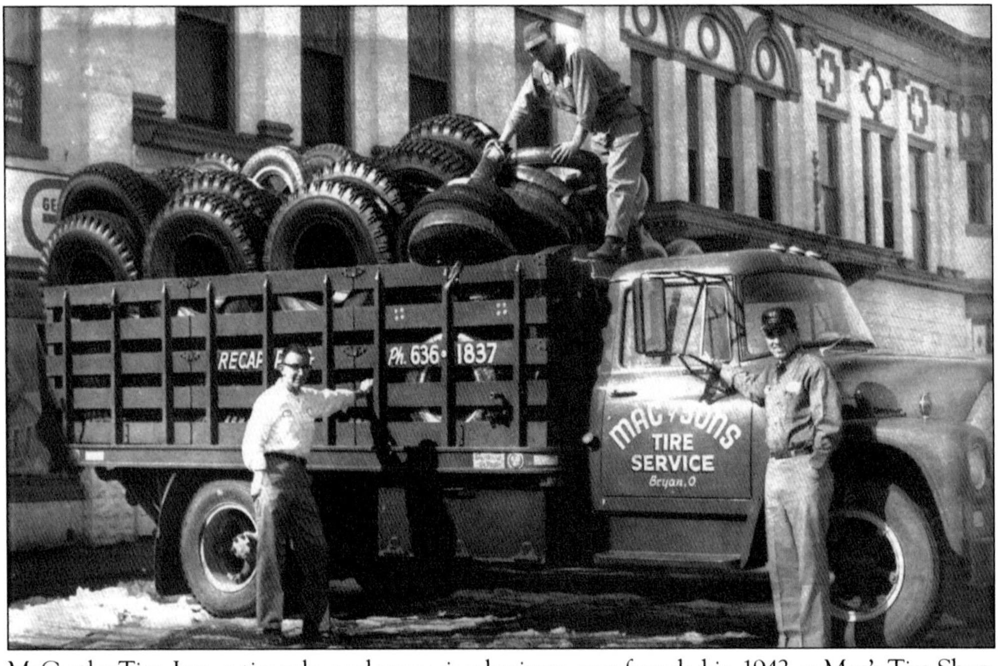

McCarthy Tire, Inc., a tire sales and recapping business, was founded in 1942 as Mac's Tire Shop. In 1946, the business moved into the former Jefferson Garage east of the Hotel Elder, shown above. In January 1967, the business relocated to 1126 Buffalo Road. McCarthy Tire was purchased by Easter Tire around 1984. (WCPL Photographic Archives.)

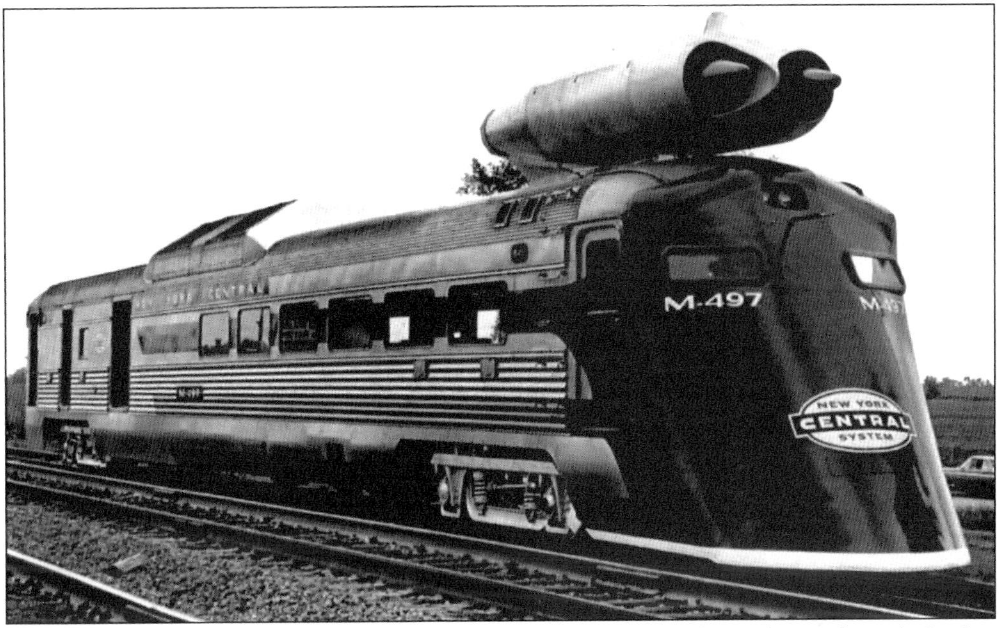

In 1966, the New York Central Railroad conducted tests from Butler, Indiana, through Stryker using the M-497 passenger railcar equipped with an aerodynamic front to reduce wind resistance and two turbojet engines to propel the car. During the M-497's second run on July 23, 1966, the North American rail speed record of 183.85 miles per hour was established. (Donald Wetzel collection.)

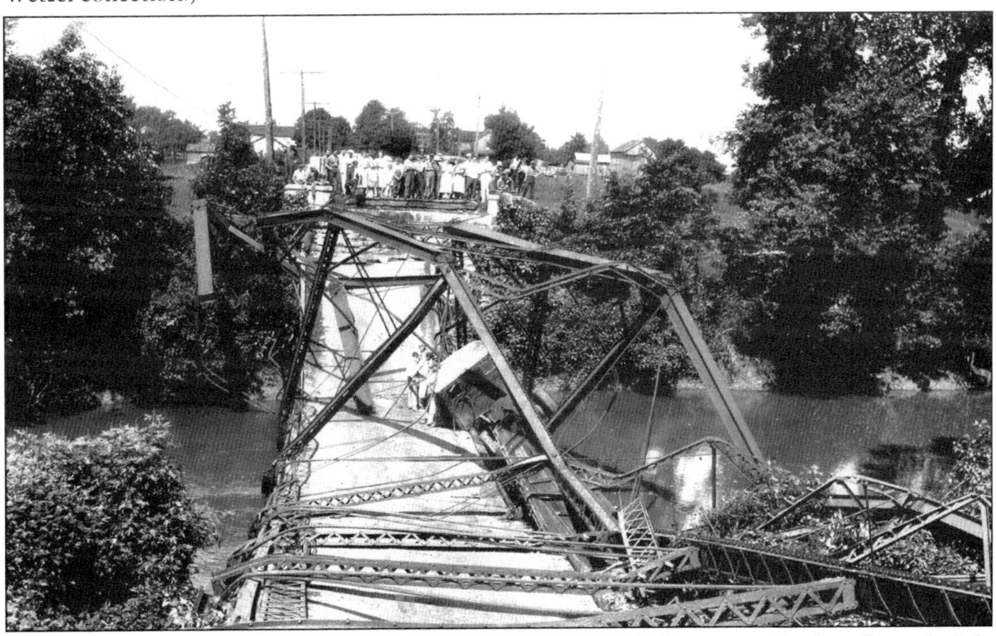

On June 10, 1939, the St. Joseph River Bridge on U.S. 6 east of Edgerton suddenly collapsed while a tractor-trailer rig was crossing, severing a three-inch natural gas line serving the community. Miraculously, the truck's driver and passenger received only minor injuries when the 142-foot, 40-plus-year-old steel span fell. A temporary wooden structure carried highway traffic until a reinforced concrete bridge was completed in 1941. (WCPL Photographic Archives.)